P9-CEJ-820
A16601180418

THE MODERN LIBRARY

OF THE WORLD'S BEST BOOKS

THE COMPLETE WORKS OF HORACE

THE COMPLETE WORKS OF

HORACE

EDITED, WITH AN INTRODUCTION BY

CASPER J. KRAEMER, JR

MODERN LIBRARY · NEW YORK

Random House IS THE PUBLISHER OF

THE MODERN LIBRARY

BENNETT A. CERF · DONALD S. KLOPFER · ROBERT K. HAAS

Manufactured in the United States of America
By H. Wolff

ACKNOWLEDGMENTS

Permission has been granted by the following authors and publishers to reprint the translations of poems on which they hold copyright:

Franklin P. Adams: Ode I.7, *Kingdoms in Cups,* translated by Franklin P. Adams.

The Forum: Ode III.28, *Celebration for Neptune,* translated by Roselle Mercier Montgomery.

Funk and Wagnalls Company: Ode I.27, *No Brawling,* translated by Lucius Morris Beebe.

Harcourt, Brace and Company: Odes I.14, I.37, III.22, IV.13, *To the Ship of State, Cleopatra Unqueened, A Pine Tree for Diana* and *Revenge,* translated by Louis Untermeyer.

Harvard Graduates' Magazine: Ode IV.8, *The Power of Verse,* translated by Alfred B. Lund.

Houghton Mifflin Company: Odes III.26, IV.9, IV.15, *One Last Touch, You Too Shall Live* and *Augustus' Peace,* translated by John Osborne Sargent.

The Living Age: Ode I.38, *No Frills!*, translated by Edward Sullivan.

New York World-Telegram: Ode I.27, *No Brawling,* translated by Lucius Morris Beebe.

Oxford University Press: Ode I.20, *To Maecenas—with an Invitation,* translated by Austin Dobson.

Scribner's Magazine: Ode II.8, *Bright-eyed Witch,* translated by John Paul Bocock.

Anna Seward: Epode 7, *Civil War,* translated by Anna Seward.

Hubert Wetmore Wells: Satires I.1-10, II.1-8, Ode I.8, *Have Mercy, Lydia,* Epodes 8, 12, *Hag, Pretty Lady,* translated by Hubert Wetmore Wells.

INTRODUCTION

by Casper J. Kraemer, Jr.

This year marks the two-thousandth year of the birth of Quintus Horatius Flaccus. For almost two millennia Horace has been loved by different generations of men as has no other ancient poet. The reason for this is not far to seek—he is essentially the poet of all of us. Speaking through the haze of years and from the midst of a civilization alien to our own, he expresses our thoughts as we would like to have thought them.

So much has been written about the man that in a brief introduction one cannot hope to say anything new. I am concerned here with but two aspects: with Horace as a personality and as a technician.

He writes to us from a stirring age when old systems had collapsed and a new order was rising hesitantly from the ashes. The reign of Augustus was the culmination of a century of heart-breaking civil war, of tumultuous political struggles which left men exhausted and crying for peace. The spirit of the age Horace feels so intimately and interprets so faithfully that we have in him not merely poetry but a historical document. In the pages which follow, one can pick up all the threads of a tangled web: the disorder, the corruption and the moral decay of an impotent political system; the dark threats of watchful enemies on the frontier; a New Deal with a slogan of peace and prosperity; the valiant struggle for the creation of a new morale based upon internal reform and harking back to the great old day; the criticism of problems as yet unsolved, like the ostentatious rage for wealth and the irrational lure of the city.

Through all this turmoil Horace moved as a man in the world but not of it. The sturdy independence which is so constantly noted as his chief characteristic kept him from being involved in the madness of the tumult. And yet, in his detached way, he loved the people who were involved. He had real warmth of friendship, perfect understanding which resolved itself frequently into genial banter, and an easy-going tolerance which made advice and reproof somehow seem the same. In a few of his earlier works, he displays a show of temper which fails to ring true. If it reflects a genuine hatred it has a slightly scared tone, but generally it derives from tradition—a poet *must* try his hand on strong subjects!

So, too, his relations to women involve a detachment which makes his passion seem quite rhetorical. His is the tone of a man too well-insulated ever to have been burned by real fire. He writes good love poetry not because, like Catullus, he feels vividly but because he writes understandingly. He knows the phrases of love, he is an interested observer of lovers rather than a participant in their thrills. From his detached point of view, a love affair is a dramatic (or perhaps picturesque) thing. In only one or two of his poems is there any hint that he may himself have been the lover, and even there he views himself so objectively that his affair loses reality. The occasional harshness toward women, which has been interpreted as the reaction of a sensitive man toward disappointment, suggests its own and different reason; he is rather disgusted with the whole business, especially when it reaches the ridiculous stage of mere emotion. He seems glad to disclaim interest in love when he reaches the mellow age of forty, and the affairs which he obediently describes thereafter are purely perfunctory. On the whole, his passion is, as it were, synthetic, composed in pleasing proportions of description, mythology, drama and playfulness.

This relative indifference to emotional stress is characteristic. Like Mendelssohn, whose music is said to be sweet because his life was so enviably happy, Horace enjoyed a tranquil, successful, happy career broken by few setbacks. Aside from a brief and undistinguished military career, his life saw little excitement and it is perhaps significant that he speaks repeatedly, if whimsically, as one of its major incidents, of the fact that he was once almost killed by a falling tree. His health was consistently good and a slight strain of weakness provides him an amiable topic of conversation which deepens occasionally to the tone of a pleasant melancholy, and robs Death, whose imminence is a favorite theme, of most of its sting. His advocacy of the simple life, of contentment with moderate means, of philosophic calm, of the "golden mean," is thoroughly part of the man. It is not the pose of the preacher but the simple faith of the man who could conceive of no other course.

Even his pleasures are naturally inhibited. The delights of drinking, which he describes so frequently, are enumerated with proper enthusiasm but also with gentlemanly restraint. To the hard-drinking American the moderation of the ancients in this respect is always startling. Horace, like all Greeks and Romans, talks with abandon when he mentions the dire results of drinking wine straight.

But if his pleasures were moderate, they were none the less genuine. One will go far to find such real delight in the countryside, not merely as an escape from the distractions of the city, but as a source of pleasurable emotion in the various phases of nature and of delight in the customs of the rural inhabitants. One cannot find better expressed an appreciation of leisure, of frank loafing, which he enjoys so much as to feel occasionally the need of a half-hearted apology.

Above all, he is lovable to us for the humor which pervades his work. His humor is in the American spirit: self-depreciation which finds its best expression in overstatement. He makes his friends or people at large the butt of his humor but never fails to imply that he, too, belongs to their group.

But Horace is not merely a man. He is a poet, and a poet quite unlike any other in the wide range of the European tradition. To the reader who must make his acquaintance with a classic solely through the medium of an English translation, any rhapsody on the author's art is no doubt a bit unfair. At the same time, no account of Horace's work can be considered adequate if it fails to call attention to his wonderful mastery of technique. The reader of the present volume will assuredly find much that is prettily turned and felicitously expressed, and the compiler should surely be the last person to minimize the literary skill of translations which he has himself selected; but yet he feels it his duty to inform the English reader that the most ingenious renderings of the most gifted translator rarely do justice to the amazing and well-nigh inimitable smoothness of Horace's verse. Latin is essentially a bald, rugged idiom well suited to certain didactic forms of literature, beautifully adapted to cases where precision is desired, as in the law, but, by and large, it is not the ideal vehicle for the expression of light and airy fancies. To one who realizes this, the deft grace and the light touch of Horace are a source of never-ending wonder.

Horace is, of course, not the only author who found the hard and rugged Latin malleable and made it a supple instrument to his hand. The same ability was possessed in varying degrees and in different fields by Vergil, Cicero, Livy and others. In his own chosen field, however, Horace is supreme. There is much justice in his claim to have been the first to adapt the Greek lyric metres to the purposes of Latin poetry, though in so saying he may seem to be doing less than justice to Catullus. A comparison of these two is almost inevitable. While undoubtedly Catullus surpasses Horace in the immediacy of his emotional appeal, Horace's superiority as a technician is beyond question. His Sapphics have a rapid flow that is absent from those of Catullus, though occasionally, in a single phrase, the earlier poet attains a haunting sweetness quite alien to Horace's nature. One is lost in admiration for the variety and smoothness of the Augustan poet's Asclepiad verses; those of Catullus are heavy and choppy and seem in comparison mere first experiments as, in justice it must be said, they were. Other forms, in which Horace had no known precursors, such as the Archilochian and above all the Alcaic, he carried to such a pinnacle of perfection that no successor (except the tame Statius) ventured to admit comparisons by carrying them on. Several of the metres used with great success by Catullus, Horace does not employ, notably the hendecasyllabic, the scazon and the elegiac couplet. Of these the first is perhaps too trivial for good lyric and all three are much better suited to epigram, as the amazing technical success of Martial reveals. To my mind, Horace is least successful in his hexameters, but it must be remembered that he uses this form only in his longer satirical and didactic pieces.

One further aspect of Horace as a workman must be touched upon. The type of criticism that delights in the meticulous analysis of literary forms and the order of words and in dubbing these with ponderous polysyllabic Greek titles will insist that Horace's odes are constructions of the highest degree of artificiality. But the wonder comes with the realization that, tortured as the writing is, it never *seems* unnatural. The spontaneous inspiration of the moment that seems at first hearing so attractive often turns out to be both naïve and shoddy on more sober reflection. Horace reverses the process; by careful elaboration he produces a result so simple and charming and natural that you often wonder why you didn't say the same thing yourself. If ever a poet possessed the high art of concealing art, Horace is that poet.

CONTENTS

PAGE

ACKNOWLEDGMENTS v

INTRODUCTION BY CASPER J. KRAEMER, JR. vii

CONVERSATION PIECES (Satires)
(Translated by Hubert Wetmore Wells)

BOOK I

1. The Golden Mean 3
2. Going to Extremes, Especially in Adultery 7
3. A Plea for Tolerance 12
4. Defense of Satire 17
5. My Trip to Brundisium 22
6. Only a Freedman's Son but Proud of It 25
7. King Meets His Match 30
8. The Hag Canidia—As Observed by Priapus 32
9. A Morning Stroll 33
10. An Answer to Critics 37

BOOK II

1. What Is a Satirist to Do? 41
2. The Simple Life 44
3. This Lunatic World 49
4. Lecture-Notes on Food 62
5. How to Get Rich Quickly 66
6. The Country Mouse 70
7. Frank Talk on Freedom 75
8. Rich Man Dines 79

REFRAINS (Epodes)

		Translated by	PAGE
1.	Dedication	Stephen Edward De Vere	87
2.	Revery of a Business Man	John Dryden	89
3.	Hymn of Hate	Francis William Newman	93
4.	Social Climber	Anonymous	94
5.	Hell-Broth	Theodore Martin	95
6.	To a Cowardly Libeler	Philip Francis	100
7.	Civil War	Anna Seward	101
8.	Hag	Hubert Wetmore Wells	103
9.	The Victory of Actium	Theodore Martin	105
10.	Good-Riddance	Francis Howes	108
11.	Love's Madness	Theodore Martin	109
12.	Pretty Lady	Hubert Wetmore Wells	111
13.	Seize the Hour	John Duncombe	113
14.	Apology	Arthur S. Way	115
15.	Inconstancy	Ofella	116
16.	The Horrors of Civil War	Stephen Edward De Vere	118
17.	Poet and Witch	Alexander Falconer Murison	121

POEMS (Odes)

BOOK I

1.	Dedication	Anonymous	127
2.	Augustus Our Saviour	Philip Francis	129
3.	Bon Voyage—and Afterthoughts	John Conington	132
4.	Impermanence	John Charles Baring	134
5.	Pyrrha's Inconstancy	E. C. Cox	135
6.	Limitations of a Poet of Love	Theodore Martin	136
7.	Kingdoms in Cups	Franklin P. Adams	137
8.	Have Mercy, Lydia	Hubert Wetmore Wells	139
9.	Kiss in Time	Roswell Martin Field	141

		Translated by	PAGE
10.	To Mercury	Alexander Falconer Murison	142
11.	Use Today, Forget To-morrow	Thomas Charles Baring	143
12.	Jove's Vice-gerent	William Dowe	144
13.	Love Unreasoning	John Conington	147
14.	To the Ship ot State	Louis Untermeyer	148
15.	Helen's Price	Elizabeth Carter	150
16.	Apology	John Conington	152
17.	Invitation to the Country	Stephen Edward De Vere	154
18.	On the Grape	John Conington	156
19.	A Belated Passion	John Conington	158
20.	To Maecenas—with an Invitation	Austin Dobson	159
21.	Hymn to Latona and Her Children	William Falconer Murison	160
22.	Purity of Soul	William Falconer Murison	161
23.	To a Mothered Girl	William Falconer Murison	162
24.	Dirge	John Conington	163
25.	After the Ball Is Over	Theodore Martin	164
26.	Praise of Lamia	John Conington	166
27.	No Brawling	Lucius Morris Beebe	167
28.	Voice from the Dead	Theodore Martin	168
29.	Scholar in Arms	John Conington	170
30.	Come, Queen Venus	Thomas Charles Baring	171
31.	Grant Me, Phoebus, Calm Content	John Conington	172
32.	The Poet to His Lyre	Edward Yardley	173
33.	Love Mocks Us All	Austin Dobson	174
34.	Converted	Stephen Edward De Vere	175
35.	Rome in Arms	William Sinclair Marris	176
36.	Our Friend's Back Again!	Theodore Martin	178
37.	Cleopatra Unqueened	Louis Untermeyer	179
38.	No Frills!	Edward Sullivan	181

PAGE

Book II

		Translated by	
1.	Book Review	Stephen Edward De Vere	182
2.	Put Wealth in Its Place	Thomas Charles Baring	184
3.	The Last Exile	J. H. Deazeley	185
4.	Love Is Like That	Theodore Martin	187
5.	Too Young for Love	Warren H. Cudworth	188
6.	Home Is Best	John Conington	189
7.	Welcome Home!	John Conington	190
8.	Bright-eyed Witch	John Paul Bocock	191
9.	Even Grief Should End	Samuel Johnson	192
10.	The Golden Mean	Margaret M. FitzGerald	193
11.	Let Your Concern Be Youth	Thomas Charles Baring	194
12.	My Theme Is Love	Anonymous	196
13.	A Narrow Escape	William Sinclair Marris	198
14.	The Shortness of Life	Stephen Edward De Vere	200
15.	Building Rage	William Sinclair Marris	202
16.	Restiveness	Enola Brandt	203
17.	United Even in Death	Warren H. Cudworth	205
18.	Vanity of Riches	T. Rutherford Clark	207
19.	Bacchus' Might	John Parke	210
20.	Success	Warren H. Cudworth	213

Book III

1.	Contentment	Charles Stuart Calverly	214
2.	Call to Youth	Hugh Vibart MacNaghten	217
3.	Strength of the Righteous	Theodore Martin	219
4.	Power of the Muses	William Sinclair Marris	223
5.	Courage—Then and Now	Stephen Edward De Vere	227
6.	How Are We Fallen!	Theodore Martin	230
7.	Keep Faith, Asterie!	Theodore Martin	233
8.	Anniversary	Warren H. Cudworth	235
9.	Reconciliation of Two Lovers	Baxter Mow	237

		Translated by	PAGE
10.	Lyce, Be Kind!	John Conington	239
11.	Bid Her Take Heed!	William Sinclair Marris	240
12.	Love Shackled	John Conington	243
13.	Fountain of Bandusia	Austin Dobson	244
14.	Glorious Homecoming	William Sinclair Marris	245
15.	Be Your Age, Chloris	Thomas Charles Baring	247
16.	Contentment Without Wealth	Stephen Edward De Vere	248
17.	Tomorrow's Rain	Theodore Martin	250
18.	Hymn to Faunus	Charles Stuart Calverly	251
19.	Now to the Feast	William Sinclair Marris	252
20.	Battle Royal	William Sinclair Marris	254
21.	To a Wine Jar	William Sinclair Marris	255
22.	A Pine Tree for Diana	Louis Untermeyer	256
23.	What Gifts the Gods Delight	H. F. B.	257
24.	The Curse of Wealth	Stephen Edward De Vere	259
25.	To Bacchus	Bryan Waller Proctor	262
26.	One Last Touch	John Osborne Sargent	263
27.	Pleasant Trip!	William Sinclair Marris	264
28.	Celebration for Neptune	Roselle Mercier Montgomery	267
29.	Invitation to a Conscientious Statesman	John Conington	268
30.	I Shall not Die	John Ordronaux	271

BOOK IV

1.	Too Old for Love	Ben Jonson	272
2.	No Pindar I	Townshend	274
3.	The Poet's Reward	Christopher Smart	276
4.	Great Scion of a Great House	Stephen Edward De Vere	278
5.	Return, Great Giver of Peace!	T. Rutherford Clark	281
6.	Thy Help, Apollo!	Stephen Edward De Vere	283
7.	Let Nature Teach	Samuel Johnson	285
8.	The Power of Verse	Alfred B. Lund	286

	Translated by	PAGE
9. You Too Shall Live	John Osborne Sargent	288
10. It Will Soon Be Too Late	Francis Wrangham	291
11. Come to the Party	George John Whyte-Melville	292
12. Invitation to a Friend, in Spring	Stephen Edward De Vere	294
13. Revenge	Louis Untermeyer	296
14. Hail, Victorious Cæsar's Sons!	Stephen Edward De Vere	298
15. Augustus' Peace	John Osborne Sargent	300

LETTERS IN VERSE (Epistles)

Book I

1. To Maecenas, Explaining His Swerve from Poetry	Alexander Falconer Murison	305
2. To Lollius, on the Practical Value of Great Literature	Philip Francis	311
3. To Florus, Asking about Personal Affairs	Philip Francis	315
4. To Tibullus, Some Reflections	Philip Francis	317
5. To Torquatus, with an Invitation to a Modest Luncheon	Philip Francis	319
6. To Numicus, on How to Be Happy	Francis Howes	321
7. To Maecenas, on Real Contentment	Francis Howes	325
8. To Celsus, Greetings and a Bit of Advice	Philip Francis	331
9. To Claudius, Introducing a Friend, Septimius	Arthur W. Fox	332

	Translated by	PAGE
10. To Fuscus, with Greetings from the Country	Alexander Falconer Murison	333
11. To Bullatius, on There Being No Place Like Home	Philip Francis	336
12. To Iccius, Advice on Adjusting Himself to His Career in Sicily	Francis Howes	338
13. To Vinius, Carrying His Master's Poetry to Augustus	Francis Howes	340
14. To Villius, His Steward, Urging Him to Be Content with His Lot	Francis Howes	341
15. To Vala, Asking after a Vacation Spot	Philip Francis	344
16. To Quinctius, Some Reflections Suggested by the Poet's Country Place	Philip Francis	346
17. To Scaeva, on How to Get on in the World	Francis Howes	350
18. To Lollius, Advice on Getting Along with the Great	Philip Francis	354
19. To Maecenas, Answering His Unfair Critics	Francis Howes	360
20. To His Book, About to Make Its Own Way in the World	Austin Dobson	363

Book II

1. To Augustus, Explaining the Modern Literary Attitude Toward the Ancient Greeks	Alexander Falconer Murison	365

	Translated by	PAGE
2. To Florus, an Excuse for Writing Poetry No Longer	Anonymous	379
JUBILEE HYMN (Carmen Saeculare)	John Duncombe	391
THE ART OF POETRY	Edward Henry Blakeney	397

Conversation Pieces
(Satires)

Colloquial chats on various subjects, serious and gay, generally in dialogue form. The first book was published about 34 B. C. in the poet's thirty-first year; the second book appeared four years later.

I· 1· *The Golden Mean*

qui fit, Maecenas

How is it, Maecenas, that no one is satisfied with his lot in life, whether he chose it himself or whether it came to him by accident, but envies those whose lot is different?

"Happy are the traders!" exclaims the soldier, weighted down with his years, his body broken in arduous service. Yet the trader, when the south wind tosses his vessel about, cries, "War is better than this! Why? When once the ranks attack you have in an instant either death or victory." The legal expert, when a client knocks at his door before cock-crow, calls the farmer lucky. But the latter, dragged from the country into the city to answer a summons, is positive that "only those are happy who live in town!" To cite the many other similar instances would wear out even talkative Fabius.

Without boring you, let me give you the conclusion. If some god should say, "See here! I will grant what you wish. You, soldier, shall be a trader; you, counsellor, a farmer. Change your lots and go your way. . . . Hurry up! Why do you hesitate?" They wouldn't do it. And yet they could! Would not Jupiter be justified in snorting with anger and saying that hereafter he would not be so indulgent as to listen to petitions?

I must not, like a jester, laugh the subject off. And still why may not one speak the truth with a smile like those kindly teachers who give candy to their pupils to induce them to learn their letters? Joking aside, however, let us be serious.

That fellow over there who turns a heavy sod with the hard plowshare, that rascally innkeeper, the soldier, the sailors who so bravely breast every sea, all of them say that they endure hardship in order that when they are old and have made sufficient provision for themselves they may retire to safety and peace. In the same way the tiny ant, that busiest of all creatures, drags in her mouth whatever she can to add to the heap she piles up, for she is aware of the future and anxious about it. When winter comes she never stirs but prudently uses the stores which she has gathered up before.

But you, neither summer nor winter, fire, sea nor sword can stop you from making money just so long as your neighbor is wealthier than you. What pleasure can it give you to dig stealthily, in fear and trembling, a hole in the ground and bury therein a huge quantity of silver and gold?

"Because if I began to spend it, I should soon have none left."

But if you don't spend it what attraction is there in the pile that you have heaped up? Suppose your threshing-floor yields a hundred thousand bushels of wheat. Your belly cannot, on that account, hold more than mine. If you were one of a line of slaves and carried on your shoulder a basket of bread, you couldn't eat more than the man who carried nothing. What difference, tell me, does it make to the man who lives a normal life whether he plows a hundred or a thousand acres?

"It is pleasant to spend from a great pile."

Well, do you think your granaries are better than our

bins if we can take just as much out of our small hoard? It is just the same as if you needed only a glass or a pitcher of water and said, "I'd rather draw the same amount from a river than from this little spring." That's why men who want more than enough are swept away, together with the bank they stand on, by the swift Aufidus River, while those who ask for only so much as they need have neither to drink roiled water nor lose their lives in the stream.

Most men, led astray by greed, say, "There is no such thing as *enough*. A man is judged by the amount he has." What can you do to people like this but tell them to be wretched since that's what they want? They are like the Athenian, as greedy as he was rich, who is said to have turned aside criticism with the remark, "People hiss me, but I congratulate myself in private when I think of all the money in my chest." Tantalus, with his thirst, strains at the waters that elude his lips.

What are you smiling at? Change names and the story fits *you!* You doze on, gloating over your money-bags whose contents you have raked and scraped together. But, as if they were holy, you don't dare to touch them, or to enjoy them any more than if they were paintings. Don't you know the value of money and its purpose? You can buy bread with it, vegetables, a bottle of wine, and other necessities from the lack of which human nature suffers. Perhaps you *enjoy* watching day and night half dead with fear, on the alert for wicked thieves, fires, or slaves who may rob you and run. Is that what satisfies you? If that is good living I want to be one of the paupers! If you go to your bed with malaria or some other sickness, is there someone who will sit by you, prepare your medicine, call in the doctor to set you again on your feet and restore you to your children and dear relatives? Neither your wife nor your son wants you to get well. All your neighbors and acquaintances, even the boys and girls, dislike you. Can you wonder, since you prefer money to everything else, that no one gives you the affection that you don't earn? If you think you can without effort keep the friends whom nature has given you, you're wasting your time, idiot! You might just as well break an ass to reins and race him in the Field of Mars.

So put limits to your money-grabbing. As your wealth grows, have less fear of poverty. Begin gradually to taper off your work as you acquire what you longed for. Don't be like that Ummidius who was so rich that he measured his money, so cheap that he never had better clothes than a slave. To the very end of his life he was afraid that he would die of hunger. Instead, his freedwoman, most courageous of Tyndareus' daughters, cut him down with an axe!

"Well, then, what do you want me to do? Live like a Navius or a Nomentanus?"

You always compare things which are utterly different. When I tell you not to be a miser, that doesn't mean that I am telling you to be a fool and a spendthrift. There is some middle ground between Tanais and Visellius, his father-in-law. There is a *mean* in things, fixed limits on either side of which right living cannot get a foothold.

So I come back to where I began to ask how it is that, like the miser, no one prefers his own lot in life, but praises those whose lot is different, pines because his neighbor's goat gives more milk, doesn't compare himself with the vast multitude of poor people, but merely strives to outdo this one and that. The man who is eager to be rich is always blocked by one who is richer, just as when in a race the barriers are raised and the chariots are flying behind the horses' hoofs, the charioteer makes for the horses that are outrunning his own, ignoring those that are left behind. And this is why we rarely find a man who can say that he had led a happy life and that, content with his path, he retires like a satisfied guest from a banquet.

Enough for now! For fear you'll think I have rifled the portfolios of blear-eyed Crispinus I will say no more.

I· 2· *Going to Extremes, Especially in Adultery*

ambubaiarum collegia

The Flute-girls' Association, the Quacks, the Beggars, the Farce Actresses, the Buffoons and the rest of that type are sorrowful and distressed at the death of the singer Tigellius. "He was so generous," they say. But then, on the other hand, my neighbor here, for fear of being called a spendthrift, will not give a needy friend the means of keeping away the cold and gnawing hunger. Ask a third man why, to gratify his thankless gluttony, he strips the fine estate of his grandfather and father, borrowing money to buy all kinds of delicacies, and his answer is that he doesn't want to be considered cheap and mean. Some people approve him, others blame.

Fufidius, rich in lands and in money which he has out at interest, is afraid of the reputation of a rake and spendthrift. When he lends money, he deducts from the principal five times the usual interest, and the more desperate a man's circumstances are the more he takes advantage of him. He hunts up accounts from young men who have just come of age and whose fathers are strict with them. "Good God," you exclaim when you hear of this, "surely such a man indulges himself in proportion to his profit!" No, you will hardly believe how far he is from being decent to himself. Why, the father, in Terence's play, who lived such a wretched life after causing his son to run away from home, did not torment himself more than he does.

Now in case anyone asks the point to all this, the answer is, *when fools avoid one kind of vice, they run into the opposite.*

Malthinus walks along with his tunic slack-girdled. Another silly chap draws it up so far as his waist. Rufillus smells of perfume, Gargonius of a he-goat. There is no middle ground. Some men will have nothing to do with women whose ankles are not hidden by a dress with trailing flounce. Others, contrariwise, will touch only those who frequent low brothels. When a well-known rake came out of a bawdy house our divine Cato greeted him with the remark, "Congratulations! When foul lust sets the blood afire it is better that young men come here rather than meddle with other men's wives." ("Well, I wouldn't like that kind of congratulation," says Cupiennius, connoisseur of matrons' parts.)

You who do not wish well to adulterers will be glad to know that they are hampered in every way, and that their pleasure, which they obtain only rarely, is accompanied with much suffering and often serious danger. One man flung himself headlong from a roof; another was beaten almost to death; another, running away, fell into a merciless gang of thieves; another paid a bribe to save himself from physical violence. Still another man was pissed upon by kitchen drudges, and matters even got to the point that one of them sliced off his privates. "Served him right," everybody said. (Everybody except Galba!)

How much safer is traffic with women of the second class! Freed-women, I mean. Sallust is just as crazy as any adulterer about them! If a man, with an eye to his property and his interest, wants to be liberal with moderation, and be called "good and generous," he should pay them just enough—not an amount that will bring down on his head ruin and infamy. But he prides himself on this one fact he loves to cite, "I never touch any matron." So in the old days Marsaeus, Origo's lover, gave his family estate and farm to an actress with the comment, "I will never have to do with other men's wives." But you have had to do with actresses and harlots, and so your good name suffers more harm than your property! Is it enough to avoid the rôle of adulterer and not to avoid that other rôle which all men despise? To lose one's good name and to squander one's inheritance, whatever rôle you assume, is terrible. What difference does it make whether you have to do with a matron, a maiden or a prostitute?

In that famous incident of Fausta, Vilius (misled, poor fellow, by his nick-name "Sulla's son-in-law") suffered more than sufficient punishment by being beaten, stabbed and thrown out of the house while Longarenus enjoyed Fausta within doors. Suppose Vilius' mind had said to him, using the words of his yard which was aware of so many evil consequences, "What do you want? Did I ever, when my passion was greatest, demand from you a woman descended from a great consul and dressed in a matron's clothes?" What could he have answered but, "The lady had an illustrious father"? How much better is the advice of nature, rich in stores of her own, if only you manage wisely and distinguish between what is to be avoided and what is desirable. Do you think it makes no difference whether your troubles arise through your own fault or from circumstances? Therefore, lest you be sorry for it, stop running after matrons. More trouble comes from that than enjoyment if you succeed. A matron, for all her pearls and emeralds, has no softer thigh or smarter leg (despite what *you* think, Cerinthus). Indeed, the prostitute is very often to be preferred. Besides, she offers her wares without disguise and openly shows what she has to sell. If she has real charm, she doesn't boast and make a show of it, while she is eager to conceal defects.

When millionaires buy horses they inspect them covered so that if, as often happens, a beautiful shape is supported by a weak hoof, it may not take in the buyer as he greedily regards the handsome back, the short head, and the stately neck. In this they are right. So don't you scrutinize perfections of person with the eyes of a Lynceus, and then be blinder than Hypsaea when you look at defects. "What a fine leg! What arms!" you may say. But note that the girl is low-hipped and short-waisted, and has a long nose and a splay foot. You can see only the *face* of a matron (except Catia) who carefully conceals the rest of her body. However, if you are out for forbidden charms that are walled about with a rampart (this is what drives you mad), there are many obstacles in your way: attendants, a litter, maids, waitresses, a dress that drops down to the ankles and a cloak thrown over it. A thousand things hinder you from getting a fair view. With the other type nothing hinders. Through her silken garment you may see, almost as well as if she were naked, that she has neither a bad leg nor an ugly foot. Your eye can take the measure of her form perfectly. Do you prefer to have tricks played upon you and your money extorted before the goods are shown?

"Just as a hunter pursues the hare in the deep snow, but disdains to touch it when it is set before him," quotes the rake, adding, "My love is like that. It overlooks easy prey and grasps at what runs away." Do you believe that by poetry like that, grief and fever and heavy cares can be exorcized? Wouldn't it be better to learn what limit nature has set to the appetites, what she can patiently forego, and what she would lament were she deprived of them, and to distinguish between the show and the substance?

When thirst parches your throat, you don't look for golden cups to drink from, do you? When you are hungry do you despise everything but peacock and turbot?

When your passions surge, and a young slave girl or a boy for whom you long is at hand, would you rather be consumed with desire than possess it? Not I. I like pleasures that are easy to obtain. To quote Philodemus: the woman who says, "By and by," "Yes, but more money," "If my husband isn't home" is fit for the castrated priests of Cybele. For myself I want a girl who neither holds out for a great price nor delays to come when she is told. She should be fair and straight, adorned only so far as not to desire to seem taller or fairer than nature made her. When I am with such a woman, she is my Ilia and Aegeria. I give her any name and am not afraid that her husband will return from the country, the door be broken open, the dog bark, the house be shaken and resound on every side with loud knocking. I needn't fear her jumping, white as a sheet, from the bed, her confidante crying, "Mercy on me," and all of us in a panic, the servant lest her legs be broken in penalty, the wife in dismay for her dowry and I, in turn, of my life, racing, with my tunic ungirded and my feet bare, to save my money, my arse or my reputation. It's an awful thing to be caught. That I could prove even if Fabius were the judge.

I· 3· *A Plea for Tolerance*

omnibus hoc vitium

There is a fault common to all singers. When they're among friends and are asked to sing they don't want to, and when they're not asked to sing they never stop. That was what Tigellius, that famous Sardinian, used to do. Augustus, who had the power to compel him, could beg him in the name of his father's friendship and his own, but could get nowhere with him. But if Tigellius happened to feel like it, he would sing "Hail Bacchus!" from beginning to end in tenor voice and in deepest bass. There was nothing consistent about the man. His pace at times was that of a fellow running from an enemy; at times, that of the bearer of Juno's sacred vessels. Sometimes he was followed by two hundred slaves, at other times by ten. At one moment his conversation was of kings and nabobs, everything in the grand style. At another time it was, "Just let me have a three-legged table, a shell of clean salt and a toga as coarse as you please if only it keeps out the cold." But give a million sesterces to this thrifty man who was content with a little, and in five days there would be nothing in his pocket. He would stay awake from night until morning and then snore the whole day through. There never was so variable a person.

Now, someone may say to me, "What about yourself? Haven't you any faults?" Of course I have, but they're different and perhaps more trivial. When Maenius railed at Novius in his absence, and someone said, "Look here, my friend, don't you know yourself, or do you think you can impose on us as if we didn't know you?", Maenius replied, "Oh, I overlook my own faults." Such complacency as that is stupid and outrageous and deserves to be censured.

When you look at your own shortcomings through bleary eyes daubed with eye-salve, why are you as keen-eyed as an eagle or as the serpent of Epidaurus in regarding the vices of your friends? That's the reason why your friends investigate *your* faults. A man may be quick-tempered, impatient of the sharp-witted sneers of our present-day critics. He may arouse amusement because of the rustic cut of his beard, because his toga doesn't hang properly or because his shoes are so loose that they will hardly stay on his feet. But as a man he is as good as the best. He is your friend, and under his rough surface a great genius lies concealed. Give yourself an overhauling. See whether nature, or perhaps bad habit, has sown the seeds of vice in you. Once you neglect your fields, there spring up in them weeds which are fit only to be burned.

Let's look at it from another viewpoint. A lover sees his mistress' defects as special beauties, as Balbinus thinks Hagna's wart charming. I wish that we made the same mistake in our friendship and that our tolerance would give deformities a kindly name. We should not act too critically to our friends if they have faults, but rather as a father does to a son. If a child squints, his father calls him "Blinky"; if he is wretchedly undersized (like that abortive Sisyphus in former days), "Chicky"; a boy with bow legs he fondly calls "Bandy"; another who can hardly stand on his twisted ankles, "Stumps." If a man is too close, call him "thrifty." It should be said of a man who is somewhat clumsily addicted to boasting, "His friends like him." A person who is too rude and free-spoken may be described as "sincere" and "courageous;" one who is too hot-headed, "high-spirited."

This, it seems to me, is what makes friends and keeps them when made. Yet we pervert even the good points and are anxious to smudge a clean bowl. One of our friends who is more retiring than the rest we call "slow" and "stupid." Another avoids every snare and lays himself open to no villain; but, since we live among people where envy is keen and slanders rife, instead of referring to him as a man of prudent sense, we call him "insincere" and "shrewd." If someone is outspoken (I dare say I must often have seemed that to you, Maecenas, on interrupting you with some meaningless chatter when you were reading or thinking) we say, "He is utterly without a sense of propriety."

It's too bad how thoughtlessly we set up harsh and unkind rules against ourselves. No one is born without faults. That man is best who has fewest. If my dear friend wishes me to love him he must be tolerant. In all fairness he must weigh my good qualities against my bad ones and tip the scales in favor of the former as being more numerous —that is, if they *are* more numerous! On this condition he shall be weighed by the same scales. If a man asks his friend not to be bothered by his own warts he should overlook his friend's pimples. It is only fair for the person who asks indulgence for his own failing to indulge the failing of another. Since no knife can remove anger or other faults that are in the nature of us poor fools, why should not reason apply its own standards and punish in proportion to actual facts? If you were to crucify a servant who, as he removed a dish, lapped up some half-eaten fish with its warm sauce, any level-headed person would call you crazier than

Labeo. How much more insane and unfair is the following? One of your friends has committed some slight offense which you would be thought ungracious not to pardon. You hate him for it and avoid him as Ruso is avoided by that unhappy debtor who, when the awful first of the month comes and he has not, by hook or crook, found interest or capital, has to offer up his throat like a prisoner of war and listen to Ruso's dreary stories. A friend of mine gets drunk and wets my couch, or knocks from the table a vase handmade by Evander, or, in his hunger takes a chicken from my side of the platter—is he on that account to be a friend less dear to me? What could I do if he stole or betrayed a trust or repudiated a pledge?

People who hold that all offenses are pretty much on a par are in trouble when they face the facts. Feelings and habits rebel, even expediency herself who is pretty nearly the mother of justice and right.

When the living creatures crawled forth upon the primal earth, dumb and unsightly beasts, they fought for their acorns and lair with nails and fists, then with clubs, and finally with arms which experience fashioned, until they discovered verbs and nouns by which they denoted ideas and sensations. Thenceforth they began to give up war, to build towns and to frame laws against stealing, robbery and adultery. There was many a wanton before Helen who was the shameful cause of war, but they died unknown deaths for, as they pursued promiscuous copulation after the manner of wild beasts, stronger men like bulls in the herd cut them down. If you study the history and records of the world you must admit that the source of justice was the fear of injustice. Nature cannot discern between what is just and unjust as she distinguishes good things from their opposites, things to be shunned from objects of desire. Neither can reason affirm that the man who breaks off a succulent cabbage in a neighbor's garden commits a sacrilege of the same degree and kind as the one who robs by night things consecrated to the gods. Let there be a sliding scale which will inflict punishments to fit crimes. Otherwise you assail with the terrible scourge what deserves only the whip. I do not believe that caning will correct one who deserves severer stripes, when you say that larceny is on a par with highway robbery and when you threaten that, if you had the power, you would prune back little and great faults with the same sickle.

If it is the philosopher alone who is rich, handsome, kingly (and a good shoemaker) why do you set your mind on what you already possess?

"You don't understand what our master Chrysippus means when he says, 'The philosopher never makes sandals for himself, even if he is a shoemaker.' "

No?

"Just as Hermogenes, even when he is uttering no sound, is nevertheless the very best singer and artist, just as that clever fellow Alfenus is a barber, even when every instrument of his craft has been laid aside and his shop closed, just so the philosopher is master of every craft, and a king."

Well, naughty boys pull at your beard, and unless you beat them off with your cane you will be jostled by the crowd, while you, poor fellow, howl and burst with rage, you, the greatest of great kings! While you, a king, go to your penny bath without a single attendant (except that ridiculous Crispinus) my tolerant friends will forgive me if in any way I make a fool of myself, while I in turn will cheerfully endure their lapses. Then I, as a private person, shall live more happily than you, the king.

I· 4: *Defense of Satire*

Eupolis atque Cratinus

The dramatists, Eupolis, Cratinus, Aristophanes and other authors of the Old Comedy, called by their frank names anyone who deserved to be represented as a rogue, a thief, an adulterer or a cut-throat, or as infamous in any other way. Upon these poets Lucilius is wholly dependent. He followed them in all but the metre—witty, penetrating, rough in the construction of his verse.

In this last respect he was at fault. Often, as a great feat, he would dictate without effort two hundred verses in an hour. Since he flowed muddily there was always something that you would like to take out. He was wordy and too lazy to endure the fatigue of writing. Of writing properly, I mean, for the amount of his poetry is beside the point.

Well, well! Here is Crispinus offering me heavy odds.

"Pick up your tablet. Pick it up, please. Have a place, a time, and proctors set over us and let's see who can write most! Thank God for making me an unproductive, unaspiring intellectual, speaking seldom and very little at that. You go ahead as you choose, act like the air shut in a goatskin bellows, puffing away until the fire softens the iron! How happy is Fannius! His works and his bust are offered for sale without his asking, while no one reads my writings. And I fear to read them in public because there are persons who dislike satire heartily. Most people deserve criticism. Pick out anyone from the crowd—he suffers from avarice or from some deplorable ambition. One man is crazy about married women, another over boys, a third about glittering silver or Albius about bronzes. Another man keeps busy trading, from the rising sun to that which warms the evening landscape, but he is hurried headlong through dangers like a column of dust in a whirlwind, in terror lest he lose some of his capital, or in order to add to his wealth. All these people have a horror of poetry and hate poets. "Keep away from him," they say. "He has hay on his horns. If only he can raise a laugh for his own diversion he will spare no friend, and whatever he has once smeared on his paper he will rejoice to have all the boys and old women know as they return from the bake shop and the lake."

But let me say a few words on the other side of the question. To begin with, I except myself from the catalogue of these I concede to be poets. One must do more than make verses scan. And you can't call a man a poet if he writes, as I do, in language more appropriate to conversation. If a man has talent, inspired genius and a grand and lofty style, you may grant him the honor of the title. Accordingly some people have questioned whether or not comedy is poetry. Neither in the words nor in the subject matter is there any inspiration or force, and, except for the fact that it is written in fixed metre, it is mere prose.

"But an angry father rages because his spendthrift son, mad about a wanton mistress, refuses a wife with a large dower, and to his great shame parades drunk through the town with torches by daylight."

Well, would Pomponius, if his father were alive, hear any milder reproofs than that? So it is not enough to write verses in plain everyday language which, if you take it apart, any father would use just as the father on the stage. If from these verses that I now write, or from those that Lucilius used to write, you take away the fixed quantities and rhythms, and if you put the last word first and the first last, you won't pull the poet's limbs to pieces as you would if you took apart the poem, "When dreadful Discord broke the iron-sheathed doors and gates of war."

So much for that! At some other time I shall enquire whether it be true poetry or not. At present I shall consider only whether this kind of writing deserves your dislike. Keen Sulcius and Caprius walk about horribly hoarse and armed with writs, each one of them a great terror to robbers. But if a man lives honestly and with clean hands he can despise them both. However true it may be that you are like the bandits Caelius and Birrus, as long as I am not like Caprius or Sulcius, why are you afraid of me? No shop or bookstand displays my books for vulgar hands (and those of Hermogenes Tigellius) to soil with perspiration. I don't recite my works to anyone but my friends, and to them under compulsion and not everywhere and in the presence of everybody. There are many poets who read their writings in the middle of the Forum, and others during the bath, the enclosed place lending melody to the voice. This pleases the vanity of men who never ask whether they act thus in bad taste or at the wrong time.

"You love to give pain," says someone, "and you do it maliciously."

Where do you find this to throw at me? Is your authority any one of my friends? A man who backbites a friend in his absence, who does not defend him when another finds fault with him, who raises unbridled laughter in company to gain the reputation of being a wit, who invents things he never saw, who cannot keep secrets, that man is a black-hearted slanderer. Avoid him, Roman!

You may often see at dinner groups of four persons on three couches. One of these delights to bespatter in any way he can everybody except the host. Presently he bespatters him too, when he is drunk and when the truth-telling god Liber reveals the hidden secrets of the heart. This man seems to you courteous and polished and frank. If I have laughed because silly Rufillus smells of perfume and Gargonius like a he-goat, do I seem to you to be spiteful and snarling?

If in your presence some mention happened to be made of the thefts of Petillius Capitolinus, you would defend him as is your habit, in your usual way, "Capitolinus has been a comrade and friend of mine from boyhood, and at my request has done me many favors, and I am happy that he lives in the city unmolested. Nevertheless I do wonder how he managed to escape conviction." This is the essence of black malignity, pure rust. Such malice, I promise you as surely as I can promise anything, will be far removed from my pages, but first of all from my heart.

If I speak too freely, with too rough a jest, you will indulgently grant me this privilege. The best of fathers taught me this habit, that by his branding them one by one by examples I might avoid all sorts of mistakes. When he wanted to urge me to live thriftily, frugally and content with what he had provided, he would say, "Don't you see how miserable is the life of Albius' son and how beggarly that of Baius? An urgent warning not to squander your patrimony!" When he wished to deter me from the vulgar love of a mistress, "Don't be like Scetanus!" he said. To keep me from running after faithless wives when I could enjoy a decent amour, he would remark, "The reputation of Trebonius who was caught in the act is not a pretty one. The philosopher may give you reasons as to what it is better to avoid and what to pursue. It is enough for me if I can preserve the custom handed down from my ancestors, so long as you need a guardian to preserve your life and reputation from harm. As soon as years have matured your body and your mind you will swim without cork." Thus by his precepts he moulded my boyhood, and whenever he told me to do something he would say, "Here is your authority for this," and point to a judge on the bench. Or again, if he forbade something, he would say, "Can you doubt that this is dishonorable or inexpedient when so-and-so stands in the blaze of ill repute?"

As a funeral in the neighborhood dispirits sick gluttons and compels them to spare themselves because of the fear of death, so others' disgraces often deter youthful minds from blunders. In accordance with this principle I am free from all vices that bring ruin, and am guilty only of lesser faults, such as you can excuse. It may be that even these may be materially reduced by a maturer age, an honest friend, and my own determination. For when I retire to my couch or go for a walk in the colonnade I do not neglect myself. "This is the truer course." "By doing so I shall live happier." "In this way I shall be a delight to my friends." "This was not very pretty. I hope that I shall not some day, in an unguarded moment, do the like." With my lips shut tight I ponder these things to myself.

When I have some leisure I amuse myself with my papers. This is one of those lesser faults of which I spoke. If you aren't tolerant toward it, a great host of poets—for we are more than half the world—shall come to my rescue and, like the Jews, we will compel you to join our crowd.

I· 5· *My Trip to Brundisium*

Egressum magna

I left great Rome behind me, came to Aricia and lodged in a modest inn. Heliodorus the rhetorician, most learned among the Greeks, was my companion. From there we went to Appius' Forum, a place crammed with boatmen and rascally innkeepers. We took two days on a leisurely trip that better travellers make in one—the Appian Way is less wearying to those who take it slowly. Because of the water which was here most vile, I proclaimed war against my belly, waiting impatiently until my companions had supped. Presently night began to spread her shadows over the earth and to scatter the stars across the heavens. A babel of voices rose, slaves abusing boatmen and boatmen abusing slaves. "Make a stop here!" "That's plenty. You've got three hundred on board, now." We wasted a whole hour paying fares and harnessing the mule. The cursed mosquitoes and frogs in the marsh made sleep impossible, while a boatman and a passenger, soused with flat wine, rivaled one another in singing to their absent mistresses. Finally the passenger became exhausted and dropped off to sleep while the lazy boatman tied the halter to a rock, turned out the mule to graze and lay on his back and snored. It was already dawn before we noticed that the craft was not moving. Then a hot-headed fellow, one of the passengers, jumped from the boat, cut himself a willow cudgel, and clubbed the mule and boatman over the head and sides. Even at that we landed only at ten o'clock to wash our hands and faces in your holy water, Feronia.

After breakfast we crawled along for three miles to arrive at Anxur which lies on a hill that can be seen from afar. Maecenas and Cocceius were to meet us here, excellent fellows, ambassadors on matters of great importance, accustomed to bring together estranged friends. Here I had to annoint my sore eyes with black salve. In the midst of the operation Maecenas and Cocceius arrived, bringing with them Fonteius Capito, a charming gentleman and a close intimate of Antony.

We were delighted to leave Fundi, where Aufidius Luscus was Judge, in amusement at the insignia of his weak-headed clerk—his bordered robe, broad stripe and pan of coals. Wearied with our journey we stopped in the city of the Mamurra's family where we had shelter with Murena and meals with Capito. Next day's sunrise was most welcome, for Plotius and Varius and Vergil met us at Sinuessa. No lovelier souls than these has the world ever produced and none is more obligated than I. What hearty greetings and rejoicings! So long as I am in my right mind there is nothing that I prefer to a delightful friend.

We found shelter in the little inn alongside the bridge as you enter Campania. Here the stewards gave us the usual fuel and salt. Our next stop was Capua, where the mules were relieved of their pack-saddles. Maecenas went off to play. Vergil and I slept, for a game of ball is bad for sore eyes and weak stomachs. Next, we were welcomed by the bountiful provisions in Cocceius' farmhouse which lies outside the inns of Caudium.

My Muse, please recount briefly the battle between the clown Sarmentus and Messius Cicirrus, and tell the ancestry of the two who engaged in the struggle. The illustrious race of Messius is Oscan. The former owner of Sarmentus is still alive. Sprung from such ancestors as these, they joined battle.

Sarmentus began, "I say, you are the picture of a unicorn." We laughed.

"All right," Messius retorted, butting his head.

"What a terrible fellow you would be if the horn hadn't been cut off your forehead! You are threatening enough crippled as you are."

An ugly scar had marred the left side of Messius' hairy forehead. With much cracking of jokes about syphilis and Messius' face, Sarmentus begged him to dance "Cyclops the Shepherd," observing that he wouldn't need a mask or dramatic boots.

Messius had much to say in answer. "Have you kept your vow and presented your chain to the household gods?" he asked. "Though you are a clerk, your mistress's property rights in you are none the less for that!" Finally, "Why did you ever run away? One pound of flour is plenty for a man as skinny and short as you."

It was certainly a jolly supper.

From that place we journeyed straight on to Beneventum where our busy host almost burned down his house while turning some scrawny thrushes on the spit. For the wavering fire, when the piled logs fell apart, spread through the old kitchen and licked the roof-tree. It was a pretty sight to see—famished guests and scared slaves grabbing their supper, and everyone trying to extinguish the flames.

Then on we went until Apulia opened up to me her familiar hills scorched by the sirocco. We could never have come through if a farmhouse near Trivicus had not taken us in for the night. Its smoke brought tears to our eyes, for the hearth burned green boughs, leaves and all. Here, like the great fool I am, I waited until midnight for a lying mistress. Sleep overcame me, however, while I was engaged in thoughts of love, and dreams agitated by dirty images stained my clothes and body.

From there we rolled downhill in carriages for twenty-four miles, to stop the night in a little town which I cannot name in verse but can describe easily by these facts: water, the cheapest thing in the world is sold here, but the bread is easily the best on the road, and the experienced traveller usually heaps up his slaves with it for the trip, because Canusium, built long ago by valiant Diomedes, has not a jugful more water and its bread is full of sand. Here Varius sorrowfully parted from his weeping friends. From this town we came, worn out, to Rubi, for the journey was long and made more difficult by rain.

Next day the weather had cleared but the road was worse, right up to the walls of Barium where there is plenty of fish. Gnatia, built under the frown of the water-nymphs, gave us occasion for laughter and joking, for they wished us to believe that at these sacred thresholds incense melts without fire! Apella the Jew may believe this. I don't, for I have been taught that the gods live a care-free life regardless of mankind, and that if Nature produces a miracle, petulant gods do not send it down from the high dome of heaven.

Brundisium is the end of a long trip—and my paper.

I· 6· *Only a Freedman's Son but Proud of It*

Non quia, Maecenas

No one of all the Lydians that ever inhabited the land of Tuscany is better born that you are, Maecenas. Your ancestors on both your mother's and your father's side were in command of great legions long ago. But you do not, as most people do, turn up your nose at lowly persons like me, the son of a freedman.

You claim, and rightly, that if a man is free-born, it does not matter who his parents are. You express your conviction that long before the reign of Tullius, who was born a slave, many men of no particular ancestry were gentlemen and were honored with high office. You point out that Laevinus, to the contrary, although he was descendant of that famous Valerius by whom haughty Tarquin was driven in flight from his throne, was not a cent more esteemed on that account, even in the people's judgment—and you know what judgment they have, how foolishly they honor the unworthy, are slaves to rumor, and lose themselves in admiring honorary titles and wax images. What, then, is your line of conduct and mine who are so far above the crowd?

I grant that the people would prefer to vote office to Laevinus rather than to the upstart Decius, and that the censor Appius would strike me from the senatorial list if I were not the son of a free-born father. This were right, too, if like the ass in Aesop's fable, I were not satisfied inside my own hide.

Glory, however, binds to the wheels of her chariot and drags behind her both the lowly and the lofty. What did it profit you, Tillius, to resume the rôle that you were forced to lay aside and to become a tribune again? Envy of you has increased, which would be less were you a private citizen. Just as soon as a man has been crazy enough to lace the calf of his leg with black buskins and has dropped the broad stripes down his breast, he immediately hears, "Who is this fellow? Who was his father?" It is just as if you labored under the same delusion as Barrus who wanted to be considered good-looking, and, wherever he went, would excite the curiosity of ladies to enquire in detail what his face, leg, foot, teeth and hair were like. In the same way if a man promises the voters to take charge of the city, the empire, Italy and the temples of the gods, he forces everyone to listen and to ask who his father was and whether he is base-born on his mother's side. Have you, the son of a mere Syrus, Dama, or Dionysius, the effrontery to execute Roman citizens or hand them over to Cadmus the hangman?

"My colleague, Novius," you say, "has his seat in the row behind me, for he is only now what my father was." Do you consider yourself then a Paulus or a Messala? Don't forget that if two hundred carriages and three funerals were to meet in the forum he could make noise enough to drown their horns and trumpets. That is the thing that counts with us.

Now let me come back to myself, the son of a freedman father. Everybody sniffs at me because I am descended from a freedman, because I am often your guest, Maecenas, and because a short while ago I was an officer in command of a Roman legion. This last reason is different from the previous one, for although anyone might perhaps be pardoned for envying me my office, it does not follow that he has the right to begrudge me your friendship, particularly in view of your care in choosing worthy friends who have no ulterior motive. It was not by luck (I am not so fortunate) that I became your friend. No mere accident brought us together. Vergil, that best of friends, and after him Varius, had long since mentioned me to you. The first time I met you I stuttered out a few words, for childish bashfulness made me speechless. I did not tell you that I was high-born nor pretend that I rode about my country place on a pony from Tarentum, but told you the facts about myself. You replied, as usual briefly, and I left. Nine months later you asked me to come again and told me to reckon myself one of your friends. It gives me satisfaction to believe that I pleased a man who discerns between honor and baseness, not on the standard of a father's social position but on my own blameless life and character.

And yet I have my father to thank for all this, if in a character generally sound the blemishes are few and slight (as you might find a mole here and there on a beautiful body), if no man can honestly accuse me of greed or sordidness or debauchery, if my life is clean and harmless and if my friends are devoted to me. Although he was poor and lived on a beggarly little farm, he would not send me to Flavius' school where went the more prominent sons of centurions, their knapsacks and writing tablets swinging from their left arms and their fee of eight coppers coming in each monthly pay-day. He boldly brought his boy to Rome to be taught the subjects that every wealthy man or senator wanted his children to learn. If anyone saw my clothes, and how many slaves attended me, as was proper in the great city, he must have imagined that expense came out of inherited wealth.

He went personally with me, a guardian who could not be bribed, among all my teachers. Is there need of more detail? He kept me clean, which is the foundation of manliness, not only from actual vice but even from the hint of scandal. He was not afraid of someone's saying that he had squandered his money on me even if in the future I had to earn a small salary as an auctioneer, or, like him, as a tax collector. Had that been the case I should not have complained. But as things have developed he deserves from me even more praise and thanks. I can never as long as I am in possession of my faculties regret a father like that.

Therefore I have no intention of protesting, as so many would, by the remark that it is no fault of their's that they had no free-born or famous parents. My way of thinking and speaking differs entirely from theirs. If nature should arrange that after we had reached a certain age we should begin life over again and choose other parents that better flattered our vanity, I, content with those that I have, would not wish for persons distinguished by curule office. Doubtless the world would think me crazy. But you, I feel sure, will believe me a rational person for being unwilling to assume a troublesome burden to which I am not used. If I did assume it I must immediately acquire a larger fortune, make and receive more morning calls, take with me this and that companion, and so never make an excursion into the country or go off by myself. I should then keep a stable of horses, and grooms for them, and maintain a collection of carriages. Under present conditions I may ride as far as Tarentum, if I feel like it, on a bob-tailed mule whose flanks are galled with saddlebags and his back with the rider. No man will call me cheap as he calls you, Tillius, when you, a judge, travel the road to Tibur with five slaves walking behind you, carrying a cooking-pot and wine-basket. So I live more comfortably than you, my dear and famous Senator, in this and thousands of other ways. I go wherever I please, afoot and alone. I inquire the price of vegetables and flour. I often ramble about at evening in the Circus Maximus where the fakirs are. I stand and listen to the fortune-tellers. Then I go home to a meal of scallions, beans and pancakes. Three slaves serve my supper. A marble slab is my table and on it stand two drinking cups, a ladle, a cheap salt-cellar, and an oil bottle and saucer made in Campania. Then to bed, untroubled by the thought that I must rise early in the morning to meet at the statue of Marsyas which is unable to bear the sight of the younger Novius. I stay in bed until nearly ten o'clock. After this I go for a stroll, or else, when I have done some quiet writing or reading as I please, I rub myself down with oil (better than the kind that disgusting Natta filches from the lamps!). About noon, wearied, I go to the bath, avoiding the Campus Martius and its handball. A moderate luncheon, just sufficient to prevent my going all day long on an empty stomach, and I busy myself at home.

That is the daily life of a man freed from the pangs and responsibilities of ambition. In that manner I comfort myself with the idea that I shall live a more happy life than if my grandfather, my father and my uncle had all of them been treasurers.

I· 7 · *King Meets His Match*

proscripti

I imagine that every blear-eyed man and every barber knows the story of the way in which that half-breed Persius paid back the venomous abuse of Rupilius.

Persius, a rich business man at Clazomenae, was engaged in a troublesome lawsuit with King. He was a hard customer and outdid even King in his repulsive manners. He was a daring braggart with a language sharp enough to outdo Sisenna or Barrus at their best.

But about King. They could come to no compromise out

of court. (All nuisances have the same rights as heroes when they meet in deadly fray. Between Hector, Priam's son, and high-souled Achilles the quarrel was mortal. Nothing but the death of either of them could end it, since each was the bravest of the brave. But if two cowards quarrel, or two that are unevenly matched, as happened with Diomede and Lycian Glaucus, the inferior of the two would quit the fight and mollify his adversary by sending presents). To get back, at the time when Brutus was governor of the wealthy province of Asia, this pair, Rupilius and Persius, had a fight. They were like the gladiators Bacchius and Bithus, and rushed eagerly into court, each of them a marvel to behold.

Persius stated his case, to the amusement of the assembly. He complimented Brutus. He complimented his staff. He called Brutus "the bright light of Asia." He called his attendants "stars of good omen." He excepted only King whose arrival he said was like that of "the dog-star, plague of the farmer." He raged on like a winter torrent through a virgin forest.

In reply the man from Praeneste hurled back abuse redolent of the vineyard, like a tough and hardy vinedresser who is often more than a match for the traveller who calls out "Cuckoo!" to him.

However, the Greek Persius, after he had been liberally besprinkled with this Italian vinegar, exclaimed, "Brutus, I beg you, by the great gods! You are in the habit of getting rid of kings. Tell me why don't you murder this King? Believe me, it's your job!"

I· 8· *The Hag Canidia—As Observed by Priapus*

olim truncus eram

Once upon a time I was the trunk of a wild fig-tree, a useless log, when a carpenter, after some doubt as to whether to make me a privy or a Priapus, decided to make me into a god. So a god I am, the greatest deterrent of thieves and birds. My right hand and the red stick projecting from my middle keep the thieves in check, while a branch fastened to the top of my head scares away troublesome birds and keeps them from alighting on the fresh gardens.

In times past slaves contracted with the undertakers to bring to this place the corpses of fellow-slaves hustled out of their cramped quarters in crude boxes. It was the public graveyard for the dregs of society, for Pantolabus the clown and Nomentanus the spendthrift. A boundary mark used to announce a frontage of one thousand feet and a depth of three hundred, and to provide that the burial place should not pass to heirs of any estate.

In these days people live on the Esquiline and find it healthful. They stroll in the sun on the rampart from which one used to catch the depressing sight of ground, sordid with bleached bones. I personally am not so much troubled by the robbers and jackals that formerly frequented this spot as by the witches who torture living souls with their incantations and drugs. I cannot in any way stay or hinder them from gathering bones and noxious herbs under the waning moon's fair face.

I myself have seen Canidia come with her black cloak fastened high, with bare feet and flowing hair, uttering her cries with the elder Sagana. Their pallor made them a horrible sight. They began by tearing up the earth with their finger nails. Then they ripped a black ewe-lamb to pieces with their teeth. The blood was poured into a ditch to evoke the spirits of the dead to give them prophetic answers. They had, in addition, a wooden image and another one of wax. The wooden one was larger so that it could inflict punishment upon the weaker; the waxen one stood in suppliant attitude, as if it were awaiting the death sentence of a slave. One of the witches called upon Hecate, the other upon dread Tisiphone. You could see snakes and hell-hounds straggling about, while the shamefaced moon hid behind the great tombs in order not to look upon such doings.

If I am lying, let my head be fouled by the white droppings of crows, and let Julius and effeminate Pediatia and the rascal Voranus come and piss upon me and defile me with excrement!

Why go into detail? Why tell how the ghosts, speaking responsively with Sagana, uttered dismal and piercing shrieks, how the witches stealthily buried in the ground the beard of a wolf and the tooth of a spotted snake, and how a raging fire blazed forth from the wax image, and how I was horrified at the voices and behaviour of the two demons? But I was a witness not incapable of revenge, for, with the sound of a bursting bladder, my fig-tree buttock popped and split. Off they scampered to the city! You would have had no end of fun seeing Canidia lose her false teeth, and Sagana her tall head-dress, and watching the herbs and the charmed bracelets drop from their arms!

I· 9· *A Morning Stroll*

ibam forte

I happened to be going along the Via Sacra, thinking, as is my wont, on some trifle—I don't remember what—and was entirely absorbed in it, when a man whom I knew only by name ran up to me and took hold of my hand, saying, "How are you, my dearest fellow?"

"Pretty well, all things considered," I answered. "And I hope that all goes well with you." When I saw that he was following me I anticipated him.

"There's nothing I can do for you, is there?"

"Yes! Make my acquaintance. I am a man of letters."

"I shall value you all the more for that," I replied. Wishing very much to be rid of him, I first quickened my pace and then stopped short, whispered something or other into my slave's ear, while perspiration ran down to my feet. "O Bolanus, you lucky man!" I murmured. Meanwhile he prattled on, praising the streets, the city, and when I did not answer, he said:

"You desire awfully to be rid of me. But I shall stick to you. I shall continue to follow you. Where are you bound?"

"There's no need of your being dragged around. I wish to call on someone—you don't know him—he lives far from here—across the Tiber near Caesar's gardens—he's sick in bed."

"My time is my own and I'm not lazy. I'll go all the way with you."

My ears dropped like an abused donkey's when he is overloaded. He began again. "If I really know myself, you will not value the friendship of Viscus or of Varius more than mine. Who can write more verses in a given time than I? Who can dance more beautifully? Even Hermogenes might envy my singing."

Here was my chance to break in. "Is your mother living, or have you no relatives to take care of you?"

"None! I have buried them all."

"How lucky they were! I am the only one left. Finish me! For the hour is come to meet the unhappy fate that the old Sabellan woman foretold of me in my childhood. She shook the lots in her urn and said, 'Neither cruel poison nor an enemy's sword, nor pleurisy, nor cough, nor crippling gout shall destroy this boy. A man who talks too much shall at some time or other finish him. If he is wise let him shun chatterers as soon as he grows up.'"

By this time we had come to Vesta's temple. It was past nine o'clock, and, as luck would have it, he was bonded to appear in Court at that hour under penalty of forfeiting his case.

"Won't you please," said he, "wait a little while to advise me?"

"I'll be hanged if I can stand so long. I know nothing about law. And besides I must hurry, you know where."

"I don't know what to do. Shall I give you up, or my case?"

"Me, I beg you!"

"I cannot," said he, and began to lead the way. As it is difficult to fight with one's master, I followed.

"How do you and Maecenas get on together?" he began again. "A man of few friends and very sound judgment—nobody uses his opportunities more cleverly. You would have a strong supporter who could play second to you if you would introduce your humble servant. Damn it, you could push all of them aside in a minute!"

"You fail to understand the relation between us. There is no house cleaner or freer from such intrigues. It never makes any difference, I tell you, that someone is wealthier or more learned than I. Each of us has his own place."

"Wonderful! I can hardly believe it."

"But it's so!"

"You make me all the more eager for his intimacy."

"You have only to wish for it. Your ability is such that you will successfully storm his citadel. He can be won—that is why he makes the first approach difficult."

"I shall not fail. I'll bribe his slaves. If I'm shut out today, I'll not give up. I'll look for favorable opportunities. I'll meet him in the streets. I'll escort him home. Life's prizes are not to be won without effort."

While all this was happening Aristius Fuscus met us, a dear friend of mine and one who knew him well. We stopped. "Where do you come from?" and "Where are you going?" was asked and answered. I began to pull his toga and to take hold of his unresponsive arm, nodding and winking for him to rescue me. The dirty joker smiled and pretended not to understand. I was raging mad!

"Surely you said that you had something to tell me in private."

"I remember it very well, but another time will do. Today is the thirtieth Sabbath. Do you want to insult the circumcised Jews?"

"I have no religious scruple."

"But I have. I am a bit weaker than you—one of the multitude. Pardon me, I'll tell you some other time."

To think that this should happen to me! The rogue ran away and left me with the knife at my throat!

By chance the plaintiff in the suit met him. "Where are you going, you scoundrel?" he cried in a loud voice. "Will you witness the arrest?" he said to me. I assented. He dragged him to court, both of them shouting, with a crowd about them. So Apollo saved me!

I· 10· *An Answer to Critics*

nempe incomposito dixi

Yes, I did say that the poetry of Lucilius does not run smoothly. What follower of Lucilius is so stupid as not to admit that? But in the same essay I praised him for flogging the city with his wit. When I pay him this tribute I do not grant him all the rest. If I did that I should have to admire the farces of Laberius as beautiful poetry.

It is not enough just to make an audience shake with laughter, although that too has its merit. There must be terseness, that the sense may flow on, unimpeded by words that burden the ears to weariness. There must be a varying style, now grave, now gay, at one time oratorical, at another poetic, at a third witty like that of a man who holds his hands and means more than he says. A jest often decides matters of importance more effectually and happily than seriousness. This was how the men who wrote Old Comedy kept their ground, and in this we should imitate them. They are the authors whom that fop Hermogenes has never read, nor that monkey whose one achievement is to drone out the poems of Calvus and Catullus.

"But he did a wonderful thing when he mingled Greek phraseology with his Latin."

You pedantic blockhead! How can you imagine it to be difficult or marvellous to do what Pitholaus of Rhodes did?

"But language nicely blended of the two improves the flavor just as when you blend Falernian with Chian wine."

Only in writing poetry? I ask you the question directly. Or does the same hold true when you are pleading a difficult case like that of Petillius? I suppose you would drop your country and its Father Latinus, and, while Pedius

Publicola and Corvinus were doing their utmost to plead their cases in pure Latin, you would interlard your native tongue with foreign words like a bilingual Canusian? Even I, although I was born on this side of the sea, once had the idea of writing Greek jingles, but Romulus himself appeared to me in the early morning hours when dreams are true, and forbade me, with the observation, "It would be as silly as carrying timber into a forest if you were to join the crowded ranks of those who write Greek."

So while the bombastic poet of the Alps murders Memnon, and calls the sources of the Rhine "muddy," I play around with trifles. Mine are not poems which can be read in the temple for Tarpa's criticism, nor plays which are good for a run on the theatrical stage. You, Fundanius, are the only one of our contemporary poets who can delight us with the conversation of the artful courtesan or of Davus as he tricks old Chremes. Pollio sings in iambic verse of the deeds of kings. Gifted Varius, in a style all his own, weaves the web of the noble Epic. The Muses that delight in rural loveliness have granted grace and charm to Vergil. Satire, which Varro, who comes from the banks of the Atax, and some other persons had unsuccessfully attempted, was what I could write better than they, but not so well as the originator. I am not the man to take from Lucilius' famous head the laurel crown placed there by the world's applause.

But I did say "that his was a muddy stream which often carried with it more that you wanted to omit than retain."

I'll leave it to you—you're a scholar. Don't you find anything in Homer which calls for criticism? Does kindly Lucilius himself ask for no change in the dramatist Accius? Does he not ridicule Ennius' poetry as undignified? He does not thereby consider himself greater than those whom he criticizes. What, then, should prevent me, as I read the works of Lucilius, from asking questions? Was it some lack in him or was it the difficulty of his subject that kept his verses from being polished? Is it for the same reason that they did not run as smoothly as those of a man who was merely satisfied with putting his ideas into correct hexameters and who was proud of having written two hundred lines every day before lunch and a like number after dinner? That was the style of the Etruscan Cassius, who was like a stream in flood, and who, as they say, was burned on a funeral pyre made of his own books in their covers.

We may admit, then, that Lucilius was a kindly and gracious writer, that at the same time he was more polished than could be expected of the inventor of a new literary style which the Greeks had never tried, and that he was superior to the crowd of early poets. But even Lucilius, if destiny had ordained his birth in our generation, would smooth out much of what he had written, would prune away everything that transgressed the bounds of perfection, and, as he worked at his poetry, would often have scratched his head and bitten his nails to the quick.

You must make frequent use of the eraser if you want to write something that deserves a second reading. You must not be concerned for the admiration of the multitude, but must be satisfied with readers who are discriminating but few. Certainly you are not so stupid as to want your poetry to be used as textbooks in cheap schools. Not I! It is sufficient for me that the better citizens applaud. I don't care about the rest, as the courageous Arbuscula said when the audience hissed her off the stage. Shall that louse Pantilius move me? Shall I suffer because, forsooth, Demetrius twits me behind my back, or because Fannius, boon companion of Hermogenes Tigellius, wants to wound me? Just let Plotius and Varius, Maecenas and Vergil, Valgius and Octavius and noble Fuscus approve these essays! Let the brothers Viscus approve them! Without flattery I may mention you, Pollio, and you and your brother, Messala, as well as you, Bibulus, Servius, and frankly generous Furnius. Also many more, connoisseurs and friends of mine, whom I will not mention here! I only wish that these essays, such as they are, may give those men pleasure, and I should be sorry if their pleasure is less than I hope. As for you, Demetrius and Tigellius, you go whine among the sofas of your lady admirers!

Go instantly, boy, and add this epilogue to my little book.

II · 1 · *What Is a Satirist to Do?*

sunt quibus in satira

HORACE. Some people think my satire is too cutting and goes entirely too far. Others think that all my poetry lacks vigor and that you could turn out verses as good as mine at the rate of a thousand a day. Give me your advice, Trebatius. Tell me what to do, Trebatius.

TREBATIUS. Nothing.

HORACE. You mean stop writing poetry completely?

TREBATIUS. Yes.

HORACE. Damned, if that isn't the best advice! Only I can't get to sleep.

TREBATIUS. Cure for insomnia: rub yourself with oil, swim the Tiber three times, take plenty of good wine at night. If you *must* write, have the courage to take as your subject the deeds of invincible Caesar. You will get ample pay for your trouble.

HORACE. I would be glad to do so, my dear sir, but I haven't the ability. It isn't everybody who can describe armies bristling with spears, Gauls breaking their lances and dying, or Parthians slipping wounded from their horses.

TREBATIUS. Well, you might describe him as a courageous, fair man in the style in which shrewd Lucilius portrayed Scipio.

HORACE. When the proper time comes I will run true to form. Unless the time is ripe no words of Horace will gain Caesar's attention. Like a spirited horse, if you stroke him the wrong way he will kick back at you to protect himself.

TREBATIUS. How much better this would be than to direct biting poetry against "Pantolabus the clown and Nomentanus the spendthrift." When you write that way you make everybody look out for himself and dislike you even though you have not touched him.

HORACE. What shall I do? Milonius starts dancing the minute wine has gone to his head and he sees double. Castor likes horses, his twin brother, boxers. There are as many preferences as there are men. I amuse myself as Lucilius did, by stringing together verses that will scan, and he was a better man than either of us. He used to entrust his intimate thoughts to his pages as if they were faithful friends and never took refuge anywhere else, regardless of success or failure. That's why the old poet's life is as clear to us as a picture painted on a votive tablet. I follow in his footsteps, being, as I am, either a Lucanian or an Apulian. (I can't tell which, for the settlers of Venusia run their ploughs on the borders of both countries—according to history, they were sent there when the Sabellians were turned out so that an enemy might not discover the place undefended and attack Roman territory if either Apulia or impetuous Lucania should threaten war.) But my pen will never attack any person. It will serve as my defense like a sheathed sword. Why should I try to draw it as long as I am safe from robbers' attacks?

O Thou, Jupiter, my father and my king, may my weapon rust where it abides and may no man injure me, a lover of peace! The man who incites me shall rue it, and as a marked man he shall be sung through the whole city. ("Better leave me alone!" is my cry).

When Cervius is offended he threatens his enemies with

the Law and the jurors' urn. Canidia reserves the poison of Albucius for her enemies. Turius' weapon is a heavy sentence if you enter court when he is on the jury. Every living thing terrifies those whom he fears with the weapon in which he is strongest. Nature powerfully compels him to do this, as we may conclude in the following way. A wolf attacks with teeth, a bull, with horns. What else is this but instinct? Entrust to the tender mercies of prodigal Scaeva his mother who has already lived too long. His loyal son's hand will commit no crime against her. Surprising? About as much so as a wolf not attacking with his hoofs or an ox with his teeth. No, the old lady will pass away from a dose of deadly hemlock put in poisoned honey.

But I must be brief. I am determined to write, no matter whether a peaceful old age awaits me, or death is now hovering over me with his sable wings, whether I am rich or poor, whether I am living in Rome, or, by unfortunate destiny, in exile.

TREBATIUS. My son, you won't live long I'm afraid. One of your influential friends is going to wither you with a frost.

HORACE. What? When Lucilius courageously invented the composition of this type of poetry and tore the mask from the faces of men who presented a fair front to the world but were inwardly corrupt, did his wit insult Laelius, or Scipio, who well deserved the title he gained in conquering Carthage? Were they hurt because Metellus was lashed or Lupus satirized? Yet he passed criticism upon aristocrats and populace alike. As a matter of fact, he had no mercy on anything but Manliness and its friends. When Scipio with his courage, Laelius with his mellow wisdom had retired from public life, they used to put formalities aside and joke with him while the cook was preparing their simple vegetable dinner. Whatever I may be, though I have not the social prestige nor the intelligence of Lucilius, even envious folk must admit that I have lived on friendly terms with the great, and in trying to set their tooth into some weakness of mine they will strike upon something hard. Do you, learned Trebatius, disagree?

TREBATIUS. No exception taken. Nevertheless, let me warn you not to get into trouble from ignorance of the Law. The courts take cognizance of and pass judgment upon any person writing ill of another.

HORACE. "Ill?" Certainly. But if they are good, if Caesar likes them, and if you merely criticize a man who deserves it while keeping yourself free from blame?

TREBATIUS. The Court will smile and you will be dismissed.

II· 2· *The Simple Life*

quae Virtus et quanta

Gentlemen, my topic for your instruction is the value of frugal living. It is not an original essay with me but comprises the teaching of the peasant Ofellus, an untrained natural philosopher. You will not hear this lecture when the gleaming of silver plate and polished tables dazzle the eye with surface glitter, and the mind, being accustomed to deceitful appearances, loses its sense of discrimination. Instead we shall discuss the subject here and now before dinner.

Why all this?

I will try to give you the answer. No judge who has been bribed weighs the facts honestly. When you come in from hunting rabbits or are wearied from training a horse, or when you play a fast game of ball (if you take to Greek games rather than the soldierly exercises of Rome) where interest in the game makes you forget its exertion, or when the game of quoits attracts you (if it does, then hurl the quoit through the yielding air)—in short, when vigorous exercise has knocked the nonsense out of you and you are thirsty and hungry, then reject if you can plain food and refuse to drink honey-wine unless the honey comes from Hymettus and the wine from Falernum!

If your steward is away, or the sea is too rough for fishing, cravings within you will be quieted with a little bread and salt. How does this come about? Most of the pleasure is in yourself, not in the odor of expensive food. Hard exercise is the best sauce. The fat, sallow gourmand cannot enjoy oysters, scar, or imported lagois. Of course, if peacock were served, I could hardly tear out of you the appetite that makes you prefer this tongue-tickler to a barnyard hen. You are spoiled by mere looks. What's the difference if a fowl is rare and expensive and makes a marvelous display with its colored tail? You don't eat the feathers that you admire, do you? Does the bird have the same striking appearance after it has been cooked? Since the meat of one fowl is just as good as the other, it is clear that you are taken in by the difference in their external appearance.

So far, so good! By what instinct can you tell whether the pike that lies here with its mouth open was caught in the Tiber or in the sea, in the stretch between the bridges, or at the mouth of the Tuscan river? It is lunatic for you to praise a three-pound mullet when you must serve it in small portions. Again, the surface appearance influences you. Moreover, you are inconsistent in disliking pike when they run *large*. In nature, the pike is large, the mullet small. It seldom happens that a hungry stomach disdains common victuals. A belly big enough for a voracious Harpy cries, "If only I can see something lying full length on an enormous platter!" Oh, ye desert winds, come and rot the dainties of such gourmets! Perhaps that remark was unnecessary. A boar and turbot, however fresh, are spoiled for a jaded appetite that is digusted at the food with which it is sated and turns gladly to radishes and pickles.

Plain fare is not yet wholly absent from the feasts of princes. Even today there is still a place on the menu for ordinary eggs and black olives. Not so long ago the dinners of Gallonius the auctioneer became unpleasantly notorious because sturgeon was served. The turbot in that day was untouched (there were just as many of them in the sea) and the stork was secure on her nest, until the prestige of a judge taught you to eat them. If a man with like prestige should announce today that roasted sea gulls are delicious, the Roman youth, ever ready to learn the wrong lesson, would acquiesce.

Ofellus used to distinguish between cheap and simple living. It is foolish to escape the one merely to run into the other. Avidienus, who deserved the nickname *Scavenger*, eats five-year-old olives and wild cherries, he won't serve wine until it has soured, and you can't stand the smell of his oil. Even in formal clothes when he celebrates a wedding, a birthday, or another holiday, he puts his oil on his salad drop by drop from a cruet that holds two pounds, and is liberal only with his cheap vinegar.

What standard of living, then, should the sensible person adopt, and which of the two lines should he follow? As the saying goes, "A wolf is on one side, a dog on the other." He will be decent enough not to offend by his meanness.

His method will not go to extremes. He will not be rough when he gives orders to his slaves, as old Albucius is, but he will not, like easy-going Naevius, let them serve greasy water to his guests. That is going too far!

I pass now to the benefits of a simple diet. The most important of these is good health. You will understand how unwholesome an assortment of dishes is when you recall how lightly a simple meal rested on your stomach in former days. When you have mixed boiled and roast foods, thrushes and shell-fish, sweet turns sour and your liver rebels. Notice how pale guests are when they rise from a banquet composed of a perplexing variety of dishes. Moreover, it is not alone the body which suffers from the indulgence of the day before, but the mind too is depressed and, instead of soaring, flies near the ground. On the contrary, the man who lives plainly wastes no time at his repast, and, after his refreshment, takes a nap and wakes thoroughly fit for his work. He will indulge himself upon occasion when a holiday comes, or if he is out of health and wishes to restore his body to normal, or when old age comes on and demands that he be more indulgent to himself in his eating and drinking. In your case, gentlemen, what safeguard have you against sickness or age if you indulge yourself in your youth and vigor? In the good old days people preferred wild boar that was high, not because they had no sense of smell, but, I fancy, because it was more proper for a guest who might drop in later to eat it when it was over-ripe than for the greedy host to dispose of it when it was fresh. If only I had lived when the world was young, with heroes like that!

You value, I presume, reputation—a good name which falls on the human ear more pleasantly than music? Enormous turbots, enormous dishes mean enormous ill repute, enormous expense. In addition, you will have a disapproving uncle, displeased neighbors, dissatisfaction with yourself, the unsatisfied longing for death when you no longer have five cents with which to buy a rope.

"Trausius is the man you should lecture to. I have a large income, as much money as three kings."

Well and good. Have you no better way of spending your surplus? Why are deserving people in want while you have abundance? Why are the ancient temples of the gods going to wrack and ruin? Why, you reprobate, don't you spend something of your vast store for your beloved country? Doubtless you are the only man to whom reverses will never come! Oh, what a laughing-stock you will someday be to your enemies! Of two given men, which will better endure the vicissitudes of life, one weakened mentally and physically with wealth, or the other who is satisfied with little, and who, in fear of what the future may bring, wisely prepares for war in time of peace?

You will have more confidence in the above arguments if I say that I remember, as a little boy, that this man Ofellus lived as moderately off his wealth as he does now when it has been reduced. You may see the sturdy farmer with his bullock and his sons laboring for hire on land once his own. He tells his own story.

"Only under exceptional circumstances did I ever have anything to eat on a work day except vegetables and a hock of smoked pork. Now and then, when an old friend visited me or a neighbor came in on a rainy day when work was impossible, we had a good time. We had a meal of a hen or a kid (not of fish bought in the city) and later enjoyed a dessert of a bunch of raisins, nuts and figs. Then we enjoyed drinking, without any regulation save not to drink to excess. We prayed that Ceres would give us a fine stand of wheat, and in the libation we forgot our cares. Let Fortune rage as she will, she cannot deprive me of all this. In what way, my sons, are we worse off since this new landlord came? Nature has made neither him nor me nor anyone else really the owner of the land. He drove us out, but his prodigality or his ignorance of the subtleties of the law will do the same for him. Even if this does not happen, an heir who is more competent will finally turn him out.

This property now goes under the name of Umbrenus. It used to be called Ofellus'. It will really never belong to anybody, but will grow its crops now for me, and presently for others. So, live a courageous life, my sons, and if things go against you, meet them undaunted."

II · 3: *This Lunatic World*

sic raro scribis

DAMASIPPUS. You write so seldom that you don't ask for clean paper four times a year. You unravel whatever you write, dissatisfied with yourself for producing nothing of value in spite of plenty. How is it going to end? You say that you ran away here from the holiday merriment. Since you are so serious then read me something to bear out your promise. Go ahead! You have nothing? Don't blame your innocent pens. Don't pound the wall—it must have been born under the displeasure of gods and poets. Your whole attitude suggested that you were about to perform many brilliant feats when you had the leisure and were safe under the comfortable roof of your little villa. What was the point of carrying into the country that tight bundle of books, those wonderful companions, Plato, Menander, Eupolis and Archilochus? Is your intention to appease envy by withholding from manliness the protection of your poetry? If so, you will deserve the contempt of your friends. Don't yield to that alluring witch, Laziness, or else be prepared to surrender, with such composure as you may, all that you have won in your better moments.

HORACE. For your good advice, Damasippus, the gods and goddesses give you—a barber! How is it that you know me so well?

DAMASIPPUS. Ever since I lost my fortune in the market and was turned out of my own business, I have minded the business of others. Time was when I loved to investigate the brass vessel in which crafty Sisyphus had washed his feet, whether a statue was unskillfully carved, or a casting more crudely done than it should be. As an expert I fixed the price of such a statue at a hundred thousand sesterces. I was the only man who knew how to buy gardens and fine houses at bargain prices. The crowds, therefore, that hang about auctions nicknamed me "Mercury's Pet."

HORACE. I am well aware of that, and I'm surprised to see you cured of that complaint.

DAMASIPPUS. It's astonishing, but a new complaint drove out the old one, as often happens when a headache or a stitch in the side becomes a stomachache, or when a drowsy patient wakes from his fit and, like a boxer, attacks his doctor.

HORACE. As long as you do nothing like that, you may do what you will.

DAMASIPPUS. My dear Sir, don't make any mistake about it. You too are mad. So is nearly everybody else, if there is any truth in what Stertinius is always saying. I faithfully took over these wonderful lessons from him, that day when he comforted me and told me to grow a philosopher's beard and sent me home from the Fabrician bridge with a will to live. For after my failure in business, when I meant to wrap my head in my cloak and throw myself into the river, he stood near me as if sent by the gods and said: (STERTINIUS) Don't be a fool. It is a false shame that tortures you. In a madman's world you are afraid of being thought mad. First of all, I ask you, what is it to be mad? If madness turns out to be peculiar to you, I will say nothing to deter you from dying bravely. The school and sect of Chrysippus affirms that anyone is mad who is driven blindly on by lamentable folly and ignorance. This applies to whole peoples and to great kings—in fact, to all except the wise man. Next let me point out that all who have branded you as "mad" are quite as mad as you. When men are lost in the woods, through some blunder one wanders this way and another that; but all are lost, though their blunder takes them in different directions. In this fashion think yourself mad, and remember that the man who laughs at you has a tail pinned to his own coat, too. There is one kind of fool who is afraid when there is nothing to fear, who complains that he has fires and rocks and rivers to contend with, when he is on an open prairie. There is another kind of person, very different from this one, but just as foolish, who runs headlong through fire and flood. His doting mother, his devoted sister, his father, his wife and all his relatives call to him, "Look out for that deep ditch, or that tall cliff!" But he will no more listen than the drunken actor Fufius did when he really fell asleep in the rôle of Ilione, though not a single Catienus, but twelve hundred of them shouted his cue, "Help me, mother!" I will show you that the whole crowd is mad with this kind of madness.

Damasippus is mad about buying ancient sculpture. Do you think that the man who lends Damasippus the money to buy them is mad too? Perhaps. But suppose I should say to you, "Here is some money. You need never return it"—would you be mad to accept it? Or wouldn't you be madder still if you declined to take what generous Mercury offers? Draw on the banker Nerius for ten thousand. It wouldn't be enough. Bind yourself, in addition, with legal documents drawn up by Cicuta, who knows all about the knotty points of law. Bind yourself in a thousand ways. The hardened debtor, like Proteus, will escape you just the same. When you drag him to court he will laugh at your expense; at his pleasure he will turn into a boar or a bird or a stone or possibly a tree. If bad management is a sign of madness, and good management a sign of sanity, the brain of Perillius is far crazier when he bids you accept money that you can never repay.

Now, dear sir, please straighten out your toga and listen. Whoever is pale from following an unworthy ambition or from love of money, whoever flushes because he desires luxuries, is darkly superstitious, or has some other mental disorder—come closer, one and all, while I prove to you that you are mad.

The largest doses of hellebore must be given to the avaricious. I am not so sure that philosophy doesn't intend the whole store of Anticyra for them. Staberius in his will ordered his heirs to engrave on his tomb the amount of his fortune, and said that if they failed to do so they must put on a show of a hundred pairs of gladiators for the people, provide a public dinner as Arrius would direct, and distribute the entire African wheat crop. "Don't censure me," he said, "regardless whether I am wrong or right in so ordering." What was in his mind when he willed that his heirs should carve upon his tomb the size of his fortune? During his life he considered poverty the worst of sins and labored industriously to escape it. Had he died poorer by a penny, he would have thought himself so much the more culpable. For all else—valor, a good name, glory, everything in heaven and earth—is secondary to the charm of riches. The man who makes a fortune is the man who will be famous, brave and just. Wise, too? Surely, and a king, and anything else he desires to be. Staberius hoped that his wealth would greatly add to his fame, as if it were some glory he had won. Did Aristippus the Greek resemble him? When this man was crossing the Libyan desert, he ordered his slaves to throw away his gold, because the burden of its weight compelled them to travel too slowly. Of these two which is the madder?

It 's a poor illustration that settles one dispute by starting another! If some one should buy lyres and, as soon as he had bought them, pile them together, without the least interest in the lyre or in any kind of music, if a man were to buy shoemakers' knives and lasts without being a cobbler, and sails for his vessel without being a trader, everybody would say rightly that he was delirious. How does he who stores up silver and gold differ from such men as these? When it is stored, he does not know how to use it, and fears to touch it, as if it were devoted to the gods.

If a man owned a great store of wheat, armed himself with a big stick, and kept constant watch over it, and although he was hungry did not dare to touch a grain of it, but fed himself instead upon bitter herbs; if he had in his cellar a thousand jars (well, that's nothing, say three hundred thousand) of old Chian and Falernian, and drank nothing but mere sour wine; again, if when he, nearing eighty, should lie upon straw, though he had plenty of bedclothes growing old and moth-eaten in his wardrobe, doubtless he would seem mad to only a few, because most men are tossed about by the same malady. You God-forsaken old man! Are you guarding your wine because you fear that you yourself will come to want, or that a son or a freedman heir will drink it up? How little will each day deduct from your capital, if you begin to pour better oil on your salads and on your hair which is uncombed and foul with dandruff? If the little you use is enough for you, why do you perjure yourself, steal, plunder everything and everybody? Oh no, you are not mad!

If you were to start throwing stones at people, and at the slaves you bought with your own money, every child would call you crazy. When you hang your wife and poison your mother, are you sound in the head? Why, yes! You never did this at Argos, or murdered your mother with a dagger, as mad Orestes did. Or do you suppose that he became mad after he killed his mother, and that the wicked Furies had not driven him out of his mind before he sank his dagger in his mother's neck? No! From the moment that Orestes was considered crazy, of unsound mind, he certainly did nothing that you can blame him for. He did not dare to use his sword on Pylades or his sister Electra, but was content to call them names—her a Fury, and him by some other name that his melancholy suggested.

Opimius, poor for all his hoard of silver and gold, drank Veientine wine from Campanian ware on holidays, and flat wine with a ladle on ordinary days. He was once overtaken by a drunken stupor so profound that his heir began rummaging delightedly among his coffers and trying his keys. His physician, who was a very resourceful man and also a faithful friend, brought him to in this way. He told them to place a table near him, empty some bags of coin on it and begin to count it. In that way he revived him. Then he said:

"If you don't take care of your money, your greedy heir will immediately run off with it."

"And I still living?"

"If you want to live, then do this."

"What?"

"Your blood will fail you, weak as you are, unless you give your failing stomach something stimulating. Do you hesitate? Come now! Take this little cup of rice gruel."

"How much did it cost?"

"A trifle."

"How much, really?"

"Eight cents."

"Ah, me! What does it matter whether I die of disease or of robbery and plunder?"

HORACE. Well, then, who is *sane*?

DAMASIPPUS. The man who is not a fool.

HORACE. How about the greedy man?

DAMASIPPUS. He is both a fool and a madman.

HORACE. Well then, if a man is not greedy, does it necessarily follow that he is sane?

DAMASIPPUS. By no means.

HORACE. Why so, my dear Stoic?

DAMASIPPUS. I will tell you. Suppose Craterus says, "This patient is not dyspeptic." Is he therefore well, and may he leave his bed? The doctor will forbid it, for lungs or kidneys may be seriously affected. A man is neither a perjurer nor a miser. Let him give a pig as thank-offering to the kind Lares! But he is ambitious and presumptuous. Let him take ship to Anticyra! What is the difference between throwing into the abyss all that you possess, and failing to use what you have been at pains to get?

It is said that Servius Oppidius, who was reckoned rich in his time, divided two farms at Canusium between his two sons, and when he was dying called his boys to his bed and addressed them thus, "When you were young, I used to see you, Aulus, carrying dice and nuts in a loose fold of your toga, giving them away and gambling with them; and you, Tiberius, counting them and anxiously hiding them away in corners. I have been afraid ever since then that two different kinds of madness might possess you, that one of you might be like Nomentanus and the other like Cicuta. Therefore I beg you both by the gods that one of you make no less, and the other of you make no more, than what your father and your common sense may prescribe as being enough for you. Lest ambition tickle you, I will bind you under oath that whichever of you becomes aedile or praetor shall forfeit his legacy and be accursed. You would waste your wealth in donations of peas, beans and lupines, for the sake of strutting in the Circus or having a statue of bronze erected to you. And meanwhile, lunatics, you would be stripped of your lands and of the money that your father left you. And all for what? So that you may get the applause that Agrippa receives—like the cunning fox who acts the part of a lion!"

Or take another example.

"O son of Atreus, why do you forbid us to think of burying Ajax?"

"Because I'm King."

"I am a commoner, so I make no further inquiry."

"My order is reasonable. However, if anyone thinks me unreasonable I will permit him to speak his mind with impunity."

"Your Supreme Majesty! May the gods grant that when Troy is taken you may bring your ships safe home! You mean that I may now ask questions, and you will answer?"

"Ask!"

"Why is it that Ajax, who for bravery was second only to Achilles, and who so often has won renown by saving the Greeks, lies unburied? Is it that Priam's people, and Priam himself, may exult in that man's lacking burial, through whom so many Trojan youths were bereft of burial in their native land?"

"Why, he ran amuck and slew a thousand sheep, yelling that he was destroying the great Ulysses, Menelaus, and myself."

"Yes, but you yourself in Aulis substituted at the altar your sweet daughter for a heifer. You strewed sacrificial flour on her head. Were *you* in your senses, you brute?"

"What's the point?"

"Well, what did mad Ajax do when he cut down the flock with his sword? He avoided harming his wife and child. He called down many curses on the sons of Atreus, but he did not lift his hand against Teucer or even against Ulysses himself."

"But I, in order to rescue my ships which were stranded on a lee shore, very wisely sought to appease the gods with blood."

"Yes, madman, with blood of your own child."

"'Own child' yes! 'Madman' no!"

Whoever has conceptions wide of the truth and distorted by passion must be considered mad. It doesn't matter whether he goes wrong through folly or through rage. Ajax is out of his mind when he kills the innocent lambs. When you "very wisely" commit a crime to gain empty titles, are you in possession of your senses? Is your heart pure when it seethes with ambition? If one were to take delight in carrying around a cosseted lamb, dressing it up like his own daughter, providing it with maids and money, calling it girls' pet names, and planning to make it the wife of a sturdy husband, the Judge by order of the courts would take from him the control of his property, and he would be put in the keeping of his relatives who were still in possession of their wits. Tell me! If a man sacrifices to the gods his daughter in place of a dumb animal, would you say that he is of sound mind? Don't admit it! Where folly confounds a man's judgment as to the value of things, there is the height of madness!

Impious people, too, are raging mad. Bellona, who delights in gory deeds, has thunder-struck him whom a glittering reputation takes captive.

The third type of madness is extravagance (its votary, Nomentanus), for reason will demonstrate that spendthrifts are both fools and madmen. Take the fellow who, the moment he received his patrimony of a thousand talents, proclaimed that the fishmonger, the fruiterer, the poultry man, the perfumer, the godless crowd of Vicus Tuscus, the sausage man and buffoons, the meat market with the whole of Velabrum, should come to his house next morning. They came in crowds, of course. A hanger-on spoke:

"Everything that I or these people have at home is yours,

sir, I assure you. Order it today or tomorrow as you please."

This was the kindly youth's answer:

"You put on hunting boots and spend the night in the snow of Lucania in order that I may have wild boar for supper. You scour the wintry seas for fish. I am an indolent chap and don't deserve to own all this fortune. You take it. Here is a million for you. Here's the same for you. Here's three million for you—your wife runs out of the house when she is called at midnight."

Aesopus' son, the actor, dissolved in vinegar a precious pearl that he took from Metella's ear, because, forsooth, he wished to drink down a million. Was he any wiser than if he had flung this same amount into a swift river or into the sewer? The sons of Quintus Arrius, a pair of notorious brothers, twins in profligacy, trifling and base desires, used to breakfast on nightingales bought at an enormous price. In which group do they belong? In the white column as sane, or in the black as mad?

If a grown-up man should find his amusement in building houses of cards, harnessing mice to a toy cart, playing at odd-and-even, or riding a hobby horse, he would be a victim of madness. Common sense will tell you that being in love is even more childish than that. There isn't any difference between playing in the dirt, as you did when you were three years old, or crying your heart out for love of a harlot. Tell me, will you act as Polemon in the story did when he was converted—throw away the symbols of your disease, leg bandages, armlets, muffler? As he was returning drunk from some party, he listened to the words of the sober Teacher and shamefacedly pulled the festal wreath from his head. Offer apples to a peevish boy and he refuses them. "Please take them, little fellow." "No!" Don't offer them and he'll yearn for them. How does the lover who has had the door shut in his face differ from the peevish boy? He debates with himself whether or not to go back to her house without being invited and hangs doubtfully in front of the door he dislikes.

To quote from the play, "Shall I not go to her now when she invites me of her own accord, or shall I consider putting an end to all this heartache? She did shut the door on me. Now she invites me again. Shall I go back? No, not if she begged me!" The lover's slave is the wiser of the two. He says, "Sir, that which has neither method nor sense cannot be dealt with in logical reason. Love always leads to quarrels, and afterwards to reconciliation. If anyone should try to get to the bottom of these things, which are as fickle as the weather, and go up and down by chance, he would get no further than if he were to be a lunatic by reason and rule."

When you shoot apple seeds at the ceiling and are delighted when you have the good luck to hit, are you sane? When you babble baby-talk from your aged palate, are you less childish than the youngster who builds card houses? Add murder to folly, and stir the fire with your sword! When the other day Marcius stabbed Hellas and then threw himself over a precipice, was he crazy? Will you acquit the man of the charge of mental disorder and find him guilty of crime, calling, as people do, the same things different names?

There was a certain old freedman who used to fast and wash his hands and run about the street-crossings and pray thus to the Lares there, "Rescue me (it is such a little thing to do), rescue me from death! Surely this is easy for the gods to grant." He had perfectly good ears and eyes, but his master, unless he wanted to risk a law-suit, would not have guaranteed his *mind* when he sold him. This crowd, too, Chrysippus includes in the category of lunatics.

"O Jupiter, who givest and takest away heavy afflictions," cries the mother of the child who has been lying ill for five months, "if he recovers from his malaria, he will stand naked in the Tiber on the early morning of the Holy Day." So if Nature or the doctor save the boy from the brink of the abyss, his silly mother will set him on the cold bank, bring back his fever and kill him. What is the matter with *her* mind? Fear of the gods."

Thus Stertinius, the eighth wise man, armed me, his friend. Consequently I shall never again be called a madman without being able to defend myself. Anyone who says I am crazy shall hear as much from me and shall learn to look into the wallet on his own back, about which he is so little aware.

HORACE. My dear Stoic, I hope you sell everything at greater profit than you did before you went bankrupt. Tell me this. In what particular way, since there is more than one, do you think that I appear crazy? I seem to myself quite sane.

DAMASIPPUS. Does even Agave, as she carries in her hands the head of her poor son that she has cut off, seem to herself a raving maniac?

HORACE. I admit, to be frank, that I am a fool—and mad, too. Make only this clear to me: with what particular mental failing do you think me afflicted?

DAMASIPPUS. All right, I will. First of all, in the matter of physique. You imitate tall people, although from the crown of your head to the sole of your foot you are a puny midget. And yet you are the same man who pokes fun at the energetic carriage of Turbo the gladiator as too great for his body. In what respect are you less absurd than he? Do you think that whatever Maecenas does is right for you to do, although you are so unlike him and so much his inferior? While their mother was absent some little frogs were crushed under a calf's foot. When one of them had made his escape he told his mother what a huge beast had crushed his brothers to death. She asked how big it was. "As big as this?," puffing herself up. "Half again as big." "What, so big?" As she puffed herself up more and more, he said: "If you puff until you burst you won't be as big." This story hits pretty close to you.

In the second place, your poetry. This is like fuel to the fire. If any man ever wrote poetry when sane, then you are sane! I say nothing about your terrible ravings—

HORACE. Stop it!

DAMASIPPUS. —about your living beyond your means—

HORACE. Mind your own business, Damasippus!

DAMASIPPUS. —those thousand passions for girls and boys—

HORACE. O my lunatic superior, have mercy, I pray you, on your lowly follower!

II· 4· *Lecture-Notes on Food*

unde et quo Catius

"Where do you come from, Catius? Where are you going?"

I can't stop. I want to set down some new precepts that will be an improvement on Pythagoras and Socrates—the man who was accused by Anytus, you know—and the learned Plato.

"It's all my fault for interrupting you at such an inconvenient time. I hope you'll excuse me. If you lose any of your ideas they'll soon come back. Your memory, whether natural or acquired, is simply marvelous."

I was just thinking how to keep all these precepts, for they were nice points and handled in fine style.

"Tell me the name of the teacher and whether he is a Roman or a foreigner."

I will repeat the precepts as I remember them, but without the author's name.

Remember to serve only eggs that are oval. They are better-flavored and whiter than the round ones; also they are firmer in texture and contain the yolk of the male bird.

Cabbage grown on dry land is sweeter than that grown in gardens near the city. Nothing is more insipid than stuff grown in a garden that has too much watering.

If a guest arrives unexpectedly in the evening, you will know what to do with a tough fowl to keep it from spoiling his appetite. Plunge it into Falernian wine mixed with water. That will make it tender.

Mushrooms that grow in the meadow are best; those grown elsewhere are not safe for eating.

The man who ends his dinner with black mulberries that he has picked from the trees before the sun is hot will keep his health through the summer.

Aufidius used to mix honey with strong Falernian. That was a mistake, for on an empty stomach you should take only something mild. It's better to begin with a sip of mild mead.

If you are constipated, limpet and common shell-fish with small-leaved sorrel will relieve you; but take them with white wine of Cos.

Slippery shell-fish are best caught when the moon is crescent, but you will not find the choicest kind in all waters. The Lucrine mussel is better than the Baian cockle. The best oysters come from Circeii; the best sea-urchins, from Misenum. Mild Tarentum boasts the biggest scallops.

No one should consider himself a connoisseur of dining until he has thoroughly learned the subtle theory of flavors. It is not enough to sweep up a mess of fish from the stall of a high-priced fish-dealer without knowing which are best for boiling, and which, if you broil them, even a sated guest will be tempted to eat.

The epicure who would avoid tasteless meat should see to it that the wild boar, which bends the round platter double, is brought from Umbria and is fattened on acorns. A boar from Laurentum is worthless, because it has been fed on sedge and rushes.

The vineyard does not always produce the most edible roes. The connoisseur will choose the forelegs of a female hare. Up to my time there has been no authoritative pronouncement on the right condition and age of fish and fowl.

There are some who devote all their talents to inventing new kinds of confectionery. It is not enough to give all your attention to one subject. No matter how good your wines are, you must also be sure that you use a high-grade oil on the fish.

You may put Massic wine outdoors in fine weather. The night air will obviate its bitterness and its annoying odor. But to strain it through linen spoils it and destroys the flavor. The connoisseur, after mixing Surrentine with the dregs of Falernian wine, can clear the sediment with a pigeon's egg. The yolk will gather the foreign matter and sink to the bottom with it.

You may cure a hangover with fried shrimps and African snails. Lettuce does not digest after over-indulgence in wine. Dried ham and sausages form an excellent stimulus, or something smoking hot from the cook-shops.

You ought to study thoroughly the nature of mixed sauces. There is the simple kind that consists of sweet olive oil. This may be mixed with rich wine, fish-brine, or Byzantine pickles. When it has been blended with chopped herbs, boiled, sprinkled with Corycian saffron, and allowed to stand, you may add Venafran olives to it.

Apples from Tibur are not so juicy as those from Picenum, but they are more attractive to look at.

Venusian grapes are suitable for preserving in jars; those from Alba are better for the smoke-house. I am in favor of serving these grapes with apples, wine-lees with caviar, and white pepper finely mixed with black salt in neat little salt-cellars.

It is a great mistake to spend three thousand sesterces in the fish-market and then to squeeze the sprawling fish into a platter too small for them.

It upsets the stomach dreadfully if the serving boy touches the drinking cup with hands greasy from morsels that he has stealthily gobbled, or if an antique goblet is covered with dust.

The cost of a cheap broom, napkin and sawdust is next to nothing; yet not to supply them is a great breach of etiquette. Would you sweep tiled pavements with a dirty palm-broom and cover your upholstery with soiled slip-covers? These things cost so little that it is inexcusable not to furnish them; it would be different if they were so expensive that only the rich could afford them.

"O learned Catius, I beg you, by our friendship and by

the gods of whom you are mindful, to take me along with you when you go to hear this man, however far it may be. For though you tell me the whole story from memory, this cannot please me so much as a personal interview. Besides, I would come to know his face and bearing. You're lucky enough to be with him all the while and so you think nothing of it. But for me it will be a great privilege to come to the distant well-springs, and to imbibe those precepts which are the secret of a happy life."

II · 5 · *How to Get Rich Quickly*

hoc quoque, Tiresia

ULYSSES. Besides what you have told me, answer me this one question, Tiresias. By what arts and methods can I repair my ruined fortunes—why do you laugh?

TIRESIAS. Is it then not enough that a man of your craftiness should be brought back to Ithaca and once more look upon his home-gods?

ULYSSES. O man that never lies to anyone, you see that, as you prophesied, I have come home stripped bare and without means. There neither storeroom nor flock has escaped the suitors. But birth and valor without substance are more worthless than seaweed.

TIRESIAS. Since poverty is what you dread, let me tell you frankly how you may become wealthy.

Suppose a thrush or some other dainty be given you for your own consumption. Let it fly away to where there is the splendor of a great fortune and an ancient owner. See to it that the rich man tastes the sweetest apples, and whatever other exceptionally fine produce your cultivated farm brings forth, before the household god tastes them, since the rich man is more to be reverenced. He may be a perjurer, of no family, stained with his brother's blood, a runaway slave; yet if he expects you to walk with him, and on the left side, do not refuse to go.

ULYSSES. The idea of my walking along as a humble dependent of filthy Damas! That wasn't my way at Troy when I held my own with the best of them.

TIRESIAS. Then you will be a poor man.

ULYSSES. I shall force my soul to bear it bravely. I have endured worse in my time. But, O prophet, go on and tell me how I shall quickly pile up wealth and a lot of money.

TIRESIAS. I have already told you, and repeat it: fish craftily everywhere for the wills of old men, and if one or two shrewd ones nibble off the bait and escape your wiles, do not give up hope or surrender your art because you are disappointed. If presently an important case, or one that is not so important, is before the Court, pick the suitor that is rich and childless. Even if he is a scoundrel who actually dares to bring his better into Court, he's the man you should defend. Forget the citizen who has a better reputation and a better cause, if he has a son at home, or a wife capable of bearing one. Say "Quintus," for example, or "Publius"—sensitive ears delight in the praenomen—"your virtue has made me your friend. I understand the uncertainties of the law and can defend a case. I will sooner let anyone pluck out my eyes than bring you into contempt or rob you of a penny. It is my business to see that you neither suffer loss nor are made a laughing-stock."

Tell him to go home and mind his health. Be his attorney. Persevere and be steadfast whether "the red Dog-star's heat split the speechless statues" or Furius, after a full supper of tripe, "spins white snow over the wintry Alps."

"Don't you see," someone will say, nudging with his elbow the person who stands next to him, "how indefatigable he is, how ready to serve his friends, how clever?" More tunnies will swim near you, and your nets will be full.

Then again, for fear you should show your hand too plainly by cultivating a bachelor, look for a fine estate where an invalid son is being reared as heir. Quietly ingratiate yourself that you may be named the second legatee, and if some accident takes him to Heaven you may have the vacant place. This procedure seldom fails.

If a man hands you his will to read, be sure to refuse and to push the legal document away from you—but in such a way that you can see out of the corner of your eye the purport of the second line of the first page. Quickly run your eye over it to discover whether you are sole heir or one of many. Sometimes an experienced scribe, who has risen from being a Quinquevir, may cheat the gaping raven, and Nasica the fortune-hunter will make sport for Coranus.

ULYSSES. Have you gone mad, or do you purposely make fun of me by uttering oracular obscurities?

TIRESIAS. O son of Laertes, whatever I say either will or will not happen, for great Apollo bestows on me the gift of prophecy.

ULYSSES. Very likely, but tell me, if you please, the meaning of that story.

TIRESIAS. What time a youth, the terror of the Parthians, offspring of noble Aeneas, shall be winning laurels by land and sea, the tall daughter of Nasica, who is unwilling to pay what she owes, shall marry brave Coranus. Then the son-in-law shall do this: he shall hand his father-in-law some papers and shall beg him to read them, and he will find that nothing has been willed to him and his but the privilege of lamenting!

I give you another hint. If by chance there is a crafty woman, or a freedman who has charge of a doddering old man, ally yourself with them. Praise them so that they shall praise you when your back is turned. This, too, helps. But to take by storm the principal himself is by far the better way. If he is a dotard and scribbles poor verses, praise them. Would he be a fornicator? See that he doesn't ask you, but of your own accord obligingly give Penelope to your better.

ULYSSES. Do you think so sober and so chaste a woman can be tempted, when her suitors could not turn her from the strait and narrow path?

TIRESIAS. Of course! The young suitors who came were too stingy of their gifts. They came not so much for amorous indulgence as for the cooking! Under such circumstances your Penelope is a good woman; but if she should have just one old man, and share the profits with you, she could no more be driven away than a dog from his bone!

I will tell you something that happened when I was an old man. A shameless old woman at Thebes was carried out to her burial as her will directed, and in this manner. Upon his bare shoulders her heir carried her corpse, which was oiled all over. She wished to see, of course, whether she might escape from him even after she was dead! I suppose that when she was alive he had pressed her too hard for money.

Begin cautiously in your approach. Err neither by defect nor by excess. If you talk too much you will offend the testy and the morose. Don't be too silent either. Be like Davus in the comedy. Stand with your head cast down as if you were deeply respectful. Get at him by flattery. If the air freshens, warn him to be careful and cover his precious head. Shoulder a way for him out of the crowd. Lend him your ear when he wishes to chatter. Is he too fond of praise? Give him more than he wants until he lifts his hands to heaven and cries "Enough!" Distend the swelling wind-bag with windy talk.

When he has released you from your long-suffering and anxiety, and when you are really awake, you shall hear, "I make Ulysses heir to one-fourth of my estate." "Then is my old friend Dama truly no more? Where shall I find another so true and worthy?" Let fall such remarks now and then; and if you can squeeze out a few tears, weep a little! You can hide your face if it betrays you. If the tomb is left to your discretion, erect a handsome one. A fine funeral will become the talk of the neighborhood. If one of your coheirs is possibly your senior and has a nasty cough, tell him that if he would like to buy an estate or a town-house that is part of your share, you will gladly let him have it at a nominal price.

But tyrannical Proserpine drags me away. May you live long and prosper!

II· 6· *The Country Mouse*

hoc erat in votis

I have always wished for a plot of ground, not too large, with a garden, and near my house a spring of living water, and a patch of woods. But the gods have done better by me than this. I only ask, O Mercury, that I may keep these gifts perpetually. If I have neither increased my estate by sharp practice, nor am likely to diminish it through my own fault or failing; if I make no foolish prayers (such as: if only I could include that adjoining corner that now spoils the shape of my little field! If only I could accidentally find a pot of gold, like the hireling who discovered the treasure and bought and ploughed in his own right the field where he found it! Hercules was a good friend to him!); if what I possess contents me and fills me with gratitude, then this is the boon I ask of you: fatten my cattle and everything else that their master has—*except his wit*—and continue to abide with me as my chiefest guardian.

So then, when I have left town for the mountains and my stronghold, what can I glorify in preference to my satires and my prosaic Muse? Here neither vaulting ambition destroys me, nor the oppressive southwind, nor the fatal autumn weather that makes a fortune for hateful Libitina.

O Father of the morning, or Janus, if you would prefer to be so addressed, with whom men begin the toils of business and the responsibities of life—so the gods will—stand at the beginning of my song! In Rome you hurry me away to give bail for a friend. "Hurry! lest some one answer the call before you." I have to go, whether the north wind sweeps the earth, or winter shortens the snowy day. Then when I have uttered "aloud and distinctly" what may one day be to my own disadvantage, I must struggle through the crowd and anger those who are slow to get out of my way. "What do you want, you fool, and what are you trying to do?" So some ruffian assails me with angry curses. "Must you bump into everything in your way because you remember your engagement with Maecenas?" (I won't deny that this remark delights me and is sweet as honey.) But as soon as I reach the gloomy Esquiline a hundred things that are no business of mine attack me on every side. "Roscius begs that you will meet him tomorrow before seven o'clock at the Puteal." "The Civil Servants urge you, friend Horace, not to forget to come in today about a new matter which is very important for our organization." "Have Maecenas put his seal to this little document!" If you say, "I'll try,", "You can if you want to," he persists.

It is going on eight years since Maecenas began to count me one of his friends—merely to the extent of offering me a seat in his carriage when he was making a trip somewhere, and of indulging in such small talk as, "What time is it?", "Do you think that the Thracian gladiator, Gallina, is a match for Syrus?", "The morning frosts sting when you are not properly clad," and other such things as one may say without fear of having them repeated. During all this time, every day and hour, I have been increasingly the object of envy. Everybody says, "He watched the games with him, and played with him in the Campus Martius. Lucky dog!" If a chilling rumor spreads from the Forum through the streets, everybody that runs into me wants to know about it. "My dear sir—you must know, since you live so close to the gods—you haven't heard anything about the Dacians, have you?" "Nothing at all." "How you always love to laugh at us!" "I tell you, I'm quite serious!" "Well, is it in the three-cornered island or on Italian soil that Caesar means to give the land to the soldiers?" When I swear that I know nothing about it, they gape at me as the only man in the world who can really hold his tongue.

In this sort of thing my day is wasted, greatly to my mortification, while all the while I sigh, "O my country home, when shall I behold you? When will it be possible for me to live among my books, to sleep, and in hours of idleness to drink the sweet draughts that make us forget life's worries? Oh! when shall I sit down to a dinner of beans, Pythagoras' kinsmen, and salad garnished appetizingly with fat bacon?" What nights! What suppers fit for the gods, at which my friends and I regale ourselves before my own hearth, with plenty left over for my saucy household servants! Each guest according to his own taste, and in disregard of foolish convention, mixes his cup of wine and water. One who is strong-headed can stand a strong draught; another delights in growing mellow with a weaker mixture. So the conversation turns, not to other people's villas and houses, nor to whether Lepos dances well or ill, but to what more immediately concerns us, and to what everyone ought to know. We debate whether wealth or virtue is the secret of happiness, whether selfish interest or nobility of character is the basis of friendship, and what is the nature of the good, and what is the chief end of life.

From time to time my neighbor Cervius recounts in his familiar way some pet story that he has heard from an old woman. For example, if someone praises the wealth of Arellius, not knowing the cares that accompany riches, he begins thus:

"Once upon a time, the story goes, a country mouse entertained in his humble abode a city mouse. They were old acquaintances. The country mouse was uncouth and thrifty, but he could be gracious upon occasion. Such a spread! He was generous with his round peas and his long oats. He even brought in his mouth a prune and some half-eaten rinds of bacon, so eager was he to tempt by the variety of fare the dainty appetite of his guest, who hardly deigned to touch with a supercilious whisker what was set before him. Meanwhile the master of the house, on his couch of fresh straw, made his own meal of spelt and darnel, leaving the delicacies to his friend. At length the city mouse addressed him. 'What pleasure can you find, my friend, in living so hard a life on this wooded ridge? Would you not prefer companionship and city life to these wild forests? Take my advice and come with me. Since all that is on earth is mortal, and there is no escape from death for either great or small, you must decide, my good sir, while there is time, to enjoy what is pleasant. Live mindful of life's brevity!'

"These words greatly impressed the country mouse. He was out of his hut in a trice. So they made their proposed journey together, wishing to creep quietly into town under cover of darkness. It was deep night when they both set foot in a gorgeous palace where scarlet coverings gleamed on ivory couches, and a pile of trays stood in baskets, the remains of a great supper on the preceding evening.

"After the city mouse had placed the country mouse comfortably upon a splendid carpet, he bustled about like a waiter with his tunic tucked up, and served course after course without pause, playing to the life the part of a pampered house-servant, and licking every dish clean before he passed it. The country mouse lay at ease, congratulating himself on the change of his circumstances, playing the part of a contented guest, when suddenly the terrific noise of slamming doors brought them both to their feet. In terror they rushed aimlessly about the dining hall, their fear increasing moment by moment, as the lofty house rang with the barking of watch-dogs. Whereupon the country mouse exclaimed:

"'I don't like this! Good-bye! My wood and my hole

with their quiet, and my simple food, are quite enough for me!' "

II· 7· *Frank Talk on Freedom*

iamdudum ausculto

DAVUS. I have been listening a long time to find out whether you were at leisure. I wish to speak with you a moment, but since I am a slave I hesitate.

HORACE. Oh, is that Davus?

DAVUS. Yes, Davus, his master's faithful and honest servant. Honest enough, at least, but not too good to live.

HORACE. Very well. Take advantage of December's privilege. Say whatever you like!

DAVUS. Some men are consistently fond of their vices and eagerly pursue them. Others drift back and forth between right and wrong. Priscus, who often attracted attention by wearing three rings, and then by wearing none, was so fickle that he would change his clothes every hour. He would suddenly leave a grand mansion and go to a neighborhood where any self-respecting freedman would be ashamed to be seen. For a time he would live a dissolute life in Rome, and then for a time he would follow the career of a philosopher in Athens. He was born under the evil influence of the God of Change. The buffoon, Volanerius, when gout had crippled his fingers as he well deserved, employed a man that he hired at so much a day to pick up the dice for him and to put them into the box. As he was the more persistent in his vicious course, so was he the less to be pitied. He was better off than one who suffers alternately from too tight or from too loose a rein.

HORACE. How long will it take you to tell me what all this is about, you rascal?

DAVUS. About you, I reply.

HORACE. How, you villain?

DAVUS. You praise the good fortune and manners of the past, but if suddenly some god offered to take you back to those times you would beg to be excused, either because you do not really mean what you say, or because you are a moral coward and, for all your vain desires to pull it out, your foot still sticks in the mire. When you are in Rome you long to be in the country, and when you are in the country you praise the distant town to the skies. Fickle man! If you are not invited out to supper, you praise your quiet meal of greens, call yourself lucky, and hug yourself because you don't have to go away from home to drink your wine—as if when you went out you went under compulsion! Should Maecenas have invited you to a late supper at lamp-lighting time, it would be—"Will no one hurry and bring the oil? Won't someone listen to me?"

So you storm and rage and are off like a shot. Mulvius and his fellow-jesters depart, too, with curses not meant for your ears.

Yes, one may say, I admit that I weakly follow where my stomach leads. I enjoy the delightful fragrance of good food. I am unstable and lazy, and, if you choose to say so, a glutton also. But since you are as bad as I am, or perhaps worse, why do you arrogantly call me to account as if you were better, and with specious phrases cover up your own shortcomings? What if you turn out to be more stupid than I, who was bought for five hundred denarii? Don't try to frighten me with your scowling. Control your hand

and your temper, while I tell you what Crispinus' porter taught me.

You desire another man's wife. Davus wants a harlot. Which of the two deserves the severer punishment? When passion inflames me, the woman who satisfies me lets me go without any sense of disgrace, or any worry lest some richer or handsomer man than I shall possess her. When you have laid aside the badge of your office, your knighthood's ring and your toga, and step out, no longer a dignitary but a low slave with your perfumed head hidden under your cape, *you really are what you pretend to be.* In great perturbation you are admitted to the house, and you tremble now with fear and now with lust. What difference does it make whether you are bound out to be a gladiator and scourged or slain with the sword, or hidden in a dirty closet by a maid who is in her mistress's confidence, with your head doubled up to your knees? Has not the husband of the offending wife a just power over both, particularly over the seducer? Yet the wife changes neither her dress nor her position, and she is not the chief sinner, since she is afraid of you and does not trust you when you say that you love her. You know perfectly well what you are doing when you put your fortune, your life, your reputation and your person into the hands of an enraged husband.

You have escaped, let me say. Then I assume that you will be afraid to offend again and will have learned to be careful. Not so. You will look for another opportunity to be terrified and to face ruin—you slave indeed! What beast, when it has burst its bonds and has escaped, deliberately returns again to captivity?

I am no adulterer, you say.

Nor am I, by Hercules, a thief when I wisely refrain from stealing your silver plate. Remove the risk, and when restraints are set aside nature will immediately assert itself and run wild. Are you my master, you that are slave to so many persons and things—you whom the praetor's rod has manumitted three or four times over, but without ever freeing you from slavish fear?

Over and above what I have said, add this, which is no less important. Whether one who takes orders from a slave is an *under-slave*, as your class names him, or a *fellow-slave*, what is my relation to you? Why, you who lord it over me are the wretched slave of someone else and dance like a wooden puppet pulled by strings in the hands of others! Who, then, is free? The wise man who is master of himself, whom poverty or death or bonds find unafraid, who bravely withstands his passions, and scorns unworthy ambition, who is at unity with himself, and so completely unafraid that nothing from without can find a resting-place on the polished surface of his life, and against whom the heaviest strokes of Fortune are futile.

Do you think that any one of these traits belongs to you? A woman asks you for five talents, worries you, slams her door in your face, throws cold water on you, and then—calls you back! Refuse to put your neck in her yoke. Come! Say "I am free! I am free!" You cannot, for it is no gentle master that commands your soul, that plies the spur to your weary side and drives you on against your will.

Or again, when you stand entranced before a picture of Pausias, how are you superior to me when I marvel at the contests of Fulvius, Rutaba, or Pacideianus with their straining legs, done in red chalk or charcoal, and as true to life as if the heroes were really brandishing their weapons, and really fighting, striking and parrying each other's blows? Davus is a "rascal and a dawdler," but you are called "an exact and accomplished critic of antiques."

If I am tempted by a smoking pie, I am a "good-for-nothing." Are *your* heroic virtue and superior soul indifferent to sumptuous suppers? Why is it any worse for me to be a glutton than it is for you? To be sure, my back pays for it. But how do you escape punishment more than I, when you set your heart on costly dainties? The fact is that rich food taken immoderately palls on the stomach, and the feet that you have fooled refuse at last to support your bloated body.

Is a slave who at the day's end swaps his master's bath-brush for some grapes any more a slave than he who squanders his estate to fill his stomach?

Say, again, that you cannot endure your own company, you cannot employ your leisure wisely, you would flee from yourself like a runaway or a vagabond, you would drown your troubles in wine and sleep. Impossible! However fast you run, black Care runs by your side or close behind you.

HORACE. Where can I find a stone—

DAVUS. For what?

HORACE. Or arrows?

DAVUS. The man is either mad or writing verses!

HORACE. If you don't get out of here, you'll be the ninth slave on my Sabine farm!

II · 8: *Rich Man Dines*

ut Nasidieni iuvit

HORACE. How did you enjoy your dinner with the rich Nasidienus?

FUNDANIUS. Vastly. I never had a better time.

HORACE. Tell me, if you don't mind, what was the first dish to appease your ravenous appetites?

FUNDANIUS. First there was a Lucanian boar, captured, so the host told us, when the south wind was softly blowing. Around it were pungent rape, lettuce, radishes, skirret, fish-pickle, Coan lees and everything to whet the appetite. When these were removed, a neatly dressed slave carefully wiped the maplewood table with a purple napkin. Another swept up the crumbs and anything that could offend the guests. Then, like an Attic maiden bearing Ceres' sacred emblems, came forward a dusky Indian with Caecuban wine, and a Greek with Chian unmixed with brine. Then said the host, "If you prefer Alban, Maecenas, or Falernian, we have both."

HORACE. Oh, the curse of being so rich! But who were your supper companions with whom you had so good a time, Fundanius? I am eager to know.

FUNDANIUS. I was at the head of the table. Next to me was Viscus of Thurii, and beyond him, if I recall, Varius. Then Vibidius and Servilius Balatro, uninvited guests whom Maecenas had brought him. Nomentanus was next to him; beyond him Porcius, who made us laugh by gulping down cheese-cakes whole. Nomentanus was there to point his forefinger at anything that might escape our notice. As for the rest of us, people of no importance, we supped on birds, shell-fish, and fish that had a flavor very different from anything we knew. I, for instance, soon discovered this when I was handed the livers of a plaice and a turbot—a dish I had never tasted before.

After this he informed me that honey-apples are red if

they are gathered when the moon is waning. What difference that makes you had better learn from him.

Then Vibidius whispered to Balatro, "We will die unavenged unless we drink him bankrupt," and called for larger cups.

At that our host grew pale, as he has a horror of hard drinkers, either because their talk is too free, or because hot wines dull a delicate taste.

Vibidius and Balatro tilted whole decanters into Allifan goblets. Everybody followed suit except the guest on the lowest coach, who took care to drink little.

Then a lamprey, with shrimp sauce, was brought in, stretched full length on a platter. At this the host remarked, "It was caught before spawning. If caught after spawning its meat is poorer. Here is the recipe for the sauce: oil of the first pressing from Venafrum; roe from the juices of the Spanish mackerel; wine five years old, but domestic, poured in while the sauce is simmering—after the sauce is cooked, Chian is the best wine to pour in—white pepper, and vinegar made from fermenting Lesbian wine. I was the first to point out that green rockets and bitter elecampane should be boiled in the sauce. Curtillus says to add sea-urchins unwashed, for the shell-fish's natural brine is better than any pickle."

Just then the canopy fell heavily from the ceiling upon the platter, bringing with it more black dust than the north wind raises on the plains of Campania. We feared something worse was about to happen, but finding there was no danger we recovered our composure. Rufus laid his head on the table and wept as if his son had been cut off in his prime. What would have been the end I don't know, if

Nomentanus had not comforted his friend by a philosopher's reflection, "Ah, Fortune, what god is more cruel to us than thou! How thou delightest ever to make sport of human life!"

Varius could hardly smother a laugh with his napkin. Balatro, who sneers at everything, remarked, "Such is life, and therefore the reward of fame will never compensate you for your labor to attain it. To think that you must be racked with every kind of annoyance to entertain me sumptuously—lest the bread be burned, or badly seasoned sauce be served, and that your slaves be properly and neatly dressed when they wait on table! Then, too, such accidents as this—the canopy's coming down as it did just now or some numbskull's falling and breaking a dish. But a host is like a general: adversity reveals his genius, prosperity hides it." To this Nasidienus replied, "Heaven grant you all that you pray for! You are so kind and considerate a guest!" and called for his sandals.

Then on each couch was heard the buzz of people whispering into each other's ears.

HORACE. I know of no play I would rather have seen. But tell me, what did you find to laugh at next?

FUNDANIUS. While Vibidius was asking the waiters whether the flagon also was broken, since the cups were not brought to him when he called for them, and while we were laughing at pretended jests, with Balatro egging us on, back came Nasidienus with changed countenance as if to mend misfortune by his art. Then followed the servants bearing on a huge platter the limbs of a carved crane sprinkled with plenty of salt and meal, and the liver of a white goose fattened on rich figs, and hares' legs torn off, much nicer so than if they were eaten with the loins. Then we saw blackbirds served with the breast burnt, and pigeons without the rumps—all nice enough if the host had not explained their laws and properties. But off we ran, taking it out on him by tasting nothing at all, as though it had all been poisoned with Canidia's breath, deadlier than African serpents.

REFRAINS
(Epodes)

Youthful miscellanies—serious, trivial and bitter—and experimental pieces, many of them echoes from the Greek. Published 30 B.C. in the poet's thirty-fifth year.

1 · *Dedication*

ibis Liburnis

You go, Maecenas, to defy
In light Liburnians bulwarks high
Of towered ships; to dare the strife,
And risk your own for Caesar's life.

You bid me stay. You bid me spend
My days in peace without my friend—
Without my friend! Such days to me
Cheerless and desolate would be.

Say which is best—a life of leisure,
Inglorious ease, and joyous pleasure,
Or that far nobler, manlier part
That tells the true and honest heart?

Be mine your toils. With you I go
O'er Alpine heights, Caucasian snow,
Or where the red sun's level ray
Spreads broadening o'er the western bay.

You say, unwarlike, feeble, frail,
My aid for you could naught avail.
True! But the bird whose tender breast
Broods o'er her young ones in the nest

Is happy, though her fluttering wing
Be powerless 'gainst the serpent's sting.
My willing service shall approve
My faith. I cling to thee for love.

Not that more numerous teams may plough
A wider tilth than mine is now;
Not that my herds may panting shun
The Dogstar's rage, the summer sun,

Changing Calabria's burning hills
For cool Lucania's shaded rills;
Not that for me a marble hall
May shine o'er Circe's storied wall.

Enough, too much, with bounteous measure
Thy hand has given. I seek no treasure
Like Chremes old to hoard and spare,
Or lavish like his slipshod heir.

2· *Revery of a Business Man*

beatus ille

How happy in his low degree,
How rich in humble poverty is he
Who leads a quiet country life,
Discharged of business, void of strife,
And from the griping scrivener free!
Thus, ere the seeds of vice were sown,
Lived men in better ages born,
Who plowed with oxen of their own
Their small paternal field of corn.
Nor trumpets summon him to war,
Nor drums disturb his morning sleep,
Nor knows he merchants' gainful care,
Nor fears the dangers of the deep.
The clamors of contentious law,
And court and state he wisely shuns;
Nor bribed with hopes, nor dared with awe,
To servile salutations runs;
But either to the clasping vine
Does the supporting poplar wed,
Or with his pruning hook disjoin
Unbearing branches from their head,
And grafts more happy in their stead;
Or climbing to a hilly steep,
He views his buds in vales afar,
Or shears his overburdened sheep,
Or mead for cooling drink prepares;
Or virgin honey in the jars;
Or, in the now declining year,
When beauteous Autumn rears his head,

He joys to pull the ripened pear
And clustering grapes with purple spread.
Sometimes beneath an ancient oak,
Or on the matted grass he lies:
No god of sleep he need invoke;
The stream that o'er the pebble flies
With gentle slumber crowns his eyes.
The wind that whistles through the sprays
Maintains the concert of the song,
And hidden birds with native lays
The golden sleep prolong.
But when the blast of winter blows,
And hoary frost invests the year,
Into the naked woods he goes
And seeks the tusky boar to rear
With well-mouthed hounds and pointed spear!
Or spreads his subtle nets from sight,
With twinkling glasses, to betray
The larks that in the meshes light;
Or makes the fearful bear the prey.
Amidst his harmless, easy joys,
No anxious care invades his health,
Nor love his peace of mind destroys,
Nor wicked avarice of wealth.
But if a chaste and pleasing wife,
To ease the business of his life,
Divides with him his household care,
Such as the Sabine matrons were,
Such as the swift Apulian's bride,
Sunburnt and swarthy though she be
Will fire for winter nights provide,

And, without noise, will oversee
His children and his family,
And order all things till he come,
Sweaty and overlabored, home.
If she in pens his flocks will fold,
And then produce her dairy store,
With wine to drive away the cold,
And unbought dainties for the poor;
Not oysters of the Lucrine lake
My sober appetite would wish,
Nor turbot, or the foreign fish
That rolling tempests overtake,
And hither waft the costly dish.
Not heathpolt, or the rarer bird,
Which Phasis or Ionia yields
More pleasing morsels would afford
Than the fat olives of my fields;
Than shards and mallows for the pot,
That keep the loosened body sound,
Or than the lamb that falls by lot
To the just guardian of my ground.
Amidst these feasts of happy swains
The jolly shepherd smiles to see
His flock returning from the plains;
The farmer is as pleased as he
To view his oxen, sweating smoke,
Bear on their necks the loosened yoke:
To look upon his menial crew
That sit around his cheerful hearth,
And bodies spent in toil renew
With wholesome food and country mirth.

This Alphaeus said within himself.
Resolved to leave the wicked town,
And live retired upon his own,
  He called his money in.
But the prevailing love of pelf
Soon split him on the former shelf:
  He put it out again!

3· *Hymn of Hate*

parentis olim

If e'er a son an aged parent's throat
 With impious hand has strangled,
His food be garlic!—worse than aconite;
 O stubborn-bowelled reapers!
What poison here within my vitals boils?
 Has viper's blood deceived me,
Brewed with these herbs? Or in the unlucky mess
 Has old Canidia dabbled?

When 'mid the Argonauts their brilliant chief
 Medea's gaze attracted,
With *this* besmeared she him, in unknown yokes
 That he the bulls might harness:
With *this* she drenched the gifts—her rival's bane—
 And fled with winged serpents.
Not, on Apulia's thirsty soil, so fierce
 The star-born vapor settles,
Nor clung more burningly the fatal boon
 On huge Alcides' shoulders.

But, O Maecenas, sportive friend! if e'er
 So foul desire possess thee,
I pray thy lass may give thee hand for lip,
 And choose the seat most distant.

4· *Social Climber*

lupis et agnis

When wolves no longer lambs pursue,
Then I'll be reconciled to you.
Still on your back and legs remain
The furrows of the scourge and chain.
Though store of wealth you now possess,
Condition changes not with dress.
Behold, when on the Sacred Way
Your gown, wide-trailing, you display,
How every free-born passer-by
Turns from the slave his scornful eye!
"Shall he who tired the lictor's hand,
Scourged by the magistrate's command,
With corn a thousand acres load,
With chariots wear the Appian Road,
And, in contempt of Otho, sit
With the knights' Order in the pit?
Why arm we, then, our coasts to guard,
And wherefore are our ships prepared
From slaves and thieves the trade to free,
While you, as tribune, rule the sea?"

5· *Hell-Broth*

at o deorum quidquid

"What, O ye gods, who from the sky
Rule earth and human destiny,
What means this coil? And wherefore be
These cruel looks all bent on me?
Thee by thy children I conjure
If at their birth Lucina pure
Stood by; thee by this vain array
Of purple, thee by Jove I pray,
Who views with anger deeds so foul,
Why thus on me like stepdame scowl,
Or like some wild beast, that doth glare
Upon the hunter from its lair?"

As thus the boy in wild distress
Bewail'd, of bulla stripp'd and dress,
So fair, that ruthless breasts of Thrace
Had melted to behold his face,
Canidia, with dishevell'd hair
And short crisp vipers coiling there,
Beside a fire of Colchos stands,
And her attendant hags commands
To feed the flames with fig-trees torn
From dead men's sepulchres forlorn,
With dismal cypress, eggs rubb'd o'er
With filthy toads' envenom'd gore,
With screech-owl's plumes, and herbs of bane,
From far Iolchos fetch'd and Spain,
And fleshless bones by beldam witch

Snatch'd from the jaws of famish'd bitch.
And Sagana, the while, with gown
Tucked to the knees, stalks up and down,
Sprinkling in room and hall and stair
Her magic hell-drops, with her hair
Bristling on end, like furious boar,
Or some sea-urchin wash'd on shore;
Whilst Veia, by remorse unstay'd,
Groans at her toil, as she with spade
That flags not digs a pit, wherein
The boy imbedded to his chin,
With nothing seen save head and throat,
Like those who in the water float,
Shall dainties see before him set,
A maddening appetite to whet,
Then snatched away before his eyes,
Till famish'd in despair he dies;
That when his glazing eyeballs should
Have closed on the untasted food,
His sapless marrow and dry spleen
May drug a philtre-draught obscene.
Nor were these all the hideous crew,
But Ariminian Folia, too,
Who with unsatiate lewdness swells,
And drags by her Thessalian spells
The moon and stars down from the sky,
Ease-loving Naples' vows, was by;
And every hamlet round about
Declares she was, beyond a doubt.

Now forth the fierce Canidia sprang,
And still she gnaw'd with rotten fang

Her long sharp unpared thumb-nail. What
Then said she? Yea, what said she not?

"O Night and Dian, who with true
And friendly eyes my purpose view,
And guardian silence keep, whilst I
My secret orgies safely ply,
Assist me now, now on my foes
With all your wrath celestial close!
Whilst, stretch'd in soothing sleep, amid
Their forests grim the beasts lie hid,
May all Suburra's mongrels bark
At yon old wretch, who through the dark
Doth to his lewd encounters crawl,
And on him draw the jeers of all!
He's with an ointment smear'd, that is
My masterpiece. But what is this?
Why, why should poisons brew'd by me
Less potent than Medea's be,
By which, for love betray'd, beguiled,
On mighty Creon's haughty child
She wreaked her vengeance sure and swift,
And vanish'd, when the robe, her gift,
In deadliest venom steep'd and dyed,
Swept off in flame the new-made bride?
No herb there is, nor root in spot
However wild, that I have not;
Yet every common harlot's bed
Seems with some rare Nepenthe spread,
For there he lives in swinish drowse,
Of me oblivious, and his vows!
He is, aha! protected well

By some more skilful witch's spell!
But, Varus, thou, (doom'd soon to know
The rack of many a pain and woe!)
By potions never used before
Shalt to my feet be brought once more.
And 'tis no Marsian charm shall be
The spell that brings thee back to me!
A draught I'll brew more strong, more sure,
Thy wandering appetite to cure;
And sooner 'neath the sea the sky
Shall sink, and earth upon them lie,
Than thou not burn with fierce desire
For me, like pitch in sooty fire!"

On this the boy by gentle tones
No more essay'd to move the crones,
But wildly forth with frenzied tongue
These curses Thyestean flung.
"Your sorceries, and spells, and charms
To man may compass deadly harms,
But heaven's great law of Wrong and Right
Will never bend before their might.
My curse shall haunt you, and my hate
No victim's blood shall expiate.
But when at your behests I die,
Like the Fury of the Night will I
From Hades come, a phantom sprite—
Such is the Manes' awful might.
With crooked nails your cheeks I'll tear
And, squatting on your bosoms, scare
With hideous fears your sleep away!
Then shall the mob, some future day,

Pelt you from street to street with stones,
Till falling dead, ye filthy crones,
The dogs and wolves and carrion fowl,
That make the Esquiline their prowl,
In banquet horrible and grim
Shall tear your bodies limb from limb,
Nor shall my parents fail to see
That sight—alas, surviving me!"

6· *To a Cowardly Libeler*

quid immerentis

You dog, that fearful to provoke
The wolf, attack defenceless folk!
Turn hither, if you dare, your spite,
And bark at me, prepared to bite;
For like a hound, or mastiff keen,
That guards the shepherd's flocky green,
Through the deep snows I boldly chase,
With ears alert, the savage race.
But you, when with your hideous yelling
You fill the grove, at crusts are smelling.
Fierce as Archilochus I glow,
Like Hipponax a deadly foe.
If any mongrel shall assail
My character with tooth and nail;
What! Like a truant boy, shall I
Do nothing in revenge—but cry?

7 · *Civil War*

quo quo scelesti

Where do ye rush, ye impious trains?
  Why gleams afar the late-sheathed sword?
Is it believed that Roman veins
  Their crimson tides have sparsely poured?
Is not our scorn of safety, health, and ease,
Shown by devastated climes, and blood-stained seas?

Those scowling brows, those lifted spears,
  Bend they against the threat'ning towers
Proud Carthage emulously rears?
  Or Britain's still unconquered shores?
That her fierce sons, yet free from hostile sway,
May pass in chains along our Sacred Way?

No! but that warring Parthia's curse
  May quickly blast these far-famed walls;
Accomplished when, with direful force,
  By her own strength, the city falls;
When foes no more her might resistless feel,
But Roman bosoms bleed by Roman steel.

O! worse than wolves, or lions fierce,
  Who ne'er, like you, assault their kind!
By what wild frenzy would ye pierce
  Each other's breast in fury blind?—
Silent and pale ye stand, with conscious sighs,
Your struck soul louring in your down-cast eyes!

The blood our rising walls that stained,
Shed by the ruthless fratricide,
High Heaven's avenging power ordained
Should spread the rage of discord wide,
Bid kindred blood in dread profusion flow
Through darkened years of expiatory woe.

8· *Hag*

rogare longo

How dare you, withered as you are
With years, ask me what saps my strength?
Your teeth are black and furrows scar
With wrinkles all your forehead's length!

Your filthy private gapes between
Shrunk buttocks like a scrawny cow's;
Your chest and wizened breasts are seen
Like horse's teats, and flabby shows

Your belly, and your lank thighs strung
To swollen calves, provoke my wrath!
Be happy! May the masks among
Your forebears' triumphs take the path

Before your corpse in funeral train!
And may no matron walk abroad
Upon whose ample breasts have lain
More perfect pearls than from your hoard.

What boots it that the Stoic's books
Sometimes 'tween silken pillows lie?
Not less robust the unlettered looks
Of those whose limbs walk lustily.

You long to stir in me desire,
And urge me to the joys of love?

Loose all the words of passion's fire
Upon me, if my heart you'd move!

9· *The Victory of Actium*

quando repostum

When, blest Maecenas, shall we twain
  Beneath your stately roof a bowl
Of Caecuban long-hoarded drain,
  In gladsomeness of soul,
For our great Caesar's victories,
  Whilst, as our cups are crown'd,
Lyres blend their Doric melodies
  With flute's barbaric sound?

As when of late that braggart vain,
  The self-styled "Son of Neptune," fled,
And far from the Sicilian main
  With blazing ships he sped;
He, who on Rome had vow'd in scorn
  The manacles to bind,
Which he from faithless serfs had torn
  To kindred baseness kind!

A Roman soldier, (ne'er, oh ne'er,
  Posterity, the shame avow!)
A woman's slave, her arms doth bear,
  And palisadoes now;
To wrinkled eunuchs crooks the knee,
  And now the sun beholds
Midst warriors' standards flaunting free
  The vile pavilion's folds!

Madden'd to view this sight of shame,
  Two thousand Gauls their horses wheeled,
And wildly shouting Caesar's name,
  Deserted on the field;
Whilst steering leftwise o'er the sea
  The foemen's broken fleet
Into the sheltering haven flee
  In pitiful retreat,

Ho, Triumph! Wherefore stay ye here
  The unbroke steers, the golden cars?
Ho! never brought you back his peer
  From the Jugurthine wars!
Nor mightier was the chief revered
  Of that old famous time,
Who in the wreck of Carthage reared
  His cenotaph sublime!

Vanquished by land and sea, the foe
  His regal robes of purple shifts
For miserable weeds of woe,
  And o'er the wild waves drifts,
Where Crete amid the ocean stands
  With cities many a score,
Or where o'er Afric's whirling sands
  The Southern tempests roar.

Come, boy, and ampler goblets crown
  With Chian or with Lesbian wine,
Or else our qualmish sickness drown
  In Caecuban divine!

Thus let us lull our cares and sighs,
  Our fears that will not sleep,
For Caesar and his great emprise,
  In goblets broad and deep!

10 · *Good-Riddance*

mala soluta

With omens ill the ship her anchor weighs
  Which loathsome Maevius hence conveys.
Wake, Southern blast! and with the swelling tide
  Lash fore-and-aft her trembling side!
Rise, Eurus! and with rattling peals of thunder
  Break down her mast—her cordage sunder!
Her beams let Boreas shiver, with a stroke
  Rude as uproots the mountain oak!
And let Orion as he sinks below,
  Dark horror o'er the waters throw,
That not a star may lend its twinkling light
  To cheer the gloomy brow of night!
Nor let him quit in calmer seas the strand,
  Than did the conquering Grecian band,
When Pallas turned from Ilium wrapt in fire
  On Ajax' impious bark her ire!
Gods! what alarm awaits the sweltering crew,
  And oh! what ashy paleness *you*—
With many a womanly lament and tear,
  And prayers to Jove averse to hear—
When murky clouds th' Ionian gulf deform,
  The surge rebellowing to the storm,
And o'er the foundered keel the big wave roars,
  Her timbers cracked—dispersed her oars!
But, should your carcass on the beach at last
  (Rich prey for cormorants) be cast,
A goat (fit victim) to the Tempests slain
  Shall, with a lamb, Jove's altar stain.

11 · *Love's Madness*

Petti, nihil

O Pettius, no pleasure have I, as of yore,
In scribbling of verse, for I'm smit to the core
By love, cruel love, who delights, false deceiver,
In keeping this poor heart of mine in a fever.

Three winters the woods of their honors have stripped,
Since I for Inachia ceased to be hypped.
Good heavens! I can feel myself blush to the ears,
When I think how I drew on my folly the sneers

And talk of the town; how, at parties my stare
Of asinine silence, and languishing air,
The tempest of sighs from the depths of my breast,
All the love-stricken swain to my comrades confessed.

"No genius," I groaned, whilst you kindly condoled,
"If poor, has the ghost of a chance against gold;
But if"—here I grew more confiding and plain,
As the fumes of the wine mounted up to my brain—

"If my manhood shall rally, and fling to the wind
These maudlin regrets which enervate the mind
But soothe not the wound, then the shame of defeat
From a strife so unequal shall make me retreat."

Thus, stern as a judge, having valiantly said,
Being urged by yourself to go home to my bed,
I staggered, with steps not so steady as free,
To a door which, alas! shows no favor to me.

And there on that threshold of beauty and scorn,
Heigho! my poor bones lay and ached till the morn.
Now I'm all for Lyciscus—more mincing than he
Can no little woman in daintiness be—

A love neither counsel can cure, nor abuse,
Though I feel that with me it is playing the deuce,
But which a new fancy for some pretty face,
Or tresses of loose-flowing amber, may chase!

12· *Pretty Lady*

quid tibi vis

What are you up to, you woman, most fit
For dark-swarthy elephants? Why do you send
Letters and gifts to me? Why would not it
Be better a youth with no nose to offend?

I smell a polypus or a rank goat
In shaggy armpits as keenly, and more,
As some clever dog smells the covert remote
That hides from the hunter the lair of the boar.

What a sweat, what a stench from her withered limbs rise
All about, when her passion she seeks to assuage—
Without moist cosmetics, and smeared with the dyes
Of crocodile's dung! And her bed, in the rage

Of her heat, and its covers she furiously tears.
She upbraids e'en my loathing in angriest plea:
"You languish far less with Inachia; there's
Three times a night for her, one time for me!

"May Lesbia be damned who, in answer to me
And my passion sent *you*—just a dull, sluggish bull!
When Coan Amyntas came, like a young tree
On its hill stood his phallus my yearning to lull.

"For whom were the fleeces in Tyrian dye
Dipped so hurriedly? Surely for you, so might be
Of the guests, of your rank, not one man that the eye
Of his wife, as she gazed, would more joyously see.

"How unhappy I am! Oh, unhappy me!
As lambs from the fiercest of wolves that they fear
As roes from the lions, so you turn and flee!
I'm the wolf and the lion, and you lamb and deer!"

13· *Seize the Hour*

horrida tempestas

See gathering clouds obscure the sky,
The air seems melting from on high
In fleecy snow, or showers of rain.
What howling tempests sweep the main
And shake the woods! While in our power,
My friends, we'll seize the hour
While youth yet revels in our veins,
And unimpaired our strength remains.
The cares of age to age resign,
But hither bring the generous wine
Laid up in my Torquatus' year,
When first I breathed the vital air.
No more of adverse fate complain,
Perhaps the gods may smile again.
Let Achaemenian essence shed
Its spicy odours round your head,
And the Cyllenian lyre compose
With soft melodious strains your woes.
Thus Chiron to his pupil sung:
"Great hero from a goddess sprung,
Fame calls thee to the Trojan plain,
To old Assaracus' reign,
Where small Scamander slowly glides,
And Simois rolls his rapid tides;
There must thou fall by Fate's decree,
Nor shall thy Mother of the Sea
Her short-lived son again receive.

Then every anxious thought relieve
By wine or music's charms, for they
Can best the cares of life allay."

14· *Apology*

mollis inertia

Why self-indulgent laziness should so completely steep
My senses in forgetfulness, and put the Muse to sleep,
As if, to slake a quenchless thirst that parched my gullet dry,
I'd drunk a bumper sleeping-draught—you daily ask me
why.
O my loyal friend you'll be
With your "whys," the death of me!
Of course it is the God of Love who stops the Muse's way.
The poems long begun,
Long promised, never done—
I cannot put the final polish on a single lay!

I'm not the first: Anacreon singed, they say, his poet-wings
At Cupid's torch; and still the wail through all his music
rings
That thrilled of old along the chords that sobbed in wood
notes wild,
His passion of despairing love for Samos' beauteous child.
In like unhappy case
Are you: no fairer face
I grant you, burnt the topless towers of Ilion long ago.
Happy man! A pert soubrette
Has caught me in her net;
And I'm wasting to a shadow—she has two strings to her
bow!

15· *Inconstancy*

nox erat et caelo

The heavens were clear, the moon was bright,
  The lesser lights stood round;
Your arms were clasped and held me tight,
  Like oak with ivy bound;
When you, predestined to defy
The solemn rulers of the sky,
  Swore,—as I swore to you:
So long as wolves shall worry flocks,
Orion's wrath put ships on rocks,
And zephyrs wave Apollo's locks
  We will be lovers true.

Neaera, you shall rue it,
  The dalliance elsewhere;
If Flaccus can't undo it,
  The slight he will not bear.
If he's a man,
He will, and can
  Disgrace the false and fair.
His pride is proof against the jilt
Who thrusts her poniard to the hilt.

And you, whoever you may be,
Whom men think luckier than me,
Who strut the taller for my woe,
Although you've wool and wheat, although
For you the golden rivers flow
And secrets of the sage you know,

Adept in transmigration, books,
And quite Homeric in good looks,
Woe! Woe! for "Shifting love!" you'll cry.
Then comes my turn, and the laughs.

altera iam teritur

Another age ground down by civil strife!
Rome by her children impious and accurst,
  Down-trampled out of life!
Great Rome, our Rome, our mother, she that erst
Rolled back the Marsian, scattered the array
Of old Etruria's monarch, Porsena;
Humbled the pride of Capua, braved the sword
Of Spartacus; the blue-eyed German horde;
The craft and fury of the Gaul;
And him abhorred by mothers, Hannibal.

Amid her streets, her temples nigh,
The mountain wolf shall unmolested lie.
O'er her cold ashes the Barbarian ride;
The war-horse spurn the tomb
Of Romulus, and from earth's sacred womb
Scatter the dust which storms and suns defied.

How meet this ruin! Swear as swore
The doomed Phocaeans' race of yore,
To leave their fields, their loved abodes,
The altars of their household gods,
To tempt new seas and stretch their sail
Full-blown before the driving gale.
Be yours, submissive still to Fate,
Like them self-sentenced yet elate,
Fearless o'er ocean's trackless waste to fly
  To lands unshamed and liberty.

Romans, is this your will? Then from the shore
Launch forth your ships; the gods approve. Obey
  Yon bird of Fate that points the way;
But first make oath: swear to return no more.

Sooner shall rocks rise from their ocean grave
And float upheaved upon the wave;
  Sooner shall Padus lave
Matinus' summit crowned with pine;
Sooner shall crown-capped Apennine
Rush to the Tyrrhene sea; tigers unite
With hinds, the ring-dove with the kite,
Than we return. Such, Romans, be your oath!
Let cowards press their beds of sloth.
Forth, manly spirits, womanish tears disdain;
Forsake the Etruscan shores and dare the boundless main!

Hence self-devoted go,
Ye who love honor best!
Visions of glory rush upon my eyes;
Prophetic voices rise:
See, see before us distant glow
Through the thin dawn-mists of the West
Rich sunlit plains and hilltops gemmed with snow,
The Islands of the Blest!

There the grey olive year by year
Yields its unfailing fruitage; there the vine
Ripens, unpruned, its clusters into wine.
There figs, ungraffed, their russet harvest grow,
And fields unplowed their wealth on man bestow.
  There from the caverned ilex sere

Wells the wild honey trickling slow;
There herds and flocks unbidden bring
At eve their milky offering;
There from the crags' embattled steep
  The laughing waters leap.
No wolf around the sheepfold striding
With mighty howl the sleeping lamb affrights;
No venomed snakes obscenely gliding
Sway the tall herbage; no destroying blights,
Nor storm, nor flood, nor scorching suns despoil,
(Such is the will of Jove) the teeming soil.

  Blest summer shores untrod
By Jason or the Colchian sorceress,
By Tyrian rover, or the wearied crew
Of sage Ulysses in their dire distress.

Merciful gift of a relenting god,
Home of the homeless, preordained for you.
  Last vestige of the age of gold;
  Last refuge of the good and bold;
From stars malign, from plague and tempests free,
Far mid the western waves a secret sanctuary.

17 · *Poet and Witch*

iam iam efficaci

Horace

Well, I surrender; to your skill I bow,
And humbly pray, by Proserpine below,
By Dian never lightly to be moved,
And by the books of incantation proved
Of virtue stars to call down from the sky,
Canidia, at length your spells let lie,
Let go, let go, turn back the speeding wheel!

Was not old Nereus' grandson moved to heal
King Telephus who dared 'gainst him to range
His Mysian troops, and darts with him exchange?
The valiant Hector's corse, delivered o'er
To dogs and vultures, Trojan matrons bore
To Ilios and anointed, when the king
Had left the walls, himself, alas, to fling
At obdurate Achilles' feet. The crew
Ulysses toilworn led their limbs withdrew
At Circe's will, from bristly hides and hard;
Then mind and voice returned, and their regard
Its former dignity resumed. For you
Whom sailor-men and pedlars so adore,
I've suffered punishment enough and more.

My youthful vigor's gone, my modest hue
Has left my bones with ghastly skin o'erlaid;
My hair with essences of yours is greyed.
My sufferings allow me no respite;

Night presses day, and day too presses night,
Nor is it in my power to ease the strain
Upon my lungs for sighing all in vain.
Therefore, poor wretch, I must at last admit
What I too hastily denied before,
That Sabine charms disturb the breast, and fit
Are Marsian spells one's head in twain to split.
There, now! What want you from me more?

O Earth, O Sea! I burn as burnt before;
Nor Hercules besmeared with Nessus' blood,
Nor fervid Aetna's flame inflaring flood;
But you a Colchian poison-worship glow,
Until the winds contemptuous me shall blow
As dust and ashes. What the end? To die?
Or what do you propose as penalty?
Speak, speak! The penalty you fix I'll pay
I pledge my honor, ready to defray,
Whether a hundred steers you may require,
Or choose the flattery of a lying lyre.

Yes, modest, honest, you shall have your station
Among the stars, a golden constellation.
Castor and Pollux, angered at the shame
Cast upon Helen, prayers yet overcame,
And to the poet they restored his sight,
Which had been taken from him. So do you,
For well you can, remove this frenzy quite,
You, sullied by no stains to forbears due,
Nor ancient hag experienced to explore
The ninth-day ashes of the buried poor.
A kindly soul you are. Your hands are clean,

And Pactomeius is your son, I ween.
Yours is the blood with which the sheets are red
Whene'er the patient springs robust from bed.

Canidia

Why pour your plaints into unheeding ears?
Not rocks more deaf to naked mariners
The wintry ocean pounds with rollers high.
Shall you reveal and flout Cotytto's rites,
Free Cupid's mysteries, and vengeance fly?
Shall you who pontiff to our orgies came
When celebrated on the Esquilian heights,
Unpunished fill the city with my name?
What good to me to empty money-bags
Into the laps of wise Pelignian hags?
What good a swifter poison to prepare?

For you a doom more lingering than you care
To hope awaits. An irksome life for you,
Poor wretch, shall be protracted, with the view
That you may ever suffer tortures new.
The treacherous father of a treacherous son,
Tantalus, Pelops' sire, who never won
The rich elusive banquet, craves respite;
Respite Prometheus to the vulture chained;
And respite Sisyphus whose rock ne'er gained
A resting place upon the mountain's height:
The laws of Jupiter forbid. And so
Shall you one time desire to leap below
From some high tower; another time your breast
With Noric sword to pierce; and sadly pressed
With heartache wearisome a noose you'll tie
About your neck, but seek in vain to die.

Then, mounted on your hated neck, I'll ride
And spurn the earth in my triumphant pride.
Shall I who have the power, as well you know
Through prying, life and feeling to bestow
On waxen images, and pluck from heaven
The moon by incantations—I who even
Can raise the buried dead though burnt in fire,
And duly mix the potions of desire—
Shall I the issues of my art bewail
Because on you its force has chanced to fail?

POEMS
(Odes)

The core of the poet's work, written in his full maturity and presenting his mellowed outlook with the polish of a carefully mastered technique. The first three books appeared in 23 B. C. when Horace was forty-two years old. The fourth book was written, somewhat as the work of a poet-laureate, ten years later

I· 1· *Dedication*

Maecenas atavis edite

Maecenas of a royal name,
O thou my earnest pride and trust,
Some men there are whose favorite game
It is to acquire Olympic dust,
And when their chariots cross the line
They feel no lower than divine.

This man is glad if fickle Rome
Him honors thrice; that if he stores
In his own silo safe at home
What's swept from Libyan threshing floors;
The farmer plows the fields—a notion
He'd not give up to plow the ocean.

The trader dreads the south-west wind
That lashes the Icarian sea;
He praises calm, and yearns to find
The homely peace of field and tree;
Yet he, unused to any hardship,
Will soon repair his sadly-starred ship.

Some love the bowls of Massic wine,
And steal the hours from business woes
Beneath a green arbute supine,

And where some prattling brooklet flows.
(Parenthesis for this translation:
A far from irksome occupation.)

Some love what makes the mothers sigh—
The wars, the camp, the clarion clear;
And out beneath a chilly sky
The hunter loves to stalk the deer,
Or trap, his tender wife forgetting,
The Marsian boar burst from his netting.

But ivy, prize of poet's brows,
Unites me with the lofty gods;
And me the grove with cooling boughs
Withdraws from all the vulgar clods—
If but Euterpe's flute may fire me
And Polyhymnia's lyre inspire me.
If as a bard thou rank'st me high
My happy head would scale the sky.

I· 2· *Augustus Our Saviour*

iam satis terris

Enough of snow and hail in tempest dire
Have poured on earth, while heaven's eternal sire
With red right arm at his own temples hurled
His thunders, and alarmed a guilty world,

Lest Pyrrha should again with plaintive cries
Behold the monsters of the deep arise,
When to the mountain summit Proteus drove
His sea-born herd, and where the woodland dove

Late perched his wonted seat, the scaly hood
Entangled hung upon the topmost wood,
And every timorous native of the plain,
High floating, swam amid the boundless main.

We saw, pushed backward to his native source,
The yellow Tiber roll his rapid course;
With impious ruin threatening Vesta's fane,
And the great monuments of Numa's reign;

With grief and rage while Ilia's bosom glows,
Boastful, for her revenge, his waters rose;
But now the uxorious river glides away,
So Jove commands, smooth-winding to the sea.

And yet, less numerous by their parents' crimes,
Our sons shall hear, shall hear to latest times,
Of Roman arms with civil gore imbrued
Which better had the Persian subdued.

Among her guardian gods, what pitying power
To raise her sinking state shall Rome implore,
Shall her own hallowed virgins' earnest prayer
Harmonious charm offended Vesta's ire?

To whom shall Jove assign to purge away
The guilty deed? Come, then, bright god of day,
But gracious veil thy shoulder beaming bright—
Oh! veil in clouds the unsufferable light.

O come, sweet queen of smiles, while round thee rove,
On wanton wing, the powers of mirth and love.
O hither, Mars, thine aspect gracious bend,
And powerful thy neglected race defend.

Parent of Rome, amidst the rage of fight
Sated with scenes of blood, thy fierce delight—
Thou, whom the polished helm, the noise of arms,
And the stern soldiers' frown with transport warms:

O thou, fair Maia's winged son appear,
And human shape in prime of manhood wear;
Declared the guardian of the imperial state,
Divine avenger of great Caesar's fate.

Oh! late return to heaven and may thy reign
With lengthened blessings fill thy wide domain!
Nor let thy people's crimes provoke thy flight
On air swift rising to the realms of light.

Great prince and father of the state, receive
The noblest triumphs which thy Rome can give;
Nor let the Parthian, with unpunished pride,
Beyond his bounds, O Caesar, dare to ride.

I · 3 · *Bon Voyage—and Afterthoughts*

sic te diva potens

So may Cyprus' heavenly queen,
So Helen's brothers, stars of brightest sheen,
Guide thee! May the Sire of wind
Opposing gales, save only Zephyr, bind!

So do thou, fair ship, that ow'st
Virgil, thy precious freight, to the Attic coast,
Safe restore thy loan and whole,
And save from death the partner of my soul.

Oak and brass of triple fold
Encompassed sure that heart that first made bold
To the raging sea to trust
A fragile bark, nor feared the Afric gust

With its northern mates at strife,
Nor Hyads' frown, nor South Wind fury-rife,
Mightiest power that Hadria knows,
Wills he the waves to madden or compose.

What had Death in store to awe
Those eyes, that huge sea beasts unmelting saw—
Saw the swelling of the surge,
And high Ceraunian cliffs, the seaman's scourge?

Heaven's high providence in vain
Has severed countries with the estranging main,
If our vessels ne'ertheless
With reckless plunge that sacred bar transgress.

Daring all their goal to win,
Men tread forbidden ground and rush on sin:
Daring all, Prometheus played
His wily game, and fire to man conveyed;

Soon as fire was stolen away,
Pale Fever's stranger host and wan Decay
Swept o'er earth's polluted face,
And slow Fate quickened Death's once halting pace.

Daedalus the void air tried
On wings to human kind by Heaven denied;
Acheron's bar gave way with ease
Before the arm of laboring Hercules.

Nought is there for man too high;
Our impious folly e'en would climb the sky,
Braving the dweller on the steep,
Nor let the bolts of heavenly vengeance sleep.

solvitur acris hiems

Sharp winter melts with Spring's delicious birth;
The ships glide down on rollers to the sea;
The herds forsake their stalls, the hind his hearth;
No more with hoar-frost gleams the whitened lea.
  Venus from Cythera the dances leads,
And hand in hand the Nymphs and Graces come,
  And tread the moonlit sward while Vulcan feeds
The fires that heat the Cyclops' busy home.
  With myrtle now 'tis time to wreathe our brows,
Or flowers up-springing from the earth let loose,
  And in the shady grove to pay our vows
With lamb or kid, whichever Faunus choose.
  Pale Death alike knocks at the poor man's house
And the King's palace. Happy Sextius! Few
  And brief the hopes our little day allows;
Dark night brings on apace the shadowy crew
  Of Pluto's dismal reign; once thou art there,
The mastership of toasts thou ne'er wilt get,
  Nor look on Lycidas, whose beauty rare
Now the young men, and soon the girls will pet.

I · 5 · *Pyrrha's Inconstancy*

quis multa gracilis

Slim, young and essenced, Pyrrha, who
On roses couched is courting you?
Whom charms in your sweet grot
The bright hair's single knot,
The choice plain dress? How oft he'll sigh
"False gods, false faith!" with tears, and eye,
Poor novice, seas that change
Storm-lashed to black and strange.

Who now enjoys you, thinks you gold,
Dreams you will love him,—still, still hold
No hand but his, nor knows
Winds change. Alas! for those
Who trust your sheen. On temple wall
My votive tablet proves to all
That Neptune earned his fee—
These dripping clothes—from me.

I· 6· *Limitations of a Poet of Love*

scriberis Vario fortis

By Varius shall thy prowess be
In strains Maeonic chaunted:
The victories by land and sea,
Our gallant troops, led on by thee,
Have won with swords undaunted.

Such themes, Agrippa, never hath
My lyre essay'd, nor bold
Pelides' unrelenting wrath,
Nor artfullest Ulysses path
O'er oceans manifold;

Nor woes of Pelops' fated line;
Such flights too soaring are!
Nor doth my bashful muse incline
Great Caesar's eulogies and thine
With its thin notes to mar.

Who, who shall sing with accents just
Mars' adamantine mail;
Or Merion, grimed with Trojan dust,
Or him who, strong in Pallas' trust,
Made even gods to quail?

Heart-whole, or pierced by Cupid's sting,
In careless mirthfulness,
Of banquets we (and maidens) sing
With nails cut, closely skirmishing,
When lovers hotly press.

I· 7· *Kingdoms in Cups*

laudabunt alii

Let others sing of famous Rhodes or chant of Mytilene,
Or let them sing about the walls of Corinth-'twixt-the-seas,
Or of Thebes for Bacchus famed, or Delphi for Apollo named, or
Celebrate the vale of Tempe, with her Thessalonian trees.

For some there be whose task it is, whose only occupation
It is, to sing unceasingly the glory of the town
(Urbs Palladis Athenae) which is Athens; and Mycenae;
And, in Juno's honor, Argos, which her horses give renown.

Me not sturdy Lacedaemon or the plain of lush Larissa
As Albunea's echoing grotto and the rushing Anio strikes,
And it also may be stated that the orchards irrigated
By the rippling rills, and Tibur's grove are what this poet likes.

Just as Notus (or the south wind) often clears the cloudy heavens,
And is fruitful not of showers that are never known to cease,
So remember to dispel, O Plancus, gloom with liquor mellow,
Whether in the flaggy camp or in Tiburnian shady peace.

Teucer, as he fled from Salamis and also from his sire,
Still, they say, tied poplar garlands round his liquor-heated brow,
And he spoke (between his swallows) to his friends about as follows:
"Let us go, my friends, wherever gentle Fortune takes us now."

"Never under Teucer's leadership or auspices despair ye,
For infallible Apollo vows a Salamis we'll gain;
O ye who shared my sadness, let wine now give ye gladness,
For to-morrow we will sail again across the boundless main!"

I· 8· *Have Mercy, Lydia*

Lydia, dic, per omnis

Tell me, Lydia, I adjure you
By the gods we both adore,
What's in Sybaris to lure you
To a love I must deplore?

Why he hates the Campus sunny,
Though he knows its dust and heat;
Why, his martial riding done, he
Shuns the bucking colt to meet;

Why in yellow Tiber's shallows
He no longer dips to lave.
Is it viper's blood he swallows
When the wrestler's oil he'd have?

And no more the discus-throwing
Stains with blue his manly wrist;
Nor his javelin in its going
Hits the mark the others missed;

Why he hides himself away
As sea-nymph Thetis' son did hide,
Ere the sad and dreadful day
When Troy was whelmed in ruin's tide,

Lest a man's garb should betray him
To the carnage that awaits,
And the Lycian squadrons slay him
Stiff and stark among his mates.

Tell me, Lydia, I adjure you
By the gods we both adore,
What has Sybaris done to lure you
To a love I must deplore?

I· 9· *Kiss in Time*

vides ut alta

Now stands Soracte white with snow,
Now bend the laboring trees,
And with the sharpness of the frost
The stagnant rivers freeze.

Pile up the billets on the hearth,
To warmer cheer incline,
And draw, my Thaliarchus, from
The Sabine jar of wine.

The rest leave to the gods who still
The fiercely warring wind,
And to tomorrow's store of good
Or evil give no mind.

Whatever day your fortune grants,
That day mark up for gain;
And in your youthful bloom do not
The sweet amours disdain.

Now on the Campus and the squares,
When evening shades descend,
Soft whisperings again are heard,
And loving voices blend;

And now the low delightful laugh
Betrays the lurking maid,
While from her slowly yielding arms
The forfeiture is paid.

I· 10· *To Mercury*

Mercuri facunde nepos

Mercurius, Atlas' grandson eloquent,
Shrewd moulder of the habitudes uncouth
Of primal man by language and the training
Whereby the wrestling-school gives grace to youth,

Thee will I sing, thou herald of great Jove
And of the gods, inventor of the lyre,
Ingenious to conceal in impish theft
Whatever to conceal thou didst desire.

When thee, the merest child, Apollo threatened
Unless his cattle stolen by fraud of thine
Thou didst restore, he could not keep from laughter
To find his quiver gone—gone with his kine.

Ay, and 't was under guidance of thy wit
That wealthy Priam, leaving Ilium lost,
Eluded Atreus' overbearing sons,
Thessalian watchfires, and the Grecian host.

The faithful souls to blissful seats thou guidest,
And with thy golden rod the shadowy throng
Thou marshallest to their place: esteemed art thou
The gods above, the gods below, among.

I · 11 · *Use Today, Forget Tomorrow*

tu ne quaesieris

Ask not, 't is not right to know it,
What last end for thee and me
Heaven has set, nor Babylonian
Numbers try, Leuconöe.

Better, whate'er comes, to bear it;
Whether many winters more
We shall see, or this our last be,
Which along the Etruscan shore

Hurls the waves in spray to perish
On the shifting shingly beach
If thou'rt wise thou'lt quaff, and quickly
Grasp the hopes within thy reach.

Even now, whilst we are talking,
Grudging time pursues his flight:
Use today, and trust as little
As thou mayst tomorrow's light.

quem virum aut heroa

Clio, what man, what hero, or what God
  Shall wake thy lyre—thy flute with sweetness thrill;
Whose name shall playful echo send abroad
  In whispers from her hill?

Whether on Helicon's umbrageous side,
  Or Pindus' height, or Haemus' peak of snow,
Whence suddenly, self-wooed, the forests glide
  As Orpheus' numbers flow.

And by the art his goddess mother gave
  He bids the rivers pause, the winds delay;
The oaks, as in gigantic strength they wave,
  Hear and his lute obey.

Father Supreme, of earth and ocean King,
  Ruler of all things human and divine,
Guide of the world, whose praises can I sing
  Before I utter thine?

None greater than thyself has sprung from thee;
  None like, none second to thy power is found;
Yet Pallas next, thy wondrous progeny,
  Is after thee renown'd.

Victorious Bacchus, how can I abstain
  To laud thy name? Or thine, thou virgin foe
Of the fierce forest tribes? Or thine refrain,
  Lord of the fatal bow?

Alcides sing I, and each royal twin,
  The wild-steed tamer and the arm of might;
When on the mariners their stars begin
  To pour their silver light,

Down from the cliffs the showers of spray distil,
  The winds are lulled, the clouds obedient flee;
The mountain waves, subservient to their will,
  Sink down upon the sea.

Shall Romulus, or Numa's tranquil reign,
  Afford the fittest theme to celebrate?
Shall Tarquin's haughty rule awake the strain,
  Or Cato's noble fate?

To Regulus, the Scauri and (of life
  Too prodigal on Cannae's bloody field)
Paulus, and old Fabricius, verses rife
  With grace their fame shall yield.

Stern poverty and the ancestral farm
  Trained these, and Curius rough with tangled hair,
For war; and nerved Camillus' mighty arm
  The battle's toil to dare.

As spreads a tree, so grows Marcellus' fame
  With every year; the Julian orb afar
Gleams bright, as when the moonbeam's lambent flame
  Outshines each minor star.

Father and guardian of the human race,
  Offspring of Saturn, thine by destiny,
Great Caesar's charge. Thou art supreme; his place
  Second to none but thee:

Whether when Parthia threatened with her hosts
  Fair Latium, their repulse his triumph gained;
Or India's tribes, or hordes from China's coasts
  His mighty hand restrained.

On thy behalf still may he rule the world;
  Shake with thy ponderous car the worlds above;
By thee the avenging bolts of heaven be hurled
  On each polluted grove!

I· 13· *Love Unreasoning*

cum tu, Lydia, Telephi

Telephus—you praise him still,
His waxen arms, his rosy-tinted neck;
Ah! and all the while I thrill
With jealous pangs I cannot, cannot check.

See! My color comes and goes,
My poor heart flutters, Lydia, and the dew
Down my cheek soft stealing shows
What lingering torments rack me through and through.

Oh! 'tis agony to see
Those snow-white shoulders scarred in drunken fray,
Or those rosy lips, where he
Has left strange marks that show how rough his play.

Never, never look to find
A faithful heart in him whose rage can harm
Sweetest lips, which Venus kind
Has tinctured with her quintessential charm.

Happy, happy, happy they
Whose living love, untroubled by all strife,
Binds them till the last sad day,
Nor parts asunder but with parting life!

I· 14· *To the Ship of State*

o navis, referent

Proud ship, the waves and winds conspire
  To drag you back to sea.
O, gain the port that we desire;
  Ride swiftly, lest you be

A hopeless wreck; for even now
  Devoid of oars you sail;
Your mast is bent and weak (a blow
  Dealt by a foreign gale).

And see the signs that from each spar
  A dire destruction spell:
Your sails in tattered ribbons are
  That catch the breezes swell.

Your keel shows signs of swift decay;
  Your cables all are bare;
No gods are left to whom you may
  Turn with a frenzied prayer.

Of Pontic pine, you boast, you came,
  Reared in a noble wood.
Think you that *this* will ever tame
  The tempest's angry mood?

'Tis little courage sailors find
  In neatly-painted boats.
Beware then, lest the howling wind
  Hurls back the boastful notes.

O, you who are my grief and care,
  Turn back to calmer seas!
Beware, oh precious ship, beware
  The shining Cyclades!

pastor cum traheret

From Sparta's hospitable shore,
His prize when faithless Paris bore,
While guilt impatient crowds his sail,
Prophetic Nereus checks the gale,
By force the flying robber holds,
And thus the wrath of heaven unfolds:

"In vain the fleet transports the dame,
Whom injured Greece shall soon reclaim,
Prepared to break the lawless tie,
And Priam's ancient realm destroy.
Behold the troops, the foaming steed,
To labors doomed, and doomed to bleed!
See! victim of thy lewd desires,
Thy country blaze with funeral fires!
See! Pallas eager to engage,
Prepares her car and martial rage:
She waves her aegis, nods her plumes,
And all the pomp of war assumes!
In vain, devoted to thy side,
Shall Cytherea swell with pride;
In vain thy graceful locks express
The studied elegance of dress;
Thy languid harp, with amorous air,
In vain shall charm the listening fair;
The palace screen thy conscious heart
In vain, against the Cretan dart,
And Ajax, nimble to pursue.
What though, concealed from public view,

The chamber guards thy nicer ear
From all the horrid din of war!
At length, adulterer! fall thou must,
And trail those beauteous locks in dust!
See! author of thy country's fate,
Ulysses, practised in deceit.
Behold the hoary Pylian sage
Against her forfeit towers engage.
Teucer and Sthenelus unite
With various skill, in various fight.
Tydides, greater than his sire,
To find thee, burns with martial fire.
But as a grazing stag who spies
The distant wolf, with terror flies;
So shalt thou fly, with panting breath,
And faltering limbs, the approach of death.
Where is thy boasted courage? Where
Thy promise plighted to the fair?
Though fierce Achilles' sullen hate
Awhile protracts the city's fate,
Heaven shall its righteous doom require,
And Troy in Grecian flames expire!

I· 16· *Apology*

O matre pulchra

O lovelier than the lovely dame
That bore you, sentence as you please
Those scurril verses, be it flame
Your vengeance craves, or Hadrian seas.

Not Cybele, nor he that haunts
Rich Pytho, worse the brain confounds,
Not Bacchus nor the Corybants
Clash their loud gongs with fiercer sounds

Than savage wrath; nor sword nor spear
Appals it, no, nor ocean's frown,
Nor ravening fire, nor Jupiter
In hideous ruin crashing down.

Prometheus, forced, they say, to add
To his prime clay some favorite part,
From every kind, took lion mad,
And lodged its gall in man's poor heart.

'Twas wrath that laid Thyestes low;
'Tis wrath that oft destruction calls
On cities, and invites the foe
To drive his plow o'er ruined walls.

Then calm your spirit; I can tell
How once, when youth in all my veins
Was glowing, blind with rage, I fell
On friend and foe in ribald strains.

Come, let me change my sour for sweet,
And smile complacent as before;
Hear me my palinode repeat,
And give me back your heart once more.

velox amoenum

Swift-footed Faunus oft delights to roam
From snow-clad peaks of Arcady, and find
Here in my soft Lucretilis a home,
Where in sequestered brake
Safe from hot suns and pitiless wind
From ledge to ledge my nimble younglings climb
Nipping fresh Arbutus and fragrant Thyme,
Fearless of prowling wolf or venomed snake,
While from Ustica's vale profound
The polished rocks the Wood-god's pipe resound

The gods protect me. They approve
My piety; my song they love.
Haste, Tyndaris, haste! partake my store
Of rural honours brimming o'er
From plenteous horn. This cool retreat
Shall guard thee from the Dog-star's heat.
Here that white hand the Teian lyre shall strike;
That sweet voice sing the old Greek melody
Of him the wand'ring Prince beloved alike
By that true wife, Penelope,
And Circe glittering as a summer sea.

Tyndaris! 'neath the arching vine
Lift to thy lips the Lesbian wine,
An innocent draught! Not here shall Mars
And Bacchus wage their customed wars;

Not here shall jealous Cyrus dare
To rend thy guiltless robe, or tear
The clinging garland from thy hair.

I· 18· *On the Grape*

nullam, Vare, sacra

Varus, are your trees in planting? Put in none before the vine,
In the rich domain of Tibur, by the walls of Catilus;
There's a power above that hampers all that sober brains design,
And the troubles man is heir to thus are quelled, and only thus.

Who can talk of want or warfare when the wine is in his head,
Not of thee, good father Bacchus, and of Venus fair and bright?
But should any dream of licence, there's a lesson may be read,
How 'twas wine that drove the Centaurs with the Lapithae to fight.

And the Thracians, too, may warn us; truth and falsehood, good and ill,
How they mix them, when the wine god's hand is heavy on them laid!
Never, never, gracious Bacchus, may I move thee 'gainst thy will,
Or uncover what is hidden in the verdure of thy shade!

Silence thou thy savage cymbals and the Berecyntine horn;
In their train Self-love still follows, dully, desperately blind,

And Vain-glory, towering upward in its empty-headed
scorn,
And the Faith that keeps no secrets, with a window in its
mind.

I· 19· *A Belated Passion*

mater saeva Cupidinum

Cupid's mother, cruel dame,
And Semele's Theban boy, and Licence bold,
Bid me kindle into flame
This heart, by waning passion now left cold.

Oh! the charm of Glycera,
That hue more dazzling than the Parian stone!
Oh! that sweet, tormenting play,
That too fair face that blinds when looked upon!

Venus comes in all her might,
Quits Cyprus for my heart, nor lets me tell
Of the Parthian, bold in flight,
Nor Scythian hordes nor aught that breaks her spell

Heap the grassy altar up,
Bring vervain, boys, and sacred frankincense;
Fill the sacrificial cup;
A victim's blood will soothe her vehemence.

I · 20 · *To Maecenas—with an Invitation*

vile potabis modicis

But common Sabine on the board
In homely ware you'll find. Yet stored
And sealed in Grecian jar 'twas first,
Dear knight, what time your praises burst
From the full circus' serried ranks,
And your own Tiber from his banks
And the great Mount, rang back reply.

No Caecuban like yours have I;
No press of Cales yet for me
Crushed the fat grape. Those cups of mine
Neither the hills of Formiae
Have tempered, nor Falernian vine.

I· 21· *Hymn to Latona and Her Children*

Dianam tenerae dicite

Ye tender maids, Diana sing;
Ye boys, let praise to Cynthius ring—
Apollo with the flowing hair;
And sing ye all Latona fair,
Whom Jupiter, of gods the king,
Beloved holds beyond compare.

Ye maids, Diana laud, who loves
The rivers, loves the waving groves
That overhang the frowning crest
Of snow-capped Algidus, or rest
Where Erymanthus' dark wood moves,
Or on green Cragus' friendly breast.

Ye boys, extol with equal fire
Apollo's Tempe of desire,
Famed Delos isle where he was born,
His quiver on his shoulder worn;
And praise his brother Hermes' lyre,
And laud his horses of the morn.

The god will hear you when you pray,
And war, plague, famine drive away,
With all their miserable train
Of ruin and distress and pain,
From Romans under Caesar's sway
To Persians' and to Britons' bane.

I· 22· *Purity of Soul*

integer vitae

The man of life unblemished ever,
Of hand unstained by evil deed,
Nor Moorish darts nor bow nor quiver
With poisoned arrows stuffed will need,

Whether it be his lot to fare
Through burning Syrtes or to brave
The Caucasus repellent, bare,
Or story-famed Hydaspes' wave.

For as I wandered fancy-free
Beyond my bounds in Sabine wood,
Singing my darling Lalage,
I met a wolf, and, though I stood

Unarmed, it fled me. Nor Apulia
Such monster in her forests rears,
Wide as they stretch, nor realm of Juba,
Dry nurse of lions, ever bears.

Place me in plains inert where ne'er
A tree is waked by summer breeze,
Or that side of the world's orb where
The chilling clouds and airs men freeze;

Place me right 'neath the sun-god's ray
In lands where no man dwells or toils;
And there I'll love my Lalage,
Her winsome prattle, winsome smiles.

I · 23 · *To a Mothered Girl*

vitas inuleo

You shun me, Chloe. Like a fawn
That seeks his timorous dam forlorn
In pathless wild,
Needlessly nervous when the breeze
Rustles the mountain forest trees,
You shun me, child.

Is it the coming of the Spring
Hath set the leaves aquivering
On all the trees?
Is it the parting of the brambles
By the green lizards? There he trembles,
His heart, his knees.

Why, Chloe, I'm no savage beast
Bent on your blood and bones to feast;
Be not so coy;
'Tis time for you to quit your mother,
Ay, now, 'tis time to seek another—
A husband, Chloe.

I · 24 · *Dirge*

quis desiderio sit

Why blush to let our tears unmeasured fall
For one so dear? Begin the mournful stave,
Melpomene, to whom the Sire of all
Sweet voice with music gave.

And sleeps he then the heavy sleep of death,
Quintilius? Piety, twin sister dear
Of Justice, naked Truth, unsullied Faith,
When will ye find his peer?

By many a good man wept, Quintilius dies;
By none than you, my Vergil, trulier wept:
Devout in vain you chide the faithless skies,
Asking your loan ill-kept.

No, though more suasive than the bard of Thrace
You swept the lyre that trees were fain to hear,
Ne'er should the blood revisit his pale face
Whom once with wand severe

Mercury has folded with the sons of night,
Untaught to prayer Fate's prison to unseal.
Ah, heavy grief! But patience makes more light
What sorrow may not heal.

parcius junctas quatiunt

Swains in numbers
Break your slumbers,
Saucy Lydia, now but seldom,
Ay, though at your casement nightly,
Tapping loudly, tapping lightly,
By the dozen once you held them.

Ever turning,
Night and morning
Swung your door upon its hinges;
Now, from dawn till evening's closing,
Lone and desolate reposing,
Not a soul its rest infringes.

Serenaders,
Sweet invaders,
Scanter grow, and daily scanter,
Singing, "Lydia, art thou sleeping?
Lonely watch thy love is keeping!
Wake, O wake, thou dear enchanter!"

Lone and faded,
You, as they did,
Woo, and in your turn are slighted,
Worn and torn by passion's fret.
You, the pitiless coquette,
Waste by fires yourself have lighted,

Late relenting,
Left lamenting,—
"Withered leaves strew wintry brooks!
Ivy garlands greenly darkling,
Myrtles brown with dew-drops sparkling,
Best beseem youth's glowing looks!"

I· 26· *Praise of Lamia*

Musis amicus

The Muses love me: fear and grief,
The winds may blow them to the sea;
Who quail before the wintry chief
Of Scythia's realm, is naught to me.

What cloud o'er Tiridates lowers,
I care not, I. O nymph divine
Of virgin springs, with sunniest flowers
A chaplet for my Lamia twine,

Pimplea sweet! my praise were vain
Without thee. String this maiden lyre,
Attune for him the Lesbian strain,
O goddess, with thy sister quire.

I· 27· *No Brawling*

natis in usum laetitiae

It is a Thracian trick to brawl in wine,
And fight with vessels dedicate to pleasure;
Bacchus will all such services decline.
Strike up the drinking, not the martial measure!

There is no bond between the lighted feast
And the accursed assassin's Median blade.
Such quarrels, Gentlemen, should long have ceased.
Be seated! Let your turbulence be stayed!

You bid me stay and drink Falernian rare?
Then let the lad, Megillia's own brother,
The source of his sweet wound to us declare:
So let him name his sweetheart and no other!

What? You refuse? I will not drink a swallow
Until I know whoever is your passion.
There is no reason for such shame to follow.
An honest love has ever been your fashion.

Whatever is the manner of your fate,
Trust it to loyal ears. Oh, cursed shame
That this Charybdis should have seized you straight,
When you, poor youth, should have less fierce a flame!

What witchcraft now can free your pinioned arms?
What god, what mystic lore of Thessaly?
From such chimerian, triple-folded charm
Winged Pegasus himself might not win free.

te maris et terrae

Thee, O Archytas, who hast scanned
The wonders of the earth by sea and land,
The lack of some few grains
Of scattered dust detains
A shivering phantom here upon Matinym's strand.
And it avails thee nothing, that thy soul,
Death's sure-devoted prey,
Soared to the regions of eternal day,
Where wheeling spheres in silvery brightness roll.

ARCHYTAS

What then! Even Pelops' sire, the guest
Of gods! to Orcus sank, by death oppressed,
And old Tithonus, too,
Though heavenly air he drew,
And Minos stern, who shared the secrets of Jove's heart.
There, too, Panthoides, once more immured,
Roams, though his spirit's pride
All save this fading flesh to death denied,
By his old Trojan shield deceitfully assured.

And he, even thou wilt grant me, was
Not meanly versed in truth and nature's laws,
But for us all doth stay
One night, and death's dark way
Must needs be trodden once, however we pause.
The Furies some to Mars' grim spat, consign,
The hungry waves devour
The shipman, young and old drop hour by hour,
No single head is spared by ruthless Proserpine.

Me, too, a headlong gust,
That dogs Orion, neath the billows thrust.
But, prithee, seaman, shed
On my unburied head
And limbs with gentle hand some grains of drifting dust!
So may the storm that threats the western deep
Turn all its wrath away,
To smite the forests of Venusia,
And thou thy course secure over the mild ocean keep!

So may from every hand
Wealth rain on thee by righteous Jove's command!
And Neptune, who doth bear
Tarentum in his care,
Bring thy rich-laden argosy to land!
Deny me this, the common tribute due,
And races to be born
Of thy son's sons in after years forlorn,
Though guiltless of thy crime, thy heartless scorn shall rue!

Nor shall thyself go free,
For Fate's vicissitudes shall follow thee,
Its laws, that slight for slight,
And good for good requite!
Not unavenged my bootless prayer shall be;
Nor victim ever expiate thy guilt.
O, then though speed thou must,
It asks brief tarrying—thrice with kindly dust
Bestrew my corpse, and then pass onward as thou wilt!

Icci, beatis nunc

Your heart on Arab wealth is set,
Good Iccius: you would try your steel
On Saba's kings, unconquered yet,
And make the Mede your fetters feel.

Come, tell me what barbarian fair
Will serve you now, her bridegroom slain?
What page from court with perfumed hair
Will tender you the bowl you drain,

Well skilled to bend the Serian bow
His father carried? Who shall say
That rivers may not uphill flow,
And Tiber's self return one day,

If you would change Panaetius' works,
That costly purchase, and the clan
Of Socrates, for shields and dirks,
Whom once we thought a saner man?

I· 30· *Come, Queen Venus*

O Venus, regina

Leave Cyprus awhile that thou lovest, and come,
Sweet Venus, of Cnidos and Paphos the queen,
Where the smoke of rich incense inviting is seen,
  To Glycera's beautiful home.

Bring thy warm-hearted boy, and the jovial crew
Of the Muses and Graces with white bosoms bare,
Bid the goddess of youth, whom thy presence makes fair,
  And Mercury come with thee, too.

I · 31 · *Grant Me, Phoebus, Calm Content*

quid dedicatum poscit

What blessing shall the bard entreat
The god he hallows, as he pours
The winecup? Not the mounds of wheat
That load Sardinian threshing floors;
Not Indian gold or ivory—no,
Nor flocks that o'er Calabria stray,
Nor fields that Liris, still and slow,
Is eating, unperceived, away.
Let those whose fate allows them train
Calenum's vine; let trader bold
From golden cups rich liquor drain
For wares of Syria bought and sold,
Heaven's favorites, sooth, for thrice a year
He comes and goes across the brine
Undamaged. I in plenty here
On endives, malows, succory dine.
Oh, grant me, Phoebus, calm content,
Strength unimpaired, a mind entire,
Old age without dishonor spent,
Nor unbefriended by the lyre.

I· 32: *The Poet to His Lyre*

poscimur, si quid

If ever, underneath the shade,
  My careless fingers I have cast
Over thy strings and something played
  A year or more to last,

Help me my Latin strain to pour,
  O lyre, that first the Lesbian strung,
Who his rocked galley to the shore
  Would fasten while he sung

The Muses, Bacchus, Venus fair,
  And him, the boy, who with her flies,
And Lycus with the deep black hair
  And with the deep black eyes.

Aid me! When I invoke thee right,
  O thou that Phoebus' glory art,
Thou givest to the gods delight
  And sooth'st the weary heart.

Albi, ne doleas

Love mocks us all. Then cast aside
These tuneful plaints, by Albius tried
  For heartless Glycera, from thee
  Fled to a younger lover. See,
Low-browed Lycoris burns denied

For Cyrus; he—though goats shall bide
With wolves ere she in him confide—
  Turns, with base suit, to Pholoë:—
    Love mocks us all!

So Venus wills, and joys to guide
'Neath brazen yokes pairs ill-allied
  In form and mind. So linked she me
  (Whom worthier wooed) to Myrtale,
  Fair, but less kind than Hadria's tide:—
    Love mocks us all!

1· 34· *Converted*

parcus deorum cultor

Wise in the love of philosophic fools
I strayed perplexed amid conflicting schools:
I worshipped not, believed not, hoped not! Now
To long-neglected gods perforce must bow,
Reverse my shattered sail, and turn once more,
Repentant, to the course I steered of yore;
For Jove, whose lightnings from Olympus hurled
Erewhile through rifted storm-clouds smote the world,
Through cloudless skies and azure depths afar
Drove now his fiery steeds and thunder-winged car.
Trembled the solid earth, the ocean floor,
The wandering rivers, and the Stygian shore,
Dark Taenarus accurst and Atlas hoar.

There is a god: his justice and his might
Adjust the balance of the world aright;
Abase the proud; exalt and glorify
The lowly grace of true humility.
Fortune at his command plucks monarchs down,
And on the humble outcast lays the crown.

o diva, gratum

Goddess of pleasant Antium,
  Whose might from lowliest place can lift
Our weak mortality, or doom
  Our proudest hours to anguish swift;

Poor struggling peasants crowd to thee
  With troubled prayers, and he who braves
In Thynian keel and Cretan sea,
  For thou art mistress of the waves.

The Dacians rude, the Scythian hordes,
  Imperious Latium, tribe and town,
And mothers of barbaric lords
  And purple tyrants fear thy frown;

Lest 'neath the heel ignobly lie
  The column that springs elate;
And loiterers rally to the cry
  "To arms, to arms!" and wreck the state.

Before thee, Doom morosely tramps,
  Her brazen fingers clenching fast
Gigantic nails and griping clamps
  And molten lead and wedges vast.

And white-veiled Honor, rare to view,
  And hope attend thee: fast they bide,
When changing mood and mantle, too,
  Thou fliest from the halls of pride.

But fickle mobs and mistresses
  Soon go, and comrades melt in air
When casks are emptied to the lees—
  Too false are they the yoke to share.

Defend our Caesar setting forth
  To fight with levies yet unworn,
The Britons of the farthest north,
  The Indian sea, and lands of Morn.

A curse on wars that brothers fought!
  What way of sin have we not trod?
Why have we left a wrong unwrought?
  And held our hands for fear of God?

What altars have we ever spared?
  O, forge anew our edgeless swords
On other anvils, to be bared
  Against the Huns and Arab hordes!

et ture et fidibus

Sing, Comrades, sing, let incense burn,
And blood of votive heifer flow
Unto the gods, to whom we owe
  Our Numida's return!

Warm greetings many wait him here,
From farthest Spain restored, but none
From him return so warm hath won
  As Lamia's chiefly dear.

His boyhood's friend in school and play,
Together manhood's gown they donned;
Then mark with white, all days beyond,
  This most auspicious day.

Bid wine flow fast without control,
And let the dancers' merry feet
The ground in Salian manner beat,
  And Bassus drain the bowl,

Unbreathed, or own the mastering power
Of Damalis; and roses fair,
And parsley's vivid green be there,
  And lilies of an hour!

On Damalis shall fond looks be bent,
But sooner shall the ivy be
Torn from its wedded oak, than she
  Be from her new love rent.

I · 37 · *Cleopatra Unqueened*

nunc est bibendum

Now let us drink and tread the earth
  With dancing mirth.
Now, comrades, let us open up
  The rare wine stored away so long,
And raise, with many a glowing cup,
  A thankful and victorious song.

A short time since all men had seen
  The Ethiop Queen
Plotting to rule on land and sea;
  Sending fresh ships on every wave,
To flood fair Rome with savagery
  And turn the Empire to a grave.

But soon her madness was dispelled.
  Her hopes were quelled
When all her ships went up in flame
  And Caesar, giving swift pursuit,
Brought back her reason as she came
  Nearer the shores she left to loot.

Hot as the hunter out to stalk
  The hare; or hawk
After a pigeon, Caesar swept
  To make his triumph greater still.
But, scorning chains, she never wept
  Or shrank from her majestic will.

She smiled at Death and dared to grasp
  The deadly asp.
Ruined and lost, she never mourned;
  She let the poison have its way.
Unqueened, she kept her throne, and scorned
  To make a Roman holiday.

I · 38 · *No Frills!*

Persicos odi, puer

No Persian pomp, my boy, for me!
No chaplets from the linden tree!
And for late roses, let them be
  Unculled, unheeded.

Naught with the homely myrtle twine
To wreathe your brows, my boy, and mine.
When drinking 'neath the pleached vine
  Naught else is needed.

Motum ex Metello

Pollio! your page records the fate
Of Rome, her crimes, her wars, her feuds,
Their causes and vicissitudes,
Since brave Metellus ruled its state,
The sport of Fortune, the array
Of leaders banded to betray,
And Roman armour crimsoned o'er
With yet unexpiated gore.
A high but perilous task! you tread
O'er fires with treacherous ashes spread.

Forsake the tragic muse severe
Awhile. When your historic pen
Has traced in characters austere
The fates of nations and of men,
Your Attic buskin wear again
Bold pleader of the sufferers' cause;
Champion of Roman arms and laws,
Pollio, the Senate's counsellor,
Crowned hero of Dalmatia's war!

Hark! As I read I seem to hear
The clarion bray; the trumpet's breath
With quivering thunder smites mine ear;
Methinks I see the war-horse quail

Before yon wall of flashing mail,
And warriors, wan with sudden fear,
  Trembling at coming death;
And chiefs careering o'er the plain
With no ignoble battle-stain,
And all that's best on earth subdued
Save Cato's iron fortitude.

Juno and gods who loved the Afric shores,
Yielding reluctant, powerless then to save,
Have laid as victims at Jugurtha's grave
The offspring of his Roman conquerors.
What soil by Daunian carnage fed
Teems not with Latin tombs? What flood
Rolls not unhallowed waters, red
  With fratricidal blood?
The Medes, the Parthians in their desert home
Exulting hear the crash of falling Rome.

Cease, cease, presumptuous shell!
The Cean's lofty dirge beseems thee not.
Once more with me a lighter descant swell
To love and laughter in Dione's grot.

nullus argento color

The treasure of the hidden mine,
My Sallust, is no friend of thine,
Unless with proper use it shine.
   Good Proculeius' name,
Who to his brethren twain did give
A father's care, shall ever live,
And history's tireless tongue shall strive
   To celebrate his fame.

He's more a king who can control
The greedy longings of his soul,
Than if wild tribes from pole to pole
   Bowed to his sovereign sway.
Dropsies indulged are aye the worst:
The puffing, pale and raging thirst
Increase, till from the system first
   The cause be driven away.

Phraates reigns on Cyrus' throne,
The crowd applauds; with angry tone
His bliss true virtue will not own;
   To teach men not to use
False names, a realm and crown secure
She grants, and bays that will endure
To him and him alone who, poor,
   Wealth without envy views.

II · 3 · *The Last Exile*

aequam memento rebus

When life is hard, your soul possess
In calm serene; when times are fair,
Refrain from triumph's haughty air,
For, Dellius, death will come no less

If length of days be wholly spanned
With grief, or if, as glad hours laugh,
You lie in quiet meads and quaff
Falernum's wine of choicest brand,

Where lofty pines and poplars white
Their boughs in friendly shade entwine
Together, and with winding line
The brooklet babbles in its flight.

Here call for wine and nard and bloom
Of roses fading all too fast,
While youth remains and fortunes last
And Fate still spares the thread of doom.

The lawns you buy you must forsake,
The home by tawny Tiber's wave;
The growing stores for which you slave
In heirship will another take.

What boots your wealth or long descent
From Inachus? As well to lie
A lowly beggar 'neath the sky
For any ruth in Death's intent.

One bourne constrains us all; for all
  The lots are shaken in the urn,
  Whence, soon or late, will fall our turn
Of exile's barge without recall.

ne sit ancillae

Nay, Xanthias, my friend, never blush, man—no, no!
  Why should you not love your own maid, if you please?
Briseis of old, with her bosom of snow,
  Brought the haughty Achilles himself to his knees.

By his captive Tecmessa was Telamon's son,
  Stout Ajax, to willing capitivity tamed:
Atrides, in triumph, was wholly undone,
  With love for the slave of his war-spear inflamed,

In the hot hour of triumph, when, quelled by the spear
  Of Celides, in heaps the barbarians lay;
And Troy, with her Hector no longer to fear,
  To the war-wearied Greeks fell an easier prey.

For aught that you know, now, fair Phyllis may be
  The shoot of some highly respectable stem;
Nay, she counts, at the least, a few kings in her tree,
And laments the lost acres once lorded by them.

Never think that a creature so exquisite grew
  In the haunts where but vice and dishonor are known,
Nor deem that a girl so unselfish, so true,
  Had a mother 'twould shame thee to take for thine own.

I extol with free heart, and with fancy as free,
  Her sweet face, fine ankles, and tapering arms.
How? Jealous? Nay, trust an old fellow like me,
  Who can feel, but not follow, where loveliness charms.

II· 5· *Too Young for Love*

nondum subacta ferre

Not yet her subject neck may wear
The yoke, not yet may she fulfill
The duties of a mate, or bear
The amorous bull's impetuous will.

In verdant meads at will to graze
Absorbs thy heifer's tranquil mind,
The heat of summer she allays
In streams, and seeks her yearling kind

In willow copses wet. Ne'er yearn
For unripe grapes: with garish reign
Comes crimson autumn, soon to turn
Each darkening bunch to purpler stain.

Soon she will come; time's mad career
Draws years from thee to give to her;
Soon boldly, when she needs a fere,
For thee will Lalage bestir.

For her shalt thou more deeply pine
Than erst for bashful Pholoë,
Or Chloris, she whose shoulders shine
Like moonbeams on the nightly sea,

Or Cnidian Gyges—scarce is read
His sex when mid the bevied girls,
And strangers well may be misled
By blooming cheeks and flowing curls.

II· 6· *Home Is Best*

Septimi, Gadis aditure

Septimius, who with me would brave
Far Gades, and Cantabrian land
Untamed by Rome, and Moorish wave
That whirls the sand:

Fair Tibur, town of Argive kings,
There would I end my days serene,
At rest from seas and travelings,
And service seen.

Should angry Fate those wishes foil,
Then let me see Galaesus sweet,
The skin-clad sheep, and that rich soil,
The Spartan's seat.

Oh! what can match the green recess
Whose honey not to Hybla yields,
Whose olives vie with those that bless
Venafrum's fields!

Long springs, mild winters glad that spot
By Jove's good grace, and Aulon, dear
To fruitful Bacchus, envies not
Falernian cheer.

That spot, those happy heights desire
Our sojourn; there, when life shall end,
Your tear shall dew my yet warm pyre,
Your bard and friend.

II· 7· *Welcome Home!*

o saepe mecum

O oft with me in troublous time
  Involved when Brutus warred in Greece,
Who gives you back to your own clime
  And your own Gods, a man of peace,
Pompey, the earliest friend I knew,
  With whom I oft cut short the hours
With wine, my hair bright-bathed in dew
  Of Syrian oils and wreathed with flowers?
With you I shared Philippi's rout,
  Unseemly parted from my shield,
When Valor fell, and warriors stout
  Were tumbled on the inglorious field.
But I was saved by Mercury,
  Wrapped in thick mist yet trembling sore,
While you to that tempestuous sea
  Were swept by battle's tide once more.
Come pay to Jove the feast you owe;
  Lay down those limbs with warfare spent,
Beneath my laurel; nor be slow
  To drain my cask—for you 'twas meant.
Lethe's true draught is Massic wine;
  Fill high the goblet; pour out free
Rich streams of unguent. Who will twine
  The hasty wreath from myrtle tree
Or parsley? Whom will Venus seat
  Chairman of cups? Are Bacchants sane?
Then I'll be sober. Ah, 'tis sweet
  To fool, when friends come home again!

II· 8· *Bright-eyed Witch*

ulla si iuris

Barine, if your loveliness
Were by one perjury the less,
If your white hand or rosy smile
Betrayed one blemish for your guile,

I'd trust you. But alas! instead,
Once you've forsworn your pretty head,
With charms that still the brighter burn
The heads of all our youth you turn.

Fair perjurer, would you be more fair,
Your mother's ashes quick forswear;
Mock heaven, night's silent pageant, aye,
The deathless god enthroned on high.

Venus will jeer, the Nymphs applaud,
While Cupid, laughing at your fraud,
Still fiercely whets his burning darts
With blood from faithful lovers' hearts.

And still young wooers stray in droves,
The slaves! not even your cast-off loves
Can bear to quit your faithless door,
Though threatening oft to come no more.

The mothers fear you for their boys;
Age dreads you! Cold amid their joys,
The young wives shudder lest your spell
Bewitch their lords who love them well.

non semper imbres

Clouds do not always veil the skies,
  Nor showers immerse the radiant plain;
Nor do the billows always rise,
  Nor storms afflict the troubled main.

Nor, Valgius, on the Armenian shores,
  Do the chained waters always freeze;
Nor always furious Boreas roars,
  Or bends with violent force the trees.

But you are ever drowned in tears,
  For Mystes dead you ever mourn;
No setting sun can ease your cares,
  But finds you sad at his return.

The wise experienced Grecian sage
  Mourned not Antilochus so long:
Nor did King Priam's hoary age
  So much lament his slaughtered son.

Leave off at length these woman's sighs,
  Augustus' numbered trophies sing;
Repeat that prince's victories
  To whom all nations tribute bring.

Niphates rolls on humbler wave;
  At length the undaunted Scythian yields,
Content to live the Roman's slave,
  And scarce forsakes his native fields.

II · 10 · *The Golden Mean*

rectius vives

Live so that you tempt not the sea relentless,
Neither press too close on the shore forbidding;
Flee extremes, and choose thou the mean all-golden.
  Treasure all priceless.

Safe, you dread not poverty's hut repellent;
Wise, you seek not mansions that men may envy;
All secure, protected by moderation,
  Fate cannot harm you.

Tallest pines are soon by the storm blasts shattered,
Turrets high may fall with the loudest clamor,
Tow'ring peaks are seared by the lightning's fury,
  Dangerous, earth's summits.

Lighten grief with hopes of a brighter morrow;
Temper joy, in fear of a change of fortune;
Bear the winters, knowing, despite their fury,
  Jove will recall them.

If, today, misfortune besiege thy pathway,
Still the future beckons a smiling promise;
Soon Apollo leaving his arrows dreaded
  Makes the Muse tuneful.

Thus in stormy days be of heart courageous
And, when waves are calm, and the danger over,
Wise man, trim your sails when a gale too prosp'rous
  Swells out the canvas.

quid bellicosus

What warlike Biscayans and Scythians plan,
Hirpinus, worry not your brain to scan;
 Salt water rolls 'twixt them and us,
 Then wherefore all this weary fuss?

Man's life requires but little. Youth, alas!
And youth's smooth comeliness too quickly pass:
 And age and its grey hairs remove
 The sweets of sleep and joys of love.

Spring's beauteous flowerets will not always seem
So fair, nor aye the same the moon's soft beam.
 Then why with thought thy spirit wear
 Unequal to incessant care?

Nay, while we can, at ease beneath the shade
Of some tall plane-tree let our limbs be laid,
 Or this dark pine, while roses rare
 And Syrian unguents scent our hair.

There let us quaff, till Evius drives away
Gnawing anxiety, while pages gay
 Shall haste our ardent wine to cool
 With water from yon limpid pool.

Let some one with her ivory cittern here
Bid Lyde haste, the wandering tymbestere,

With locks that know not plaits nor curls,
Plain-knotted like a Spartan girl's.

II· 12· *My Theme Is Love*

nolis longa ferae

Dire Hannibal, the Roman dread,
Numantian wars, which raged so long,
And seas with Punic slaughter red,
Suit not the softer lyric song;

Nor savage centaurs, mad with wine;
Nor Earth's enormous rebel brood,
Who shook with fear the powers divine,
Till by Alcides' arms subdued.

Better, Maecenas, thou in prose
Shalt Caesar's glorious battles tell;
With what bold heat the victor glows,
What captive kings his triumphs swell.

Thy mistress all my muse employs;
Licymnia's voice, her sprightly turns,
The fire that sparkles in her eyes,
And in her faithful bosom burns.

When she adorns Diana's day,
And all the beauteous choirs, advance,
With sweetest airs, divinely gay,
She shines, distinguished in the dance!

Not all Arabia's spicy fields,
Can with Licymnia's breath compare;
Nor India's self a treasure yields,
To purchase one bright flowing hair:

When she with bending neck complies
To meet the lover's eager kiss,
With gentle cruelty denies,
Or snatches first the fragrant bliss.

II · 13 · *A Narrow Escape*

ille et nefasto

Accursed his hand that made thee grow,
And black the day he planted thee,
Foredoomed to work his children woe,
And shame the village, vicious tree!

Who set thee upon my estate,
Disastrous log, to tumble on
The master's undeserving pate?
I dare not think what he has done.

He broke his father's neck; he smote
His guest beside the midnight hearth;
With dark Medea's drugs he wrought
And every bane devised on earth.

From hour to hour not one of us
Takes thought of his peculiar doom;
Bold sailors dread the Bosphorus
Nor heed what other fate may loom.

We fear the Mede who shoots and flies,
And he the prison walls of Rome,
And still in unimagined guise
Comes Death on man, and aye will come.

How near the sombre Queen of Hell
And Aeacus the judge was I!
The mansions where the blessed dwell,
And Sappho wailing dolefully

Of her unloving maids: and thee,
Alcaeus, as thou chantest o'er
With golden quill the toils of sea,
The toils of exile, toils of war.

The shades attend in solemn awe
As meet they may when either sings,
But keener list and closer draw
To songs of fights and banished kings.

Nay, e'en the hundred-headed hound
Slinks every ear and listens thrilled;
And all the snakes that writhe around
The Furies' heads are charmed and stilled.

Prometheus, too, amid his woes,
And Pelops' sire have rest a space;
Orion hearkens and foregoes
The lion and the lynx to chase.

?heu fugaces, Postume

Alas, my Postumus, our years
Glide silently away. No tears,
No loving orisons repair
The wrinkled cheek, the whitening hair
That drop forgotten to the tomb.
Pluto's inexorable doom
Mocks at thy daily sacrifice.
Around his dreary kingdom lies
That fatal stream whose arms infold
The giant race accurst of old:
All, all alike must cross its wave,
The king, the noble, and the slave.
In vain we shun the battle's roar,
And breakers dashed on Adria's shore;
Vainly we flee in terror blind
The plague that walketh on the wind,
The sluggish river of the dead,
Cocytus, must be visited;
The Danaids' detested brood,
Foul with their murdered husbands' blood,
And Sisyphus with ghastly smile
Pointing to his eternal toil.
All must be left; the gentle wife,
Thy home, the joys of rural life:
And when thy fleeting days are gone
Th' ill-omened cypresses alone
Of all thy fondly cherished trees
Shall grace thy funeral obsequies,
Cling to thy loved remains, and wave

Their mournful shadows o'er thy grave.
A lavish but a nobler heir
Thy hoarded Caecuban shall share,
And on the tessellated floor
The purple nectar madly pour—
Nectar more worthy of the halls
Where pontiffs hold high festivals.

II· 15· *Building Rage*

iam pauca aratro

Soon princely palaces will make 2 1-
Ploughed acres rare, and ponds will spread
As wide as is the Lucrine lake,
And lindens that no vine has wed

Will rout the elms; while gardens rich
In violet and myrtle pour
A world of scent o'er olives which
Gave elder owners goodly store,

And thickly-matted laurel boughs
Keep out the sun. Ah, other ways
Had Cato wrought and Romulus
In those untidy, good old days!

With them the state was rich, the man
Was poor—he had no colonnade
Set north and stretching many a span
To pamper him with air and shade.

Their laws allowed no man to scorn
The wayside turf for building; stone
The state provided to adorn
The temples and the towns alone.

"I sent my soul through the Invisible,
Some letter of that After-life to spell:
And by and by my soul returned to me,
And answered, 'I myself am Heav'n and Hell'—"

* * *

otium divos rogat

When storm clouds veil the moon's pale glow, and stars
No longer shine with light serene to guide
The pilot in his course, what sailor bold . . .
The victim of an open, grasping sea . . .
Invokes not all his gods for quiet then?
For peace, Grosphus, the Thracian cries, now crazed
By war's mad strife; 'tis peace the Mede, too, craves,
Adorned with quiver, bow, and deadly dart . . .
The peace not bought with gems, nor gold, nor dyes.

To quell the tumult of the soul and drive
Away the cares from panelled doors of state
Both wealth and pow'r are far too small and weak.
He lives well in his poverty for whom
His father's silver gleams with lovely glow
On frugal table; fear and base desire
Can never rouse him from his restful sleep.

Why, then, in life which soon must end, do we
Undaunted, strive for all things known to men . . .
Or restlessly our fatherland exchange
For lands warmed by another sun? What man,
An exile from his native soil, can flee

Himself, his cares, his fears, his driving woes?
Still morbid Care will mount the ships of bronze,
Will keep her pace with throngs of horsemen fleet,
Outrun the deer, outspeed the Eastern wind.

The mind rejoicing in today's glad store
Will scorn to fret about tomorrow's cares,
And temper all its sorrows with a smile;
In all this world no perfect good exists.
Yet Nature's law of compensation works:
Achilles felt death's unexpected blow,
Tithonus lived in life a lingering death;
And what Time gives to me, perhaps it will
Deny to you, who proudly may possess
Your herds of lowing cattle, mares, and fields,
Your woolen garments dipped in purple dye.
To me, just Fate has granted one small farm,
The tender spirit of the Grecian muse,
And pow'r to shun the malice of the mob.

cur me querelis

Why must these tiresome bodings be?
Earlier for thee in death to wend
Suits not, Maecenas, gods nor me,
My fortune's prop, my worthiest friend!

Of thee, my soul's best part, bereft,
Shall I, the other half, delay,
With all ties gone and nothing left
Save cheerless life? That fatal day

Shall wreck us both. No idle vow
I utter; we shall go, shall go
Whene'er thou journey, I and thou,
Companions on the road below.

Though rose Chimera belching fires,
Or Gyas with his hundred hands,
'Twould part us not—so Fate requires,
And powerful Justice so commands.

Though Libra ruled when I was born;
Though baleful Scorpio held his reign
With aspect fell, or Capricorn,
The tyrant of the western main.

Our horoscopes in wondrous style
Agree. Thee Jove, thy guardian blest,
Rescued from Saturn's wicked wile
And brought death's rapid wings to rest

When from the theatre densely filled
The glad ovation thrice outbroke.
I, badly stunned, was all but killed
When fell the tree, but Faun the stroke

With right hand brushed aside; the god
Of poets he. A fane must tell
Thy thanks while victims dye the sod;
Blood from my humble lamb must well.

II · 18 · *Vanity of Riches*

non ebur neque aureum

My ceiling shows not brave
  With gold or ivories;
No marble architrave
  On quarried pillars lies,
Which utmost Libya gave.

No despot did devise
  On me, a stranger heir,
His royal treasuries;
  No dames of birth prepare
For me Laconian dyes.

Pure faith is all my store,
  Faith, and so rich a vein
Of poet power and lore
  That wealth itself is fain
To seek this humble door.

I ask not Heaven to send
  Aught else; I never pressed
For more, my puissant friend,
  Who am entirely blessed
One Sabine farm to tend.

To-morrow ousts to-day;
  Young moons grow large and less;
Death dogs thy steps; but aye
  On marble palaces,
O fool, thy fancies stray,

Who, reckless of the tomb,
  Dost build, and 'mid the roar
Of Baian surf presume
  On the great sea, whose shore
Yields not ambition room.

What, shall this lust of gain
  Not even the landmarks keep
Which that is thine contain?
  This avarice o'er-leap
Thy client's scant domain?

Thence the poor exiles fare,
  Husband and wife; and, strained
To their sad bosoms, bear
  Young babes all squalor-stained,
And gods, their father's care.

Natheless no other hall
  More surely shalt thou find,
Thou gilded prodigal,
  Than that by Death designed,
  The greediest of us all.

What would'st thou? Earth's embrace
  Impartial shall enfold
King's son and peasant base;—
  Prometheus' guile and gold
From Charon gained no grace.

Proud Tantalus, he wears,
  He and his race, the chains
Of Death, who needs no prayers
  To lighten of their pains
The world's worn laborers.

II · 19 · *Bacchus' Might*

Bacchum in remotis

Let future times the wondrous tale believe!
I saw the mighty god of wine,
Mid rocks remote erect his shrine,
And holy lectures give;
Attended by a Sylvan train;
Goat-footed satyrs list'ning stood,
With guardian nymphs from every wood,
Well-pleased to hear the great instructive strain.

E'en I, who worship with a heart sincere;
Yet tremble at the awful nod
And bow before the mighty God
With reverence and fear:
My breast the sacred influence feels:—
Then drop the spear,—abate thy rage,
For lo! fierce anger to assuage,
Thy humble, supplicating vot'ry kneels!

Permit the adventurous bard to sing thy praise,
Thy priestesses with zeal inspired,
Their num'rous train with frenzy fired,
And stubborn Thyades:
What streams of luscious wine, for thee;
For thee, what milky fountains pour,
Increasing still thy plenteous store
With honey, dropping from the hollow tree.

Of Ariadne's num'rous charms I tell,
Who, beauteous with her silver hairs,

Adorned the skies with added stars;
And how Lycurgus fell:
How Pentheus felt thy angry frown!
Who impiously profaned thy name;
For which his palace wrapped in flame
Tumbled, with hideous, spreading ruin down.

Thy power does o'er remotest realms extend;
Oceans that feel Barbaric sway,
Thy guardian Deity obey,
And mighty rivers bend:
O'er craggy mountain-tops with speed,
(While snakes hang peaceful down each back,
Or harmless twist around the neck)
The joyous train of Bacchanals you lead.

You, when the giants dared to climb on high,
With impious force to tumble down
Your sire from his almighty throne,
And hurl him from the sky:
In lion's form you joined the fight;
The dreadful conflict dauntless stood,
With feet and jaws besmeared with blood,
And Rhoetus, with his monsters put to flight.

More skilled to rule the dancing merry choir,
You seemed; as formed for sloth and ease,
In softer sports alone to please,
Unused to war's uproar:—
But when in battle you appear,
In danger's front you fearless shone,
The bloody art soon made your own;
Though mild in peace, yet terrible in war.

When rising glorious from Hell's drear abode,
  The shining horns that grace thy head,
  A beamy lustre round thee spread:
    And awed before the god,
  In humble posture, as was meet,
  Grim Cer'brus saw with fear amazed,
  Grew kinder as he fondly gazed,
And fawning, wagged his tail, and licked thy feet.

non usitata

On neither weak nor vulgar wing
  Shall I be borne thro' liquid air
A two-formed bard, nor shall I cling
  To earth, but, proof 'gainst envy, fare

From towns. Not I, the lowly-born,
  Not I, thine intimate, shall die,
Maecenas dear, and dwell forlorn
  Where melancholy Styx flows by.

E'en now rough scales invest each shin,
  My frame a bird's white form assumes
Above, and back and arms begin
  To be arrayed in fluffy plumes.

A tuneful swan, on safer vanes
  Than Icarus', I soon shall soar
O'er Lybian deserts, Arctic plains,
  And Bosporus' tumultuous shore.

Colchian and Goth that masks his dread
  Of Marsian troops my spell shall own;
Far Scyths shall know me, scholars bred
  In Spain, and he that drinks the Rhone.

Around my empty bier suppress
  Unseemly grief, the moan, the dirge;
Give o'er the final call; no less
  A tomb's vain honors cease to urge.

III · 1 · *Contentment*

odi profanum vulgus

I scorn and shun the rabble's noise.
Abstain from idle talk! A thing
That ear hath not yet heard, I sing,
The Muses' priest, to maids and boys.

To Jove the flocks which great kings sway,
To Jove great kings allegiance owe.
Praise him: he laid the giants low:
All things that are, his nod obey.

This man may plant in broader lines
His fruit trees: that the pride of race
Enlists a candidate for place:
In worth, in fame, a third outshines

His mates; or, thronged with clients, claims
Precedence. Even-handed fate
Hath but one law for small and great:
That ample urn holds all men's names.

He o'er whose doomed neck hangs the sword
  Unsheathed, the dainties of the South
  Shall lack their sweetness in his mouth:
No note of bird or harpischord

Shall bring him Sleep. Yet Sleep is kind,
  Nor scorns the huts of laboring men;
  The bank where shadows play, the glen
Of Tempe dancing in the wind.

He, who but asks 'Enough,' defies
  Wild waves to rob him of his ease;
  He fears no rude shocks, when he sees
Arcturus set or Haedus rise:

When hailstones lash his vines, or fails
  His farm its promise, now of rains
  And now of stars that parch the plains
Complaining, or unkindly gales.

In straitened seas the fish are pent;
  For dams are sunk into the deep:
  Pile upon pile the builders heap,
And he, whom earth could not content,

The Master. Yet shall Fear and Hate
  Climb where their Master climbs; nor e'er
  From armed trireme parts black Care;
He sits behind, the horseman's mate.

And if red marble shall not ease
  The heartache; nor the shell that shines
  Star-bright nor all Falernum's vines,
All scents that charmed Achaemenes:

Why should I rear me halls of rare
  Design, on proud shafts mounting high?
  Why bid my Sabine vale good-bye
For doubled wealth and doubled care?

angustam amice pauperiem

Let every Roman boy be taught to know
Constraining hardship as a friend, and grow
  Strong in fierce warfare, with dread lance and horse
Encountering the gallant Parthian foe.

Aye, let him live beneath the open sky
In danger. Him from leaguered walls should eye
  Mother and daughter of th' insurgent king,
And she for her betrothed, with many a sigh,

Should pray, poor maiden, lest, when hosts engage,
Unversed in arms he face that lion's rage
  So dangerous to trust what time he gluts
His wrath upon the battle's bloody stage.

For country 'tis a sweet and seemly thing
To die. Death ceases not from following
  E'en runaways. Can youth with feeble knees,
That fears to face the battle, scape his wing?

Defeat true manliness can never know;
Honors untarnished still it has to show.
  Not taking up or laying office down
Because the fickle mob will have it so.

'Tis Manliness lifts men too good to die,
And finds a way to that forbidden sky:
  Above the thronging multitudes, above
The clinging mists of earth it rises high.

Nor less abides to loyal secrecy
A sure reward: I would not have him be
  Neath the same roof, the babbler who reveals
Demeter's secret things, or launch with me

A shallop frail: The god of heav'n has blent
Oft in one doom th' unclean and innocent:
  Seldom the miscreant has scaped the slow
And sure pursuit of halting punishment.

justem et tenacem

He that is just, and firm in will
Doth not before the fury quake
Of mobs that instigate to ill,
Nor hath the tyrant's menace skill
His fixed resolve to shake;

Nor Auster, at whose wild command
The Adriatic billows dash,
Nor Jove's dread thunder-launching hand.
Yea, if the globe should fall, he'll stand
Serene amidst the crash.

By constancy like this sustained,
Pollux of yore, and Hercules
The starry eminences gained
Where Caesar with lips purple-stained,
Quaffs nectar, stretched at ease.

Thou, by this power, Sire Bacchus, led,
To bear the yoke thy pards didst school,
Through this same power Quirinus fled,
By Mar's own horses charioted,
The Acherontine pool.

What time the gods to council came,
And Juno spoke with gracious tone,
"That umpire lewd and doomed to shame,
And his adulterous foreign dame
Troy, Troy have overthrown;

"Troy doomed to perish in its pride
By chaste Minerva and by me,
Her people, and their guileful guide,
Since false Laomedon denied
The gods their promised fee.

"The Spartan wanton's shameless guest
No longer flaunts in brave array,
Nor screened by Hector's valiant breast,
Doth Priam's perjured house arrest
My Argives in the fray.

"Protracted by our feuds no more,
The war is quelled. So I abate
Mine anger, and to Mars restore
Him, whom the Trojan priestess bore,
The grandchild of my hate.

"Him will I suffer to attain
These realms of light, these blest abodes,
The juice of nectar pure to drain,
And be enrolled amid the train
Of the peace-breathing gods.

"As long as the broad rolling sea
Shall roar 'twixt Ilion and Rome,
Wherever there wandering exiles be;
There let them rule, be happy, free;
Whilst Priam's, Paris' tomb

"Is trodden over by roving kine,
And wild beasts there securely breed,

The Capitol afar may shine,
And Rome, proud Rome her laws assign
Unto the vanquished Mede.

"Yes, let her spread her name of fear,
To farthest shores; where central waves
Part Africa from Europe, where
Nile's swelling current half the year
The plains with plenty laves.

"Still let her scorn to search with pain
For gold, the earth hath wisely hid,
Nor strive to wrest with hands profane
What is to man forbid.

"Let earth's remotest regions still
Her conquering arms to glory call,
Where scorching suns the long day fill,
Where mists and snows and tempests chill
Hold reckless bacchanal.

"But let Quirinus' sons beware,
For they are doomed to sure annoy,
Should they in foolish fondness e'er
Or vaunting pride the homes repair
Of their ancestral Troy.

"In evil hour should Troy once more
Arise, it shall be crushed anew,
By hosts that over it stride in gore,
By me conducted, as of yore
Jove's spouse and sister too.

"Thrice rear a brazen wall, and though
Apollo's self his audience lent,
Thrice shall my Argives lay it low,
Thrice shall the captive wife in woe
Her lord and babes lament."

But whither would'st thou, Muse? Unmeet
For jocund lyre are themes like these.
Shalt thou the talk of gods repeat
Debasing by thy strains effete
Such lofty mysteries?

III· 4· *Power of the Muses*

descende caelo

Calliope, the heavens forsake,
And fill with lingering song the flute:
Or lift thy silvery voice, or wake
The chords of Phoebus' lute.

O listen! Are these mocking dreams,
That she is bidding me to rove
Where pleasant airs and pleasant streams
Caress the holy grove?

Once, when a child on Voltur's steep
Beyond Apulia's bounds I strayed,
And, tired of play was fain to sleep,
The fairy ring-doves made

My bed of leaves—a marvel told
By folk along the Bantine dale,
From Acherontia's craggy hold,
To rich Forentum's vale;

How safe from deadly snake or bear,
'Neath bay and holy myrtle piled,
I slumbered sure, the gods had care
Of such a daring child!

So, when I seek bright Baiae's shores,
Low Tibur, or Praeneste chill,
Or climb my Sabine uplands, yours,
Yours, Muses, am I still.

I love your choirs and founts, and ye
  Have kept me safe through divers harms:
Philippi's rout, yon fatal tree,
  And Palinurus' storms.

If ye be still at my right hand,
  I'll trudge with willing heart across
Assyria's waste of scorching sand,
  Or sail wild Bosphorus,

'Mid savage Britons go unhurt,
  And Basques who drink of horses' blood,
Or Scythians with quivers girt,
  Where rolls the Volga's flood.

So, when his war-worn companies
  Great Caesar hath to quarters brought,
And turns to rest, ye give him ease
  In your Pierian grot,

Good Nine, who give and love to give
  Your counsel soft. We know full well
How on the Titans' monstrous hive
  The crashing levin fell

Of Jove, who sways the windy seas,
  Dull earth, and towns and realms of gloom,
And throngs of men and deities,
  With one impartial doom.

Yet cause enough had Jove to dread
The bristling arms of those proud foes,
Who strove on dark Olympus' head
Huge Pelion to impose.

But what could lusty Mimas do,
Or what Porphyrion's front of scorn,
What Rhoetus, or his twin who threw
Like spears the trees uptorn,

'Gainst Pallas' changing shield? and there
With Jove stood Vulcan, hungry-eyed,
And Juno Queen, and he who ne'er
Shall lay his bow aside,

Who bathes his hair in crystal floods
Of Castaly, and aye doth guard
His native Lycia's brakes and woods—
Delos' and Patara's lord.

Blind force of its own might is spent;
Self-tempered force the gods prolong
To higher ends; but they resent
A power that works for wrong.

Let hundred-handed Gyas be
My witness, and Orion who
Attempted Dian's purity
And whom her arrow slew.

Earth, piled above her brood, may fret
  And moan for them the thunder cast
To pallid Hell; no quick flame yet
  Hath gnawed through Etna vast;

And still o'er wanton Tityus' veins
  The vulture perches at his post;
And still Pirithous lies in chains
  And pays the price of lust.

caelo tonantem

Jove rules the skies, his thunder wielding:
Augustus Caesar, thou on earth shalt be
  Enthroned a present Deity;
Britons and Parthian hordes to Rome their proud necks
    yielding.

Woe to the Senate that endures to see
(O fire extinct of old nobility!)
The soldier dead to honor and to pride
  Ingloriously abide
Grey-headed mate of a Barbarian bride,
Freeman of Rome beneath a Median King!

Woe to the land that fears to fling
Its curse, not ransom, to the slave
Forgetful of the shield of Mars,
Of Vesta's unextinguished flame,
Of Roman garb, of Roman name;
The base unpitied slave who dares
From Rome his forfeit life to crave!
In vain;—Immortal Jove still reigns on high:
Still breathes in Roman hearts the Spirit Liberty.

With warning voice of stern rebuke
Thus Regulus the Senate shook;
He saw, prophetic, in far days to come,
The heart corrupt, and future doom of Rome.
"These eyes," he cried, "these eyes have seen

Unbloodied swords from warriors torn,
And Roman standards nailed in scorn
  On Punic shrines obscene;
Have seen the hands of free-born men
Wrenched back and bound; th' unguarded gate;
And fields our war laid desolate
By Romans tilled again.
What! will the gold-enfranchised slave
Return more loyal and more brave?
  Ye heap but loss on crime!
The wool that Cretan dyes distain
Can ne'er its virgin hue regain;
And valour fallen and disgraced
Revives not in a coward breast
  Its energy sublime.
The stag released from hunter's toils
From the dread sight of man recoils.
Is he more brave than when of old
He ranged his forest free? Behold
In him your soldier. He has knelt
To faithless foes; he too has felt
The knotted cord; and crouched beneath
  Fear, not of shame, but Death.
He sued for peace, tho' vowed to war!
Will such men, girt in arms once more,
Dash headlong on the Punic shore?
No! they will buy their craven lives
With Punic scorn and Punic gyves.
O mighty Carthage, rearing high
Thy fame upon our infamy,
A city, aye, an empire built
On Roman ruins, Roman guilt."

From the chaste kiss and wild embrace
Of wife and babes he turned his face,
  A man self-doomed to die;
Then bent his manly brow, in scorn,
Resolved, relentless, sad, but stern,
  To earth, all silently;
Till counsel never heard before
Had nerved each wavering Senator;
Till flushed each cheek with patriot shame,
And surging rose the loud acclaim;—
Then, from his weeping friends, in haste,
To exile and to death he passed.

He knew the tortures that Barbaric hate
Had stored for him. Exulting in his fate
  With kindly hand he waved away
  The crowds that strove his course to stay,

He passed from all, as when in days of yore,
  His judgment given, thro' client throngs he pressed
  In glad Venafrian fields to seek his rest,
Or Greek Tarentum on the Southern shore.

delicta maiorum

Ye Romans, ye, though guiltless, shall
Dread expiation make for all
The laws your sires have broke,
Till ye repair with loving pains
The gods' dilapidated fanes,
Their Statues grimed with smoke!

Ye rule the world, because that ye
Confess the gods' supremacy;
Hence all your grandeur grows:
The gods, in vengeance for neglect,
Hesperia's wretched land have wrecked
Beneath unnumbered woes.

Twice have Monaeses, and the hordes
Of Pacorus withstood the swords
Of our ill-omened host.
No more in meagre torques equipped,
But decked with spoils from Romans stripped,
They of our ruin boast.

Dacian and Ethiop have well-nigh
Undone our Rome distracted by
Intestine feud and fray:
This by his fleet inspiring fear,
That by his shafts, which far and near
Spread havoc and dismay.

Our times, in sin prolific, first
The marriage-bed with taint have cursed,
And family and home;
This is the fountain-head of all
The sorrows and the ills that fall
On Romans and on Rome.

The ripening virgin joys to learn
In the Ionic dance to turn
And bend with plastic limb;
Still but a child, with evil gleams,
Incestuous loves, unhallowed dreams,
Before her fancy swim.

Straight, in her husband's wassail hours,
She seeks more youthful paramours,
And little seeks, on whom
She may her lawless joys bestow
By stealth, when all the lamps burn low,
And darkness shrouds the room.

Yea, she will on a summons fly,
Nor is her spouse unconcious why,
To some rich broker's arms,
Or some sea captain's fresh from Spain,
With wealth to buy her shame, and gain
Her mercenary charm.

She did not spring from sires like these,
The noble youths who dyed the seas
With Carthaginian gore,
Who great Antiochus overcame,

And Pyrrhus, and the dreaded name
Of Hannibal of yore;

But they, of rustic warriors wight
The manly offspring, learned to smite
The soil with Sabine spade,
And fagots they had cut to bear
Home from the forest, whensoever
An austere mother bade;

What time the sun began to change
The shadows through the mountain range,
And took the yoke away
From the overwearied oxen, and
His parting car proclaimed at hand
The kindliest hour of day.

How time doth in its flight debase
Whatever it finds! Our fathers' race,
More deeply versed in ill
Then were their sires, hath borne us yet
More wicked, duly to beget
A race more vicious still.

III · 7 · *Keep Faith, Asterie!*

quid fles, Asterie!

Why weep, Asterie, for the youth,
That soul of constancy and truth,
  Whom from Bithynia's shore,
Rich with its wares, with gentle wing
The west winds shall in early spring
  To thy embrace restore?

Driven by the southern gales, when high
Mad Capra's star ascends the sky
  To Oricum, he keeps
Sad vigils through the freezing nights,
And, thinking of his lost delights
  With thee, thy Gyges weeps.

Yet in a thousand artful ways
His hostess' messenger essays
  To tempt him, urging how
Chloe—for such her name—is doomed
By fires like thine to be consumed,
  And sighs as deep as those.

Narrating how by slanders vile
A woman's falsehood did beguile
  The credulous Proetus on,
To hurry, with untimely haste,
Into the toils of death the chaste,
  Too chaste, Bellerophon.

Of Peleus then she tells, who thus
Was nigh consigned to Tartarus,
  Because his coldness shamed
Magnesia's queen Hippolyte,
And hints at stories craftily
  To sap his virtue famed.

In vain! For he, untouched as yet,
Is deafer than the rocks that fret
  The Icarian waves; but thou
Keep watch upon thy fancy too,
Nor to Enipeus there undue
  Attractiveness allow!

Though no one on the Martian Mead
Can turn and wind a mettled steed
  So skilfully as he;
Nor any breast the Tuscan tide
And dash its tawny waves aside
  With such celerity.

At nightfall shut your doors, nor then
Look down into the street again
  When quavering fifes complain;
And though he call thee, as he will,
Unjust, unkind, unfeeling, still
  Inflexible remain!

III· 8· *Anniversary*

Martiis caelebs

A bachelor, March Calends see me fill
My thurible with incense, pluck bouquets,
And heap the living turf with coals, but still
  Thou standest in amaze,

Though in the lore of both our tongues well read,
A toothsome feast and snowy goat in fee
To Liber erst I vowed, when nearly sped
  By blow of falling tree.

Each rolling year this day with mirth and joke
Shall draw the pitch-smeared cork from out the lip
Of flagon set to mellow mid the smoke
  In Tullus' consulship.

Drink, dear Maecenas, to thy friend's escape
A hundred toasts, till morning's sunbeams fall!
Let watchful cressets flare! Far hence the shape
  Of strife and angry brawl!

No longer worry over weal of state.
The force of Dacian Cotiso is quelled;
The noxious Medes, embroiled at home of late,
  In mortal feuds are held;

The Cantabri upon the Spanish coast,
Our ancient foes, late fettered, humbly bow;
Within their steppes the Scyths withdraw their host
  And slack their bowstring now.

Reck not though danger o'er the city lower;
Lay public care aside with all its stings;
Enjoy the blessings of the present hour
And drop all weightier things.

donec gratus eram

HE:

Whilst yet my love thy favor graced
And no preferred youth embraced
Thy snowy neck, then I to sing
More honored was than Persia's king.

SHE:

Whilst thou another hadst not wooed,
Nor Lydia after Chloe stood,
I, through thy verses known to fame
Was honored more than Ilia's name.

HE:

Me now deft Chloe captivates,
On lyre sweet melodies creates;
For her I should not fear to die,
If fate would spare my dearest tie.

SHE:

Me noble Calais in turn
With torch of mutual love doth burn.
For him I twice should die with joy,
If fate would spare my charming boy!

HE:

What if our former love revive?
Would parted lovers' prospects thrive?
Wouldst thou, were Chloe bid depart,
Regain the portal of my heart?

SHE:

Though he is fairer than a star,
And thou than cork less stable far,
More wrathful than sea billows high,
With thee I choose to live and die.

extremum Tanain

Ah, Lyce! though your drink were Tanais,
  Your husband some rude savage, you would weep
To leave me shivering on a night like this,
      Where storms their watches keep.

Hark, how your door is creaking, how the grove
  In your fair courtyard, while the wild winds blow,
Wails in accord, with what transparence Jove
      Glazes the driven snow!

Cease that proud temper; Venus loves it not;
  The rope may break, the wheel may backward turn;
Begetting you, no Tuscan sire begot
      Penelope the stern.

Oh, though no gift, no "prevalence of prayer,"
  Nor lovers' paleness deep as violet,
Nor husband, smit with a Pierian fair,
      Move you, have pity yet!

O harder e'en than toughest heart of oak,
  Deafer than uncharmed snake to suppliant moans!
This side, I warn you, will not always brook
      Rain-water and cold stones.

III · 11 · *Bid Her Take Heed!*

Mercuri—nam te docilis

O Hermes, by whose teaching once
Amphion's singing moved the stones:
O shell, endowed with seven-fold strings
Wherein such wondrous music rings—

Once dumb and scorned, but welcome now
In palaces and fanes art thou—
Inspire me with a song shall bend
You, wilful Lyde, to attend.

Like some young filly that careers
About the meadows free, and fears
The touch of man, she recks not of
A mate—as yet o'er young for love.

But thou canst draw the beasts and woods
To follow thee, and stay the floods:
The porter of the gate of Hell,
Grim Cerberus, confessed thy spell,

Though round his Gorgon head he shakes
His fillet of a hundred snakes,
And though from out his triple mouth
Pour fetid breath and bloody froth,

Ixion, too, was forced to smile,
And Tityus: the urn awhile
Stood empty as the Danaïd throng
Drew comfort from thy soothing song.

Tell Lyde of their tragedy;
The famous weird these maidens dree—
Filling their jar, whence night and day
The wasting water leaks away.

So doom awaiteth at the last
The sinner dead, and who surpassed
Their infamy, that with the sword
Could slay each one her wedded lord.

Yet one deserved the name of bride;
One only, who superbly lied
To her deceitful father—Fame
Shall ever consecrate her name.

"Awake!" she cried, "my lord, my love!
Ere from a snare thou think'st not of
Come longer slumber! Up, and go
Before my sire and sisters know.

"Lo! they are lions, lighting on
A herd, and rending one by one:
But I am softer—I'll not wound
Nor hold thee fast in prison bound.

"My sire may load me down with chains;
Or far to Africa's domains
May ship me, for that I, your wife,
Was pitiful and spared thy life.

"Go, get thee gone, o'er land and flood
While Night and Love are kind, and good
The omens; grave upon my tomb
One word of sorrow for my doom.

III · 12 · *Love Shackled*

miserarum est

How unhappy are the maidens who with Cupid may not
play,
Who may never touch the wine-cup, but must tremble all
the day
At an uncle and the scourging of his tongue!
Neobule, there's a robber takes your needle and your thread,
Lets the lessons of Minerva run no longer in your head;
It is Hebrus, the athletic and the young!
Oh, to see him when anointed he is plunging in the flood!
What a seat he has on horseback! Was Bellerophon's as
good?
As a boxer, as a runner, past compare!
When the deer are flying blindly all the open country o'er,
He can aim and he can hit them; he can steal upon the boar
As it couches in the thicket unaware.

o fons Bandusiae

O babbling Spring, than glass more clear,
Worthy of wreath and cup sincere,
Tomorrow shall a kid be thine
With swelled and sprouting horns for sign—
Sure sign—of loves and battles near.

Child of the race that butt and rear:
Not less, alas! his life-blood dear
Shall tinge thy cold wave crystalline,
O babbling Spring!

Thee Sirius knows not. Thou dost cheer
With pleasant cool the plow-worn steer,
The wandering flock. This verse of mine
Shall rank thee one with founts divine;
Men shall thy rock and tree revere,
O babbling Spring!

III · 14 · *Glorious Homecoming*

Herculis ritu

Of late we spake how Caesar sought,
Like Hercules, the laurels fraught
With death—To-day, ye folk of Rome,
From Spain he comes triumphant home.

Rejoicing in her peerless spouse
His wife shall go and pay her vows,
With her our hero's sister too,
And, decked with votive fillets due,

The dames of Rome their thanks to pour
For sons and daughters safe once more.
O youths and wedded girls, take care
To utter words of omen fair!

This day shall be in truth a day
Of joy to hunt black care away;
No mobs I dread, nor death by sword,
While Caesar o'er the earth is lord.

Bring wreaths and perfumes, and a jar
That can recall the Marsic war,
And pitcher be, that 'scaped the hands
Of Spartacus' marauding bands.

And bid Neaera, sweet-voiced maid,
Her scented tresses quickly braid;
But if her porter makes delay—
That surly menial—come away!

Hairs growing grey compose a mind
To feuds and quarrels once inclined;
When Plancus ruled and I was hot
And young, I would have brooked it not.

III · 15 · *Be Your Age, Chloris*

uxor pauperis Ibyci

O thou pernicious dame
Of penniless Ibycus, 'tis time to cease
Thy toilsome life of shame,
And make thee ready to depart in peace.
Shake not thy palsied foot
Amongst the girls; nor sully with thy cloud
Their bright stars. What may suit
Pholoë becomes not Chloris. To knock loud
At youthful nobles' door,
Like Thyiad maddened by the tambour's sound,
Beseems thy daughter more,
Who like a roe for Nothus' love doth bound.
The silky wool that grows
Near rich Luceria, not the cithern's strain,
Is thine: the damask rose
Give up, nor strive the cask's last dregs to drain.

inclusam Danaen

A tower of brass held Danae immured;—
Strong oaken doors and watch-dog's mid-night bay
'Gainst love too bold the royal maid secured;
But Jove and Venus smiled
Mocking her Sire, for gold will work its way
Through guarded gates and sentinels beguiled.

Gold cleaves the fortress and the rock
With force more potent than the thunder's shock.
The Argive augur, sold
By his false wife, Eriphyle, for gold,
Died with his sons. The man of Macedon
Subdued with bribes proud kings in arms arrayed:
And Menas, won
By Roman gold, a Roman fleet betrayed.

Maecenas! knighthood's boast! thou knowest how
Like thee I shrank from lifting of my brow
Above my peers. To him whose modest thrift
Denies itself, Heaven sends its ampler gift.
Naked I fly the standard of the great,
And seek the ranks of those who nought desire,
More honored thus despising vulgar state
Than if I should my bursting garners fill
With rich Apulia's grain heaped daily higher,
Sitting 'mid worthless wealth, a beggar still.

Enough for me my little wood, my spring
Where Zephyr's cooling wing

Fans the crisp stream; my garden plot
Whose promised crop deceiveth not;—
The Afric despot knows no happier lot.

What though Calabrian bees for me
No honey filch from flower or tree—
What though no Gallic flocks increase
For me their wealth of snowy fleece—
What though the Formian vine
Ripens not in my bin its mellowing wine—
Content I live; not rich; yet free
From harsh unfortunate penury:
If more I claimed thou would'st not more refuse.

True riches mean not revenues:
Care clings to wealth: the thirst for more
Grows as our fortunes grow. I stretch my store
By narrowing my wants; far wealthier thus
Than if the treasures of Alyatteus
And Phrygia's plains were mine. We are not poor
While nought we seek. Happiest to whom high Heaven
Enough—no more—with sparing hand has given.

III · 17 · *Tomorrow's Rain*

Aeli vetusto nobilis

Aelius, sprung from Lamus old,
That mighty king who first, we're told,
  Ruled forted Formiae
And all the land on either hand
Where Liris by Marica's strand
  Goes rippling to the sea;

Unless yon old soothsaying crow
Deceive me, from the East shall blow
  To-morrow such a blast
As will with leaves the forests strew,
And heaps of useless sea-weed, too,
  Upon the sea-beach cast.

Dry faggots, then, house while you may;
Give all your household holiday
  To-morrow, and with wine
Your spirits cheer; be blithe and bold,
And on a pigling two moons old
  Most delicately dine!

Faune, nympharum fugientum

Wooer of young nymphs who fly thee,
  Lightly o'er my sunlit lawn
Trip, and go, nor injured by thee
  Be my weanling herds, O Faun,

If the kid his doomed head bows, and
  Brims with wine the loving cup,
When the year is full; and thousand
  Scents from altars hoar go up.

Each flock in the rich grass gambols
  When the month comes which is thine;
And the happy village rambles
  Fieldward with the idle kine;

Lambs play on, the wolf their neighbor;
  Wild woods deck thee with their spoil;
And with glee the sons of labor
  Stamp upon their foe, the soil.

quantum distet

How Codrus brave, who died to save
His native land, was sprung
From Inachus: of Peleus' line,
Of battles fought round Troy divine,
All these thy lyre hath sung;
But what a Chian cask will cost,
Who'll make our water hot,
And where we are to find our host,
And when escape this Arctic frost,
Of these thou tellest not.
Boy! bear a cup to greet the Moon,
For Midnight one, and haste!
Bear to the seer Murena one;
With ladles nine or three of wine,
As suits each toper's taste.
Mad bards who love the Muses band
For three times three may shout:
The naked Graces, hand in hand,
To touch no more than three command,
Lest revel end in rout.
I'm for a rouse! why tarry mute
The pipes of Cybele?
Why silent hang the lyre and lute?
No niggard hands for me!
Strew roses! Surly Lycus there,
Unfit to wed a wife so fair,
Shall hear our revelry—
Ah, Telephus! thick-haired and bright
As Hesper at the fall of night,

To thee doth Rhode turn,
And proper mate of thine is she·
But Glycera has kindled me;
For her I slowly burn.

non vides quanto

Pyrrhus! at peril of thy life
  Wouldst rob a tigress of her young?
O thou wilt fly the deadly strife,
  Faint-hearted thief, ere long;

When through the press of lads she hies
  To claim Nearchus fair to see,
And battle rages, ere the prize
  Fall unto her or thee.

Yet, while she whets her fearsome teeth
  And thou art bearing shafts to shoot,
They say the judge has crushed the wreath
  Below his naked foot,

And lets the cooling breezes rough
  The scented locks about his cheek,
Like Nireus, or the boy borne off
  From fountained Ida's peak.

o nata mecum

Twin-born with me in Manlius' year,
O thou who bringest men good cheer,
Or grief or brawl or passions wild,
Or easy sleep, my pitcher mild;

Whate'er thy end, 'tis meet to call
Thy Massic to our festival;
Come down—it is Corvinus' whim:
I need my ripest wines for him.

Deep-dyed in Plato's lore is he,
But not too stern to relish thee;
Why, good old Cato, so they tell,
Would warm unto his wine right well.

Thou hast a gentle rack to strain
The stiffest wits: to thee are plain
The sage's cares and secret thoughts
By grace of Him that loosens knots.

Reviving hope to anxious minds,
Thou givest horns of strength to hinds
Who, filled with thee, no longer pale
At crested kings or men in mail.

May Bacchus and the Graces still
Close-linked, and Venus if she will,
Prolong thy rounds neath lantern gay
Till flee the stars at dawn of day.

III · 22 · *A Pine Tree for Diana*

montium custos

Oh virgin queen of mountain-side and woodland,
Blessed protector of young wives in travail,
Who snatches them from death if thrice they call thee—
Goddess and guardian;

To thee I dedicate this slender pine-tree;
And each year with a boar's blood I shall bless it—
A youngling boar just dreaming of his first thrust,
Savage and sidelong.

III · 23 · *What Gifts the Gods Delight*

caelo supinas

If, Phidyle, in country-wise
Thy hands thou raisest to the skies,
If beneath the crescent moon
Thou cravest of the gods a boon,
Bringing, as thy sacrifice,
Snouting porker, grain, and spice,

Never shall thy fruitful vine
Neath the Afric blast decline,
Nor the cornfields, thy delight,
Sicken with the barren blight,
Nor heavy airs of apple-tide
Hurt the yearling flock, thy pride;

For snowy oak and ilex groves
Of Algidus supply the droves
Of victims vowed to powers divine;
While Alban pastures breed the kine
Whose dedicated necks must feel
The stroke of sacerdotal steel,

There's lordly need for thee to heap
A holocaust of slaughtered sheep
To tempt thy little gods to grant
The boon for which thou'rt suppliant;
Let but their modest chaplets be
Of myrtle mixed with rosemary.

If all unsullied be the hands
Of him who at the altar stands,
No offerings of costlier price
Can be more meet for sacrifice
To deprecate celestial ire
Than flour and salt flung on the fire.

intactis opulentior

Though India's virgin mine,
And hoarded wealth of Araby be thine,
Though thy wave-circled palaces
Usurp the Tyrrhene and Apulian seas;
When on thy devoted head
The iron band of Fate has laid
The symbols of eternal doom,
What power shall loose the fetters of the dead?
What hope dispel the terrors of the tomb?

Happier the nomad tribe whose wains
Drag their rude huts o'er Scythian plains;
Happier the Getan horde
To whom unmeasured fields afford
Abundant harvests, pastures free:
For one short year they toil;
They claim once more their liberty,
And yield to other hands the unexhausted soil.

The tender-hearted step-dame there
Nurtures with all a mother's care
The orphan babe: no wealthy bride
Insults her lord, or yields her heart
To the sleek suitor's glozing art.
The maiden's dower is purity,
Her parents' worth, her womanly pride,
To hate the sin, to scorn the lie,
Chastely to live, or, if dishonored, die.

Breathes there a patriot brave and strong
Would right his erring country's wrong,
Would heal her wounds and quell her rage?
Let him with noble daring first
Curb Faction's tyranny accurst!
So may some future age
'Grave on his bust with pious hand
"The father of his native land":
Virtue yet living we despise,
Adore it lost, and vanished from our eyes.

Cease, idle wail!
The sin unpunished, what can sighs avail?
How vain the laws by man ordained
If Virtue's law be unsustained!
A second sin is yours! The sand
Of Araby, Gaetulia's sun-scorched land,
The desolate realms of Hyperborean ice,
Call with one voice to wrinkled Avarice:
He hears; he fears nor toil, nor sword, nor sea,
He shrinks from no disgrace but virtuous poverty.

Forth! mid a shouting nation bring
Your precious gems, your wealth untold;
Into the seas, or Temple, fling
Your vile unprofitable gold.
Romans! Repent, and from within
Eradicate your darling sin;
Repent! and from your bosom tear
The sordid shame that festers there.
Bid your degenerate boys to learn
In rougher schools a lesson stern.

The high-born youth mature in vice
Pursues his vain and reckless course,
Rolls the Greek hoop, or throws the dice,
But shuns the chase, and dreads the horse;
This perjured sire, with jealous care,
Heaps riches for his worthless heir;
Despised, disgraced, supremely blest,
Cheating his partner, friend, and guest.
Uncounted stores his bursting coffers fill,
But something unpossessed is ever wanting still.

quo me, Bacche

Where dost thou drag me, son of Semele,
  Me who am lost in wine?
Through what love-groves, through what wild haunts of
    thine
Am I, in this strange frenzy, forced to flee?
From what deep caverns (as I meditate
On peerless Caesar's fame and deathless fate)
Shall I be heard, when my exulting cries
Proclaim him friend of Jove, and star in yon bright skies?
Something I'll shout, new, strange, as yet unsung
  By any other human tongue!

Thus, stung by thee, the sleepless Bacchanals ever
Grow mad whilst gazing on the Hebrus river,
On snow-white Thrace, and Rhodope, whose crown
  Barbarian footsteps trample down.
  And oh! like them it joys my soul
  To wander where the rivers roll,
To gaze upon the dark and desert groves.

O thou great power, whom the Naiad loves
And Bacchant women worship (who o'erthrow
  The mighty ash-trees as they go).
  Nothing little, nothing low,
  Nothing mortal, will I sing.
'Tis risk, but pleasant risk, O king,
To follow thus a god who loves to twine
His temples with the green and curling vine.

III · 26 · *One Last Touch*

vixi puellis

I lived for the girls and was true to their charms,
And I battled it not without glory;
But discharged from the war with my lute and my arms,
This wall here shall rubric my story.

It guards the left side of the Venus who rose
From the sea, so enchantingly gracious.
Here hang up your torches and crowbars and bows,
To the doors shut against them mendacious.

Holding Memphis the snowless and Cypress thine isle,
Venus, goddess, accept the oblation.
The most leal of thy subjects, Queen, give me thy smile-
And proud Chlöe a slight flagellation!

impios parrae

May sinners meet all omens ill!
The bitch with cubs; the owlet's tongue;
The dun wolf stalking down the hill;
The vixen great with young!

May adders o'er the roadway glide
And scare their steeds with arrow dart,
But I, diviner, eagle-eyed
For her who hath my heart,

Will pray the raven e'er he hies
Back to the stagnant marshes where
He calls the rain, at morning-rise
To croak an omen fair.

Be happy, wheresoe'er thou art,
And think on me, my lady, still;
No roaming crow delay thy start,
No daw that bodeth ill!

Yet see! Orion sinks and reels
With tempest. Well I know the mien
Of inky Adria when it feels
The west wind lashing keen.

For wives and children of our foes
Such terrors be! When Auster roars
And whips the surges black, whose blows
Convulse the solid shores.

E'en bold Europa when she gave
Her snowy limbs to yon false bull,
Grew pale, beholding ocean's wave
Of beasts and terrors full.

Of late, intent on meadow flowers,
She plaited wreaths the Nymphs to please.
Now she discerns through night's dim hours
Only the stars and seas.

Anon to mighty Crete she came,
With all its hundred towns, and cried,
"O Sire! I may not speak thy name
Since folly love defied.

"O whence, O where? Mere death—no more—
Were doom too light for maid's offence.
Am I awake and sinning sore,
Or all in innocence,

"By phantoms from the ivory gate
Bemocked? To pluck the buds new-blown,
Or wander o'er yon weary strait—
Ah! which were better done?

"Give me that steer of ill repute
To hew in pieces with the sword,
To wrench the horns from off the brute
That once I so adored!

"Shameless I left my father's home;
Shameless I shrink from death. This prayer

Hear, some kind god, and let me roam
Mid lions, lone and bare!

"Ere wasting mars my comely cheek,
Ere withers all my sap away,
While I am seemly yet, I seek
To be the tiger's prey.

"Die, die thou base Europa! Haste!
(Far off my father chideth me)
For noose the good zone at thy waist,
For gibbet yon tall tree.

"Or haply climb yon airy scaur,
And fling thee on the jagged rock
To death; unless it likes thee more,
Thou child of kingly stock,

"To card thy wool the slaves among
And serve a foreign master's dame."
Now Cupid, with his bow unstrung,
And Venus, mocked her shame,

Till, tired of jibes, the goddess spake:
"Refrain from rage and railing, when
Thy hated bull shall bring thee back
His horns to rend again.

"Wife of unconquered Jove thou art,
And know'st it not! Learn not to shame
Thy honours; hush thy sobs! A part
Of earth shall bear thy name!"

festo quid potius die

How now to make of this a festal day?
This that is Neptune's own. Quick! Lyde mine,
The cellar keys, the hoarded Caecuban!
We'll wage a war on wisdom in good wine!

The noonday sun is sinking to the west;
Make haste, make haste! Think you day will not pass?
You shrink to tap the bins of Bibulus?
Come now! Fetch forth the lingering wine jars, lass!

Now music! Well, then, I will take first turn.
Of Neptune and his Nereids I will sing,
Combing their green locks underneath the sea.
Then, Lyde, you your curved lyre must string.

Touch it to music in Latona's praise,
And sing of Cynthia's arrows far and fleet,
But save your sweetest singing for the last—
For Venus' praise the best alone is meet,

The queen of Cnidus and the Shining Isle,
Who visits Paphos with her yoked swans white
Deserves a hymn. Night, too, her meed of praise
In tuneful song let lyre and lips unite!

Tyrrhena regum progenies

Heir of Tyrrhenian kings, for you
 A mellow cask, unbroach'd as yet,
Maecenas mine, and roses new,
 And fresh-drawn oil your locks to wet,
Are waiting here. Delay not still,
 Nor gaze on Tibur, never dried,
And sloping Aesule, and the hill
 Of Telegon the parricide.
O leave that pomp that can but tire,
 Those piles, among the clouds at home;
Cease for a moment to admire
 The smoke, the wealth, the noise of Rome!
In change e'en luxury finds a zest:
 The poor man's supper, neat, but spare,
With no gay couch to seat the guest,
 Has smooth'd the rugged brow of care.
Now glows the Ethiop maiden's sire;
 Now Procyon rages all ablaze;
The Lion maddens in his ire,
 As suns bring back the sultry days;
The shepherd with his weary sheep
 Seeks out the streamlet and the trees,
Silvanus' lair; the still banks sleep
 Untroubled by the wandering breeze.
You ponder on imperial schemes,
 And o'er the city's danger brood:
Bactrian and Serian haunt your dreams,
 And Tanais, toss'd by inward feud.
The issue of the time to be

Heaven wisely hides in blackest night,
And laughs, should man's anxiety
Transgress the bounds of man's short sight.
Control the present: all beside
Flows like a river seaward borne,
Now rolling on its placid tide,
Now whirling massy trunks uptorn,
And waveworn crags, and farms, and stock,
In chaos blent, while hill and wood
Reverberate to the enormous shock,
When savage rains the tranquil flood
Have stirr'd to madness. Happy he,
Self-centered, who each night can say,
"My life is lived: the morn may see
A clouded or a sunny day:
That rests with Jove: but what is gone,
He will not, cannot turn to nought;
Nor cancel, as a thing undone,
What once the flying hour has brought."
Fortune, who loves her cruel game,
Still bent upon some heartless whim,
Shifts her caresses, fickle dame,
Now kind to me, and now to him:
She stays; 't is well: but let her shake
Those wings, her presents I resign,
Cloak me in native worth, and take
Chaste Poverty undower'd for mine.
Though storms around my vessel rave,
I shall not fall to craven prayers,
Nor bargain by my vows to save
My Cyprian and Sidonian wares,
Else added to the insatiate main.

Then through the wild Aegean roar
The breezes and the Brethren Twain
Shall waft my little boat ashore.

III · 30 · *I Shall Not Die*

exegi monumentum

I've reared a fame outlasting brass,
  Which in its more than kingly height
Shall Egypt's Pyramids surpass,
  Unharmed by countless seasons' flight.
The wasting rain, the North wind's rage,
  On it shall leave no lasting trace,
Nor shall it e'er grow dim with age
  While Time runs his unfinished race.
Not all of me shall die. For Death,
  Though he should still my beating heart,
Takes but a fragment with my breath
  And leaves untouched the greater part.
My fame, by future ages still
  Shall be renewed from day to day,
While up the Capitolian hill
  Both Priest and Vestal take their way.
Where Aufidus with rapid wave
  Sweeps on, and droughty Daunus rules
A sluggish stream that scarce can lave
  The land of rustics he controls.
Raised from my former low degree,
  All future nations shall rehearse
The glorious union due to me,
  Of Latin with Aeolic verse.
Then wear, Melpomene, with pride,
  The mien your merits high should bear,
And weave, by willing fingers tied,
  The Delphian laurel in my hair.

IV · 1 · *Too Old for Love*

intermissia, Venus, diu

Venus, again thou mov'st a war
  Long intermitted; pray thee, pray thee spare!
I am not such, as in the reign
  Of the good Cynara I was: refrain
Sour mother of sweet Loves, forbear
  To bend a man, now at his fiftieth year
Too stubborn for commands so slack:
  Go where youth's soft entreaties call thee back.
More timely hie thee to the house
  (With thy bright swans) of Paulus Maximus:
There jest and feast, make him thine host
  If a fit liver thou dost seek to toast,
For he's both noble, lovely, young,
  And for the troubled client fills his tongue:
Child of a hundred arts, and far
  Will he display the ensigns of thy war.
And when he, smiling, finds his grace
  With thee 'bove all his rivals' gifts take place,
He'll thee a marble statue make,
  Beneath a sweet-wood roof, near Alba lake;
There shall thy dainty nostril take
  In many a gum, and for thy soft ear's sake
Shall verse be set to harp and lute,
  And Phrygian hautboy, not without the flute.
There twice a day in sacred lays,

The youths and tender maids shall sing thy praise!
And in the Salian manner meet
Thrice 'bout thy altar, with their ivory feet.
Me now, nor girl, nor wanton boy,
Delights, nor credulous hope of mutual joy;
Nor care I now healths to propound
Or with fresh flowers to gird my temples round.
But why, oh why, my Ligurine,
Flow my thin tears down these pale cheeks of mine?
Or why my well-graced words among,
With an uncomely silence, fails my tongue?
Hard-hearted, I dream every night
I hold thee fast! but fled hence with the light,
Whether in Mars his field thou be
Or Tiber's winding streams, I follow thee.

Pindarum quisquis studet

The poet whose too flattering hopes aspire
To reach the noble heart of Pindar's fire;
Like the famed boy, by no persuasion won,
Opposes waxen pinions to the sun;
The feeble wings dissolve in searching light,
And drop the mad adventurer from his flight;
Whose sad attempts to gain forbidden fame
Disgrace his fall with a more signal shame,
And only serve to give the sea a name.
As headlong floods, swoln with perpetual rain
No more their once-surmounted banks restrain,
Deep streams of eloquence, in Pindar's page,
Swell with such uncontrolled, impetuous rage;
Worthy the laurel's consecrated prize
As oft as his obedient pen he tries,
Whether his pompous dithyrambic song
In arbitrary numbers rolls along;
Or if of God he sings in god-like words,
Or heaven-born heroes, and their acts record;
No bards so fit the immortal men to tell
By whom the fires were quenched or monsters fell
Or if his muse embalms the victors' names,
Renowned for godlike deeds at Pisas' games;
Describes the champion and the fiery steed,
Measuring the extended plain with winged speed;
Each action with peculiar lustre shines,
And warms us o'er again in Pindar's lines,
In whose eternal volume there to live,
In greater praise than thousand statues give.

Not less successful when the style he turns,
And some brave youth's too early funeral mourns;
Who might without the muse compassion move,
Untimely snatch'd from the new joys of love:
The widowed bride admits of no relief,
No intervals break off the endless grief;
Till Pindar with the power of numbers tries
To bring the lovely image to her eyes;
Whom he describes, so virtuous and so brave,
That in his nobler part he triumphs o'er the grave.

IV · 3 · *The Poet's Reward*

quem tu, Melpomene

He on whose natal hour you glance
  A single smile with partial eyes,
Melpomene, shall not advance
  A champion for the Olympic prize,
Nor, drawn by steeds of managed pride,
In Grecian car victorious ride.

Nor honor'd with the Delphic leaf,
  A wreath for high achievements wove,
Shall he be shown triumphant chief,
  Where stands the Capitol of Jove,
As justly raised to such renown
For bringing boastful tyrants down.

But pleasing streams that flow before
  Fair Tibur's flowr'y-fertile land,
And bow'ring trees upon the shore
  Which in such seemly order stand,
Shall form on that Aeollic plan
The bard, and magnify the man.

The world's metropolis has deigned
  To place me with her darling care;
Rome has my dignity maintained
  Amongst her bards my bays to wear;
And hence it is against my verse
The tooth of envy's not so fierce.

O mistress of the golden shell!
  Whose silence you command, or break;
Thou that canst make the mute excel,
  And ev'n the sea-born reptiles speak;
And, like the swan, if you apply
Your touch, in charming accents die.

This is thy gift, and only thine,
  That, as I pass along, I hear—
"There goes the bard, whose sweet design
  Made lyrics for the Roman ear."
If life or joy I hold or give,
By thee I please, by thee I live.

qualem ministrum fulminis

Like the fierce bird with thunder-laden wing
That bore to Jove his gold-haired Ganymede,
  And from the Monarch dread
Of gods and men obtained supreme dominion
O'er all that fly; lured by the breath of Spring,
A fledgling first he spreads his fluttering pinion:
Soon fired by youth, impelled by inborn might,
Through cloudless skies he wings his daring flight;
He soars, he swoops, and on the fold descends;
  Or, hungry for the fight
With sanguine beak the writhing dragon rends;
Or, as the Lion, from his tawny dam
Late weaned, on some glad mead descries
The roe-deer, or the unsuspecting lamb
Contented grazing; on, with flashing eyes,
And fangs new-fleshed he bounds; the victim dies:

So Drusus swooping from the Rhaetian snows
Smote the Vindelici; nor helm, nor sword,
Nor Amazonian battle-axe could ward
From Roman vengeance Rome's barbaric foes;
  Victors in every field till now
Suppliant before a Roman youth they bow.
They know at last what hearts undaunted, fed
Beneath the roof of an auspicious home,
  What Nero's sons, by Caesar bred
With all a father's love, can do for Rome.
The strong and good beget the brave and true:
Deep in the cavern of the infant's breast

The father's nature lurks, and lives anew:
The steer, the generous steed inherit
Parental beauty, strength, unconquered spirit:
The stock dove springs not from the Eagle's nest.

But inborn virtue still requires
Culture to shape what nature's self inspires;
Leave it unformed, unaided, guilt and shame
Shall stain the noblest heart, the most illustrious name.

How deep the debt your fathers owed,
O Rome, to Nero's race, to Nero's blood!
Witness Metaurus' purple flood;
Witness that day when through the clouds of night
Refulgent burst, a living light,
The glorious sun that smiled to see
A grateful nation's jubilee,—
For Hasdrubal lies low, and Rome again is free!

Through the fair fields of Italy once more
The people grew: the voice of toil was heard:
And where the Punic conqueror
So long o'er smoking plains his war-horse spurred
Fierce as the flame that wraps the forest trees,
Or storms careering over Sicilian seas;
Once more the Nation's heart awakened stirred,
And in the desecrated fane
Adoring Rome beheld her banished gods again.

Then spake perfidious Hannibal,—
"Unwarlike deer, the wolf's predestined food,
We seek a foe 'twere triumph to elude,

That race heroic, which of yore
Their gods, their babes, their aged fathers bore
From Ilion's burning wall
Through Tuscan billows to Ausonia's shore:
So the broad oak that spreads its dusky shade
On Algidus, shorn by the woodman's knife,
Wounded and lopped, bourgeons again to life,
And draws, refreshed, new vigor from the blade.

"Great nation! fierce as Hydra when she sprung
Severed yet scathless, full on Hercules!
Great Roman people, strong
As Colchian monsters, Theban prodigies!
Plunge them 'neath Ocean's lowest depths, they rise
More bright, more glorious: fell them to the earth,
They start to life: the vanquished victor dies;
And Roman dames for aye blazon their husbands' worth.

"Tidings of victory
I send no more. I send a wailing cry:
Our Punic name, our hope, our fortune, all
Have died with Hasdrubal!"

Valiant and wise, 'neath Jove's benignant care
What man can do the Claudian race shall dare:
They too with counsels sage shall staunch the wounds of war.

IV · 5 · *Return, Great Giver of Peace!*

divis orte bonis

God-given guardian of Quirinus' sons,
  The sacred Senate holds thy promise dear;
Return, return; too long his absence runs
  Who spake of brief delay and is not here.

Restore to Rome the radiance of that face
  Which, smiling on us like the budding year,
Can lend to gracious day a novel grace,
  And gift the sunshine with a warmer cheer:

For as some mother hungering for her son—
  Fast bound beyond the far Carpathean swell
By jealous gales till all the year be done,
  In exile from the home that loves him well,—

Calls him with vows and prayers and augur's art,
  Her eyes still set toward the sinuous sand,
So from a grateful people's faithful heart
  A cry for Caesar echoes through the land.

For safe the cattle range the peaceful mead,—
  Ceres the mead and glad abundance bless;
O'er bloodless seas the flying galleys speed;
  And faith is fearful of unfaithfulness.

Our homes are pure and happy, every one;
  Good laws, good customs cleanse our leprosies;
The father's face is imaged in the son;
  Immediate vengeance follows hard on vice.

Who recks of dwellers in the Scythian snows?
  Who dreads the Mede? Who fears, if Caesar reign,
Yon savage brood the Teuton forest knows,
  Or who is troubled for the war with Spain?

Each sees the sun down in his native glen,
  There wedding widower elm and tender vine;
Then blithely hies him homeward, and again
  Crowns his glad cup and bids thee bless the wine.

Thee with all prayer, with all libation thee,
  Thee in the number of his Lares set
He worships; so Hellenic piety
  To Castor and Alcides paid its debt.

Good chief, with years of joy thy country dower!
  This at the dawn of days not yet begun
Dry-lipped we pray; and thus in wassail hour
  When couched in ocean sleeps the weary sun.

dive, quem proles

Apollo! thou whose vengeful dart
Slew the fair sons of vaunting Niobe,
Quivered in Tityos' wanton heart,
And smote Achilles, sea-born Thetis' son,
When with uplifted spear, alone,
Greater in war than all save thee,
He shook the Dardan ramparts well-nigh won:
Like the felled Pine or Cypress wrenched by storm,
Dying, on Ilion's dust he stretched his stately form.

He would have scorned to shroud his might
Hid in that lying Horse: in darkness rise
And steal like skulking thief of night
On ill-starred revelries.
In light of day
His blood-stained hand had wrapt in flame
The captive host, the monarch grey,
All, all, alas! the sin, the shame!
Babbling lips of children torn
From dying breasts, infants, and babes unborn.

Not such the will of Jove!
Apollo's prayer, and her's the Queen of Love
Prevailed: the Father God
Relenting gave the nod,
And bade Aeneas rear on high
New Walls on Western hills with happier augury.

Phoebus! who on Thaba's lyre
Breathest the soul of Grecian fire,
Leave Lycian Xanthus who caresses
With his soft wave thy golden tresses,
Inspire, protect, our Latin song
Beardless Agyieus, ever young!
The Poet's name thou gavest long since to me,
The art, the spirit of Poesy.

Noble virgin, noble youth,
Scions of old Roman race,
Loved of Dian who pursueth
Stags and panthers in the chase,
Keep the Lesbian measure true,
Mark my finger on the string,
Sing the hymn to Phoebus due,
Cynthia's crescent glory sing,
Hymn to Leto's son be given,
Hymn to her whose gracious light
Gilds the harvest; who in Heaven
Speeds the circling season's flight.

When the glad feast comes again,
Maids, then wedded, ye shall say
"To gods well pleased we sang that strain
In youth, and Horace taught the lay."

diffugere nives

The snow, dissolved, no more is seen;
The fields and woods, behold, are green;
The changing year renews the plain;
The rivers know their banks again;
The sprightly Nymph and naked Grace
The mazy dance together trace;
The changing year's successive plan
Proclaims mortality to man.
Rough Winter's blasts to Spring give way;
Spring yields to Summer's sovereign ray;
And Winter chills the world again.
Her losses soon the moon supplies,
But wretched man, when once he lies
Where Priam and his sons are laid,
Is nought but ashes, and a shade.

Who knows if Jove, who counts our score,
Will rouse us in a morning more?
What with your friend you nobly share,
At least you rescue from your heir.

Not you, Torquatus, boast of Rome,
When Minos once has fix'd your doom,
Or eloquence, or splendid birth,
Or virtue, shall restore to earth.
Hippolytus, unjustly slain
Diana calls to life in vain;
Nor can the mighty Theseus rend
The chains of Hell that hold his friend.

donarem pateras

I'd give to my friends costly presents of plate
Or tripods, the spoils of the brave and the great
In our war with the Greeks, Censorinus, and you
Not the least of these gifts should bear off as your due,
Were I rich; if Parrhasius or Scopas, whose skill
Could depict now a man, now a God at their will,
Whether painted in colors or sculptured in stone,
Had produced a great work, you're the one who should own
That work if I had it; but you do not care,
But songs you delight in and songs I can give,
And tell you their value in verse that will live.
Not marble, though chiselled by sculptor of worth,
Whose fame reaches out to the ends of the earth,
Though such spirit and life to dead heroes it give
That we're almost persuaded they're breathing and live;
Not Hannibal, threatening, back-driven in flight,
Nor impious Carthage, with torch fires alight,
Imparted a lustre so bright to his name
Who, Africa conquered, victorious came
To our shores, as the Muses of poetry. None,
If their pages are silent, for what he has done
Shall bear off his recompense! What had we known,
If the poets a mantle of silence had thrown
O'er Ilia's story, or Romulus' fame?
'Twas the poets who told us how Aeacus came,
Caught back from the waves of the Styx, till he rest,
By the power of their song, in the isles of the blest.
The man of true worth is forbidden to die
By the Muses, they find him his place in the sky.

So Hercules shares in the banquets of Jove,
While Castor and Pollux, bright shining above
As clear stars in heaven, from shipwreck can save
Our fleets that are whelmed by the storm and the wave;
And Bacchus, becrowned with the chaplet of palm,
Hears the prayers of the faithful and saves them from harm.

ne forte credas

Think not the words will perish that I sing,
  Born where the waters of Ofanto roar;
  Words which, by poet's art unknown before,
Set to the lyre are echoed to its string.

Maeonian Homer holds the upper seat,
  But palms to Pindar we do not refuse;
  Not to the Cean or Alcaeic muse,
Nor grave Stesichorus laudation meet.

Nor gay Anacreon's song of olden days
  Has age destroyed; the words that love inspires
  Outlive their utterance; and still live the fires
Aeolian Sappho kindled in her lays.

Helen of Lacedaemon not alone
  Has lusted for a paramour's smooth tresses,
  Enamoured of the gold-inwoven dresses,
The retinue and splendor of a throne.

Troy more than once was vexed; from bow of Crete
  Teucer was not the first his shafts to aim,
  Nor Sthenelus the first to conquer fame,
Nor grand Idomeneus by material feat;

But the Muse told their story. Not the brave
  Deïphobus and not the fiery Hector,
  Of modest wives and children the protector,
Was first with thousand wounds to find a grave.

Of valiant men a countless multitude
  Lived before Agamemnon—yet none weep
  Their fate; no sacred bard disturbs their sleep
And night's long, silent shadows o'er them brood.

Valour unsung, unknown, from obscure sloth
  Differs but little; should I silent be,
  Nor on my page the tribute render thee
Due thy deserts, 'twere grievous wrong to both.

Thy many labors, Lollius, for the State
  Oblivion must not hide; thou hast a mind
  Wise in affairs; to no excess inclined,
Firm in bad fortune, nor in good elate;

Stern foe of fraud and avarice, abstaining
  With care from that solicitude for pelf
  Which seeks to center all things in itself,—
Not consul one year only, but remaining

At all times consul, while the proffered bribes,
  Loyal and true, the magistrate rejects,—
  The honest, not the gainful way elects,
And routs, victorious, sin's opposing tribes.

The man of wealth we do not rightly call
  A happy man; much happier he who knows
  How to enjoy the good that Heaven bestows,
Accepts its gifts and wisely uses all;

Endures in patience cruel poverty,
  And deems dishonor worse by far than death;
  For friends and country yields his latest breath,—
Living for them, he dares for them to die.

IV · 10 · *It Will Soon Be Too Late*

o crudelis adhuc

Vain of thy charms, and cruel still,
When winter's unexpected chill
Thy pride shall humble; when the hair,
Now floating on thy shoulders fair,
Shall fall; and the bright flush that glows
With tint surpassing damask rose
On thy soft cheek, by sure decay
Shall roughen, fade, and die away,
How oft before thy glass thou cry,
As the sad change appals thine eye:
"Why, when in early youth I shone,
Wore not my mind its present tone?
Or why, since now such tone is mine
Wear not my cheeks their youthful shine?"

est mihi nonum

Phyllis! a cask I have of Alban wine
Now more than nine years old; my garden shows
Fresh parsley, chaplet for the feast to twine;
  And ivy grows

In plenty,—gaily shall it deck thine hair;
Glitters the house with plate; chaste vervains round
The altar, thirsting for its votive share
  Of blood, are bound;

All hands are busy; lads and lassies hie
Now here, now there, each mingled task to claim,
While through the sullying smoke that rolls on high
  Leaps the bright flame.

But why we bid thee here I must explain,
Our joys to share. We keep glad April's Ides,
The month of Venus, daughter of the main,
  This day divides.

Right sacred 'tis to me, almost more dear
Than birthday of my own; since from its light
Maecenas reckons each revolving year
  In passing flight.

Young Telephus another fair hath seized,
Above thy rank thou follow'st him in vain;
Wealthy and wanton is the lass; well pleased
  He hugs his chain.

Scorched Phaëthon bids ambitious minds beware;
From Pegasus the striking warning heed;
Mortal Bellerophon he scorned to bear,
That winged steed.

Do thou desist from the degrading chase;
Hopes that amount to guilt do thou resign;
Shun the unequal match, my home to grace,
Last love of mine.

Come thou with me; I'll woo no other fair.
Come learn the strains shall suit that winning voice;
Lulled by soft music's charm, e'en gloomy care
Must needs rejoice.

IV · 12 · *Invitation to a Friend, in Spring*

iam veris comites

Now Thracian airs, companions of the Spring,
Temper the seas, and with Etesian wing
Fan the expanded sail. Released from snow
The earth awakes; late raging rivers flow
With noiseless course. Once more the voice is heard
As sad she builds her nest, of that poor bird
Who grieves for Itys—her, the dire disgrace
(Though foul the sin avenged) of Cecrop's race.
The shepherd stretched on tender herbage trills
Strains like his native mountains wild and free,
Charming the god who haunts those pine-dark hills,
And loves the peaceful flocks of Arcady.

Thirst comes with summer. Vergil, haste,
Comrade of noble youths, and taste
Choice wines of Cales. My reward
One little shell of Syrian nard.
The mellowed cask long stored within
The depths of the Sulpician bin
Shall then be thine, that nectar rare
Which brightens hope and drowns dull care.
Come! taste my wine, but ere thou try it
Remember, friend, that thou must buy it:
I cannot, like the rich man, give
Largess to all and nought receive.

Hence, sordid cares! Hence, idle sorrow!
Death comes apace, to-day, tomorrow.

Then mingle mirth with melancholy.
Wisdom at times is found in folly.

audivere, Lyce, di

The gods have heard me, Lyce,
The gods have heard my prayer.
Now you who were so icy
Observe with cold despair
Your thin and snowy hair.

Your cheeks are lined and sunken;
Your smiles have turned to leers;
But still you sing a drunken
Appeal to Love who hears
With inattentive ears.

Young Chia with her fluty
Caressing voice compels.
Love lives upon her beauty;
Her cheeks, in which he dwells,
Are his fresh citadels.

He saw the battered ruin,
This old and twisted tree;
He marked the scars, and flew in
Haste that he might not see
Your torn senility.

No silks, no purple gauzes
Can hide the lines that last.
Time, with his iron laws, is
Implacable and fast.
You cannot cheat the past.

Where now are all your subtle
Disguises and your fair
Smile like a gleaming shuttle?
Your shining skin, your rare
Beauty half breathless—where?

Only excelled by Cinara,
Your loveliness ranked high.
You even seemed the winner, a
Victor as years went by,
And she was first to die.

But now—the young men lightly
Laugh at your wrinkled brow.
The torch that burned so brightly
Is only ashes now,
A charred and blackened bough.

quae cura patrum

How shall the senate, how shall Rome
On sculptured bust, or history's page, record
Thy virtues, Caesar, and their just reward
Stamped on the heart of ages yet to come?
Greatest of chiefs where'er the Lord of Day
Levels o'er peopled shores his morning ray!

Strangers to Roman law till now
The rude Vindelici have learned to bow
To Caesar's warlike might. His sword,
Wielded by Drusus, quelled the Breunian horde,
When Alpine citadels in ashes laid
Saw Rome in blood avenged by slaughter thrice repaid.

Claudius by happy auspice led
Through Rhaetian ranks his onset sped;
Conspicuous in the field of blood,
With what fell ruin he pursued,
Unsated still, that giant brood
Who dared a patriot's death to die
  Martyrs to liberty.

Fierce 'mid the living and the dead,
O'er flaming plains he spurred his steed blood-red;
So southern storms the restless billows smite
When the sad Pleiads, rising through the night,
From bursting clouds send forth their baleful light;
  Or so, in Daunia's ancient realm
  Bull-headed Aufidus amain

Rolls down his raging flood to overwhelm
The harvest ripening on the Apulian plain.

Thus through the Rhaetian's steel array
In front, in rear, young Claudius mowed his way.
On the red earth in serried ranks they lie,
And yield to Rome a bloodless victory.
Thine were the hosts, the counsel, and design,
Caesar! The tutelary gods were thine.
Since that proud day when Alexandria's port
Her vacant halls and her deserted court
Lay'd at thy feet—since that auspicious day
Our stubborn foes a master's hand obey.
For three long lustres, reconciled,
On noble deeds benignant Fortune smiled,
Then gave to Rome the boon long sought in vain,
The grace, the glory of a peaceful reign.

The proud Iberian, slow to yield,
The Scythians flying o'er the field,
The monster-teeming seas that roar
Round distant Britain's rock-bound shore,
The Gaul in peril unalarmed,
Sygambri peaceful and disarmed,
The Nile that hides his mystic source,
Ister, and Tigris' headlong course,
The Median in his mountain home,
Wondering, adore in thee, Caesar, the shield of Rome

IV · 15 · *Augustus' Peace*

Phoebus volentem proelia

On siege and battlefield I mused,
  Of martial themes I wished to sing,
But Phoebus chid—my lyre refused
  To speak, and mute was every string;
He bade me furl my little sails,
Nor rashly tempt Tyrrhenian gales.

'Tis thine, O Caesar, to restore
  To wasted fields their wealth of corn;
And standards that we lost of yore,—
  From haughty Parthia's columns torn,—
Bring back in triumph to our shrine,
Of Jupiter Capitoline.

Beneath thy sway we live in peace,
  The double gates of Janus close,
Outbursts of vagrant license cease,
  And all is order and repose;
Thy hand that stays the people's crimes
Restores the arts of olden times:

Arts which have spread the Latin name,
  Increased the might of Italy,
Founded the empire's matchless fame
  And all embracing majesty,
Till they have spanned the earth's extent
From sunset to the Orient.

While we have Caesar at our head,
  Serene custodian of the State,
No civil fury shall we dread,
  Nor feuds that cities desolate;
The rage that fires barbarian hordes
Shall never sharpen Roman swords.

Not they who dwell upon its banks
  And the deep Danube's waters drink,
No faithless Parthian's quivered ranks,
  No natives of the Tanais' lake,
The Julian edicts dare to break.

These themes I leave: the lot be mine
  On common and on festal days,
With Bacchus' gifts of flowers and wine,
  To mingle my congenial lays,—
And while our wives and children share
In offerings of peace and prayer,

We'll, like our fathers, celebrate—
  In songs that blend with Lydian pipes—
The men in simple virtues great,
  Our captains of the ancient types;
Anchises, Troy, our themes shall be,
And genial Venus' progeny.

Letters in Verse
(Epistles)

Open letters, yet retaining their individual appeal, on subjects primarily literary and philosophical but also warmly personal. Written at various times between 20 B. C. and 13 B. C. when the poet was turning fifty.

I · 1 · *To Maecenas, Explaining His Swerve from Poetry*

prima dicte mihi

Theme of my first, theme of my latest, lay,
You seek, Maecenas, still to make me toil
Within the old lists, though adequately proved
And long discharged with gift of freedom's foil.
My age, my mind, have undergone a change.
There is Veianius: him it behoved
On Hercules' door-post his arms to range,
And in the country lies he hidden away,
So that upon the arena's edge he may
Not be obliged so often to implore
The people's favor on his freedom's score.
In my well-rinsed ears oft rings the rede:
"Be wise in time and loose the ageing steed,
Lest in the end he fail, while men deride,
And break his wind." So now I lay aside
Not only verses but all other toys:

I want to find the true and fitting joys,
And all engrossed in this pursuit am I.
I treasure and arrange what by and by
I may draw forth for guidance from my store.
And, should you ask what leader I adore,
What school I follow, this my answer be:
Where'er the tempest chances to drive me,

I'm carried as a guest, not bound to swear
In terms prescribed by master whatsoe'er.
Now turn I practical, and with a lunge
Into the waves of politics I plunge,
True Virtue's guard and sentinel severe;
Again I slide back—ere I know it, caught—
Into the maxims Aristippus taught:
And I essay neath my control to bring
All things, nor be controlled by any thing.

As night seems long to him a mistress blinks,
And day is slow to him that works and swinks,
As lazy moves the year with minors galled
To be by mothers' oversight enthralled,
So tedious and distasteful flows for me
The time my hope and my design I see
Delayed, when I desire in strenuous mood
To execute some project for the good
Of poor and rich alike, whose loss will hold
An equal detriment to young and old.
Remains myself I govern and console
By simple rules like these: one's eye may see
Less far than Lynceus', yet, if bleared one be,
One won't despise the ointment's soft control;
Nor, since one can't have Glycon's limbs so stark,
Should one be careless to ward off the gout.
There is a point whereto we may reach out,
If yet we cannot go beyond that mark.

Does avarice and wretched vague desire
For more and more one's bosom set afire?
Spells are there, strains, the torment to allay

And much of the distemper charm away.
Swell you with love of fame? Then remedies
Unfailing are there to restore your ease,
Once you have read thrice over with pure mind
The treatise where the formulae you find.
The envious, passionate, slothful, drunken, lewd—
No man so savage but he drops the mood,
Lend he but patient ear to counsel good.

First step in virtue is from vice to flee;
First step in wisdom, to be folly-free.
You mark how much your mind and body strain
To shun the ills you think give greatest pain—
A narrow fortune, or a base defeat.
To furthest Ind you run on eager feet
A pushing merchant, over seas, rocks, fire,
In flight from poverty—condition dire!
Will you not learn and listen and believe
In some one wiser, so you may conceive
'Twere well no more your mind on things to set
You foolishly admire and want to get.
What bruiser that parades the hamlets round
And crossways would disdain to have him crowned
At great Olympia, had he—hope so sweet—
The proffered palm without the dust and heat?

Of less account is silver than is gold,
Of less account is gold than virtue. "Hold!
O citizens, O citizens, get money,
Get money first, and virtue after money."
These maxims first and foremost the Exchange
From end to end holds forth, through all its range;

Old men repeat them, echo them the young
With slate and satchel o'er the left arm slung.

Brains, morals, speech, good faith you've at your back,
But of four hundred thousand sesterces you lack
Some six or seven: plebeian still you'll be,
But boys at games, as any day you see,
Cry: "Play you fair, you shall be king, pardie!"
Be this our wall of bronze: a conscience clear,
No guilt to turn us pale, to cause us fear.
Now, tell me, pray, which of the two is better,
The Roscian statute or the children's patter
Offering the realm to those that do the right,
From age to age pronounced by men of might
Like Curius and Camillus? Do you take
As sounder the advice: "Go, money make,
Make money, fairly make it, if you may,
But, if not fairly, then in any way"—
So you may get yourself a closer view
Of Pupius' doleful plays: or his that you
With ever present help exhorts and fits
To face, erect and free, haught Fortune's hits?

Now, should the folk of Rome the question pose
Why, as I use the self-same porticos,
I don't adopt their views—don't flee from what they
hate—
I'll cite the answer to the lion sick
Made by the fox suspicious of a trick:
"The footprints fright me: all go to your den,
But ne'er a one of them comes back again."
You are indeed a monster many-headed.

For, what am I to follow, whom to credit?
Some men are keen for contracts with the State,
And some hunt greedy widows with a bait
Of fruits and tit-bits, and old men ensnare
To put in their preserves; for many, fair
Their fortune grows by usury's secret care.
But granted different men are occupied
With different objects, different pursuits,
Can the same persons for an hour abide
In liking of a thing that once them suits?
"In all the world there's no more charming bay
Than Baiae," if some wealthy man should say,
The lake and sea feel at the very word
The eagerness of their impatient lord;
And, if a morbid fancy clinch the whim,
"To-morrow, workmen," is the word of him,
"Off to Teanum with you, tools and all!"
The marriage-bed is standing in the hall:
"A single life's the thing," he says; "compare
Can nought with that." If 'tis not there,
He swears the married only bliss attain.
What noose such changeful Proteus can restrain?

"The poor man, what does he?"

Oh! have your smile;
He changes pub, bath, barber, garret vile;
He hires a boat and is by sickness caught
As is a rich man on his private yacht.
I meet you with my hair unevenly dressed:
You laugh; and, if I wear a threadbare vest
Beneath a glossy tunic, or my gown

Hangs all awry and slips from shoulder down,
You laugh. What do you when my judgment wars
Against itself, rejects what once it sought,
And seeks again what it just dropt as naught,
Sways like the sea, and all consistence mars
Through life's whole system, builds, pulls down,
Turns round to square and square to round anon?
You think my madness is the general one,
And so not laugh. For you do not believe
I need a doctor, or I should receive
A guardian from the praetor; nay, you take
Upon you charge of my affairs, and wake
Your umbrage at a wretched ill-pared nail
Of one that leans on you and loves you well.
It comes to this: the wise man bears the gree,
Neath Jove alone; he's wealthy, he is free,
Honored, and handsome—king of kings is he:
And, best of all, he's sound—unless, suppose,
A nasty rheum has caught him by the nose.

I · 2 · *To Lollius, on the Practical Value of Great Literature*

Trojani belli scriptorem

While you, my Lollius, on some chosen theme,
With youthful eloquence at Rome declaim,
I read the Grecian poet o'er again,
Whose works the beautiful and base contain;
Of vice and virtues more instructive rules
Than all the sober sages of the schools.
Why thus I think, if not engaged, attend,
And, Lollius, hear the reasons of your friend.
  The well-wrought fable, that sublimely shows
The loves of Paris, and the lengthened woes
Of Greece in arms, presents, as on a stage,
The giddy tumults and the foolish rage
Of kings and people. Hear Antenor's scheme;
Cut off the cause of war; restore the dame.
But Paris treats this counsel with disdain,
Nor will be forced in happiness to reign.
While hoary Nestor, by experience wise,
To reconcile the angry monarch tries.
His injured love the son of Peleus fires,
And equal passion, equal rage inspires
The breasts of both. When doating monarchs urge
Unsound resolves, their subjects feel the scourge.
Trojans, and Greeks, seditious, base, unjust,
Offend alike in violence and lust.
  To show what wisdom and what sense can do,
The poet sets Ulysses in our view,
Who conquered Troy, and with sagacious ken
Saw various towns and polities of men;
While for himself, and for his native train,

He seeks a passage through the boundless main;
In perils plunged, the patient hero braves
His adverse fate, and buoys above the waves.
  You know the sirens' songs and Circe's draught,
Which had he, senseless, and intemperate, quaffed,
With his companions, he, like them, had been
The brutal vassal of an harlot queen;
Had lived a dog, debased to vile desire,
Or loathsome swine, and grovelled in the mire.
But we, mere numbers in the book of life,
Like those who boldly wooed our hero's wife,
Born to consume the fruits of earth; in truth,
As vain and idle, as Phaeacia's youth;
Mere outside all, to fill the mighty void
Of life, in dress and equipage employed,
Who sleep till mid-day, and with melting airs
Of empty music, soothe away our cares.
  Rogues nightly rise to murder men for pelf.
Will you not rouse you to protect yourself?
But though in health you doze away your days,
You run, when puffed with dropsical disease.
Unless you light your early lamp, to find
A moral book; unless you form your mind
To nobler studies, you shall forfeit rest,
And love or envy shall distract your breast.
For the hurt eye an instant cure you find;
Then why neglect, for years, the sickening mind?
  Dare to be wise; begin; for once begun,
Your task is easy; half the work is done:
And sure the man, who has it in his power
To practise virtue, and protracts the hour,
Waits, like the rustic, till the river's dried;

Still glides the river, and will ever glide.
  For wealth and wives of fruitfulness we toil;
We stub the forest, and reclaim the soil.
Blessed with a competence, why wish for more?
Nor house, nor lands, nor heaps of labored ore
Can give their feverish lord one moment's rest,
Or drive one sorrow from his anxious breast;
The fond possessor must be blessed with health
Who rightly means to use his hoarded wealth.
  Houses and riches gratify the breast,
For lucre lusting, or with fear depressed,
As pictures, glowing with a vivid light,
With painful pleasure charm a blemished sight;
As chafing soothes the gout, or music cheers
The tingling organs of imposthumed ears.
Your wine grows acid when the cask is foul.
Learn the strong sense of pleasure to control.
With virtuous pride its blandishments disdain;
Hurtful is pleasure when it's bought with pain.
He wants for ever, who would more acquire;
Set certain limits to your wild desire.
  The man who envies must behold with pain
Another's joys, and sicken at his gain:
Nor could Sicilia's tyrants ever find
A greater than an envious mind.
  The man, unable to control his ire,
Shall wish undone what hate and wrath inspire:
To sate his wrath, precipitate he flies,
Yet in his breast his rage unsated lies.
Anger's a shorter madness of the mind;
Subdue the tyrant, and in fetter bind.
  The docile colt is formed with gentle skill

To move obedient to his rider's will.
In the loud hall the hound is taught to bay
The buckskin trailed, then challenges his prey
Through the wild woods. Thus in your hour of youth
From pure instruction quaff the words of truth.
The odors of the wine, that first shall stain
The virgin vessel, it shall long retain.
Whether you prove a lagger in the race,
Or with a vigorous ardour urge your pace,
I shall maintain my usual rate; no more;
Nor wait for those behind, nor press on those before.

I· 3· *To Florus, Asking about Personal Affairs*

Iuli Flore

Florus, I long to know where Claudius leads
The distant rage of war; whether he spreads
His conquering banners o'er the Thracian plains,
Or near the Heber, bound in snowy chains.
Or does the Hellespont's high-tower'd sea,
Or Asia's fertile soil his course delay?
What works of genius do the youths prepare,
Who guard his sacred person? Who shall dare
To sing great Caesar's wars, immortal theme!
And give his peaceful honors down to fame?
How fares my Titius? Say, when he intends
To publish? Does he not forget his friends?
He, who disdains the springs of common fame,
And dauntless quaffs the deep Pindaric stream.
But will the muse her favorite bard inspire
To tune to Theban sounds the Roman lyre?
Or with the transports of theatric rage,
And its sonorous language, shake the stage?
  Let Celsus be admonish'd o'er and o'er,
To search the treasures of his native store,
Nor touch what Phoebus consecrates to fame,
Lest, when the birds their various plumage claim,
Stripp'd of his stolen pride, the crow forlorn
Should stand the laughter of the public scorn.
What do you dare, who float with active wing
Around the thymy fragrance of the spring?
Not yours the genius of a lowly strain,
Nor of uncultur'd, or unpolish'd vein,
Whether you plead with eloquence his cause,

Or to your client clear the doubtful laws;
And sure to gain, for amatorious lays,
The wreaths of ivy, with unenvied praise.
  Could you the passions, in their rage, control,
That damp the nobler purpose of the soul;
Could you these soothing discontents allay,
Soon would you rise where wisdom points the way;
Wisdom heaven-born, at which we should all aim,
The little vulgar, and the known to fame,
Who mean to live within our proper sphere,
Dear to ourselves, and to our country dear.
  Now tell me whether Plancus holds a part
(For sure he well deserves it) in your heart?
Or was the reconciliation made in vain,
And like an ill-cured wound breaks forth gain,
While inexperienced youth, and blood inflamed,
Drive you, like coursers to the yoke untamed?
Where'er you are, too excellent to prove
The broken union of fraternal love,
A votive heifer gratefully I feed,
For your return, in sacrifice to bleed.

I · 4 · *To Tibullus, Some Reflections*

Albi, nostrorum sermonum

Albius, in whom my satires find
A candid critic, and a kind,
Do you, while at your country seat,
Some rhyming labors meditate,
That shall in volumned bulk arise,
And even from Cassius bear the prize;
Or saunter through the silent wood,
Musing on what befits the wise and good?
  Thou art not form'd of lifeless mould,
With breast inanimate and cold;
To thee the gods a form complete,
To thee the gods a fair estate
In bounty gave, with art to know
How to enjoy what they bestow.
  Can a fond nurse one blessing more
Even for her favorite boy implore,
With sense and clear expression bless'd,
Of friendship, honor, health possess'd,
A table, elegantly plain,
And a poetic, easy vein?
  By hope inspired, depress'd with fear,
By passion warm'd, perplex'd with care
Believe, that every morning's ray
Hath lighted up the latest day;
Then, if tomorrow's sun be thine,
With double lustre shall it shine.
  Such are the maxims I embrace,

And here, in sleek and joyous case,
You'll find, for laughter fitly bred,
A hog by Epicurus fed.

I· 5· *To Torquatus, with an Invitation to a Modest Luncheon*

si potes Archiacis

If, my Torquatus, you can kindly deign
To lie on beds of simple form, and plain,
And sup on herbs alone, but richly dress'd,
At evening I expect you for my guest.
Nor old, I own, nor excellent, my wine,
Of five years vintage, and a marshy vine;
If you have better, bring th' enlivening cheer,
Or from an humble friend this summons hear.
In hopes my honor'd guest to entertain,
My fires are lighted, my apartments clean:
Then leave the hope, that, wing'd with folly, flies;
Leave the mean quarrels that from wealth arise;
Leave the litigious bar, for Caesar's birth
Proclaims the festal hour of ease and mirth,
While social converse, till the rising light,
Shall stretch beyond its length the summer's night.
Say, what are Fortune's gifts, if I'm denied
Their cheerful use? for nearly are allied
The madman, and the fool, whose sordid care
Makes himself poor to enrich a worthless heir.
Give me to drink, and, crown'd with flowers, despise
The grave disgrace of being thought unwise.
  What cannot wine perform? It brings to light
The secret soul; it bids the coward fight;
Gives being to our hopes, and from our hearts
Drives the dull sorrow, and inspires new arts.
Is there a wretch, whom bumpers have not taught
A flow of words, and loftiness of thought?

Even in th' oppressive grasp of poverty
I can enlarge and bid the soul be free.
  Cheerful my usual task I undertake
(And no mean figure in my office make),
That no foul linen wrinkle up the nose;
That every plate with bright reflections shows
My guest his face; that none, when life grows gay,
The sacred hour of confidence betray.
  That all in equal friendship may unite,
Your Butra and Septicius I'll invite,
And, if he's not engaged to better cheer,
Or a kind girl, Sabinus shall be here.
  Still there is room, and yet the summer's heat
May prove offensive, if the crowd be great:
But write me word how many you desire,
Then instant from the busy world retire,
And while your tedious clients fill the hall,
Slip out at the back door, and bilk them all.

I· 6· *To Numicius, on How to Be Happy*

nil admirari

To look at nothing with admiring eyes,
In this short precept, dear Numicius! lies
The art of human happiness compressed,—
The one sure way to make and keep us blest.
Yon moon and stars that shoot a trembling ray,
The glad vicissitudes of night and day,
The sun, the seasons true to nature's law—
There are who view untouched with wondering awe.
What deem you then of earth's inferior stores,
Of ocean's treasures poured on Indian shores,
Of place and pomp, and Rome's applauding noise—
With what indifference should we view these toys!
  Who fears their opposites, or who desires
The things themselves, in either case *admires*.
Each fixing on vain show a vacant eye
Stares at he knows not what—he knows not why:
Whether we loathe or covet, laugh or mourn,
No matter, if alike, by passion borne,
Each object that belies what fancy drew
Entrance the senses and arrest the view.
  Ev'n virtue followed beyond reason's rule
May stamp the just man knave, the sage a fool.
Hear this, ye vain! then greet with fond applause
The sculptured silver or the Parian vase:—
Pore on some bronzed antique with ravished eye,
Or grasp the glittering gem, or Tyrian dye:—
Rejoice that at the waving of your hand
With eager gaze a listening rabble stand:—
Off to the courts betimes at interest's call,

Nor thence retire till evening's shadows fall,
Lest upstart Mutus (oh the foul disgrace!)
Eclipse the glories of your nobler race,—
His dotal your paternal farms outdo,
And so you crouch to him—not he to you.
All-changing time now darkens what was bright,
Now ushers out of darkness into light.
Flaunt in the mall and flutter as you may,
Or scour with whirling wheel the Appian way,—
Known or obscure, you must with all your care
Descend where Numa and old Ancus are.
If sharp distemper riot in your veins,
You seek by medicine's aid to soothe its pains;
Would you (who would not?) live by reason's laws
And gain true bliss?—first ascertain the cause.
Can Virtue only grant the wished-for end,
Rouse and to her your manliest efforts bend.
Is she but words which fools would strive to fix,
As hallowed groves are after all but sticks?
Be first to run to port, spread all your sails,
Forestall the market, watch your Phrygian bales;
Add use to principal, sum to sum,
And toil till you have raised a fair, round *plum:*
Proceed to double this—nay stop not there;
Triple it then—and then complete the square.
For why—a portioned wife, fair fame, and friends,
Beauty and birth on sovereign WEALTH attends;
Blessed is her vot'ry throned his bags among!
Persuasion's self sits perched upon his tongue;
Love beams in every feature of his face,
And every gesture beams celestial grace.
Avoid the Cappadocian monarch's curse,

Who, rich in slaves, is penniless in purse.
Lucullus once being asked (the story goes)
For five-score cloaks of frize to grace the shows,—
Five-score! he cried: *you over-rate my powers:*
But I'll enquire; and what I have are yours.
Next day he writes—"There were within his call
"Five thousand—they might take a part or all!"
No house is rich but that, where much o'erflows
Which varlets rifle and no master knows.
If wealth, then, leads to pure and lasting bliss,
This be your earliest task—your latest this!
  If influence and the people's favour claims
The prize, let's hire a slave to tell their names,
And prompt as when to bow and whom to greet
With ready smile across the crowded street:
"These in the Fabian tribe some votes command,
"Those in the Veline; prithee stretch your hand.
"This great man gives the fasces; that—beware—
"From whom he will withholds the ivory chair."
Caress them all: call one friend; another
Hail *father,* as the years may suit, or brother.
  If he alone lives well who is well-fed,
See, morning dawns; up, sluggard, from your bed!
Forth to the shambles; fish and flesh provide,
True bliss your aim and gluttony your guide!
Hunt as Gargilius did, who through the throng
With nets and poles each morning pushed along,
That that same throng might see the long-drawn train
With one poor purchased boar sneak back again.
Then bathe replete with undigested food,
Deaf to the censure of your wife and good.
Forfeit your franchise: Let Ulysses' crew,

Who scorned their home for luxury, yield to you.
 If without love and dalliance life can give
(As sings Mimnermus) no delight, why—live
In love and dalliance: In a word, whate'er
Can make life happiest, point your efforts here.
Farewell! and if my doctrine seem amiss,
With candor set me right:—if not, take this!

I· 7· *To Maecenas, on Real Contentment*

quinque dies

Pledged in the country but five nights to stay,
August is past, and lo! I still delay,
False to my word. But if, dear sir, you care
To see me in good plight and debonair,
That license which you grant me sick, I know
You'll not deny me fearing to be so;
Now that pale autumn marshals forth again
The undertaker with his rueful train,
While each fond mother with distraction wild
Hangs o'er the pillow of her sickening child;
While levees thronged and law-courts never still
Let loose the fever and unseal the will.
But when autumnal drought to winter yields,
And drifting snows have bleached the Albanian fields,
Down to the sea your poet will retire
To read in comfort crouched beside the fire;
Anon, when zephyrs breathe and swallows sing,
To greet his patron with returning Spring.
  Your kindness, sir, to me, is really kind;
Not like the boons of some Calabrian hind
With fulsome zeal that will not be repressed
Forcing his pears upon his sated guest.
"Come, eat them, pray!" "I've eaten all I would."
"Then pocket what you please." "You're very good."
"Your infant tribe would deem them no bad store."
"I'm as obliged as if I took a score."
"Well, please yourself; but know what you disdain
Will fall ere night a portion to the swine."
The spendthrift and the fool are so polite,

They give to others what they hate or slight;
And where love's seed is sown with hand so rude,
No wonder of the crop's ingratitude.
The good and wise, though anxious to uphold
True worth, yet know that lupines are not gold.
For me, I ever shall be proud to raise
My worth in justice to my patron's praise:
But, would you have me never quit your side,
First give me back those locks whose jetty pride
Once clustered o'er my brow in gallant trim;—
Give back the well-strung nerve and vigorous limb;—
With that gay converse and those spirits light
That o'er the bowl deplored coy Cynara's flight.
  A fox's whelp one day half-famished stole
Into a corn-bin through a narrow hole;
Where, having gorged his fill, he strove in vain
To squeeze his bloated carcass out again;
  "Friend," cried a weazel near, "first mend your shape;
You entered lean, and lean you must escape."
Should fortune ever, on this footing, call
Her favors back, I could resign them all;
Nor, capon-fed, with hypocritic air
Would I preach up the peasant's frugal fare;
Nor should the wealth of all Arabia please,
Taxed with the loss of liberty and ease.
Oft have you praised me as of modest views,
More prompt to laud your bounty than abuse;
Oft in your presence, nor less oft away,
As my liege-lord, I've hailed your gentle sway.
Try me—and (though with thanks received) you'll find
Your gifts can be with cheerfulness resigned.
Well did Ulysses' son, as poets sing,

Thank for his proffered steeds the Spartan King:—
"The rocky island whence I drew my birth,
"Albeit to me the loveliest spot on earth,
"Nor stretched in plain, nor rich in grassy food
"Is ill-adapted for the equine brood:
"Wherefor I would renounce, if you permit,
"Those boons, good monarch! for yourself more fit!"
Small things become the small: for me Rome's noise
And pomp imperial present no joys,
Far more disposed to dream away the hours
In Tibur's peaceful shades or soft Tarentum's bowers.
  Philippus, for his pleadings famed afar,
Alert and bold, returning from the Bar
About the hour of two one sultry day,
And now complaining that the length of way
Grew for his years too much, espied ('tis said)
A smug-faced cit beneath a barber's shed—
Paring his nails with easy unconcern;—
Then called his lackey—"Boy, step in and learn
"Who this may be—his family, his fame,
"Where he resides, and what's his patron's name."
The lad (by name Demetrius) lacked not skill
Or promptness to dispatch his master's will.
He flies, returns, informs him in a trice,
" 'Twas one Vulteius Mena, pure from vice,
Of humble means, by trade an auctioneer,
Who bustled to and fro to raise the gear,
Lounged when his daily toils were at an end,
Was fain to get, but not afraid to spend;
Mixed with acquaintance of his own degree,
Had a fixed dwelling, and enjoyed with glee
The public shows; or, when his work was done,

In Mars's field at tennis would make one."
"Troth, I should like to know the wight; go, say
I should be glad he'd dine with me today."
Mena, the message heard, in mute surprise
Stares, and can scarce believe his ears and eyes;
Begs his devout acknowledgements, in sum
Feels flattered and obliged, but cannot come.
"How! does the wretch then slight me?" "Even so,
And through contempt or shyness answers, no!"
Next morning, as Philippus strolls along,
He spies Vulteius to a tuniced throng
Vending cheap wares, and, having crossed the street,
Makes toward his client, and is first to greet.
He, humbly bowing, pleads the ties of trade
And business, that he had not early paid
His compliments; e'en now, in toils immersed,
Is shocked to think he had not hailed him first.
"On one condition be your pleas allowed—
"Dine with me today." "Sir, I shall be proud."
"Enough—you'll come at the ninth hour; 'till which
Go, ply your trade and labor to be rich."
The hour arrives—he goes—and, having said
Some wisdom and some foolery, hies to bed.
Day after day where thus he kindly took
The flattering bait and nibbled round the hook,
A morning dangler now and constant guest;
What time the Latin festival gives rest
To wrangling law-courts, he's invited down
To see his patron's seat nor far from town
Perched in the chaise, he lauds in terms most high
The golden crops, green lawns, and Sabine sky.

Philippus, much diverted, all the while,
Sees his scheme work and sees it with a smile,
Resolved with all chance pastime care to drown.
In short, seven thousand sesterces paid down,
With seven thousand more proffered at an easy rate,
Tempt him to buy and farm a snug estate.
'Tis bought (and not to spin my story out)
The smart cit drops into the rustic lout;—
He prattles of his tilth and vines—prepares
His elms—and launches in a sea of cares,
Stung to the quick with gain's elusive itch
And pining with the thirst of getting rich.
Soon after (mark the change!) night-plunderers seize
His lambs; his she-goats perished with disease;
Now blighted harvests mock his hopes; and now
The jaded ox drops dead beneath his plow.
Teased with his losses, cursing Fortune's spite,
Snatching his nag at the mid hour of night,
Half-frantic to his patron's seat he goes,
Unshorn, in squalid garb that speaks his woes.
"How now!" Philippus cries, "Your looks are such
"I fear you drudge too hard, and toil too much."
Troth, patron! to this merit I've no claim;
Wretched I am, and that's my proper name!
Then oh! by all the ties of faith and love,
By all your boons, and by the powers above,
Kind sir, I do conjure you and implore,
Replace me in my pristine state once more!
  The moral of my tale is briefly this:
Let him who finds that he has changed amiss,
And that his promised joy turns out but pain,

With all convenient speed change back again!
'Tis a sound rule that each man has his pleasure,
And each should mete himself by his own measure.

I· 8· *To Celsus, Greetings and a Bit of Advice*

Celso gaudere

To Celsus, muse, my warmest wishes bear,
And if he kindly asks you how I fare,
Say, though I threaten many a fair design,
Nor happiness, nor wisdom, yet are mine.
Not that the driving rains my vineyards beat;
Not that my olives are destroyed by heat;
Not that my cattle pine in distant plains—
More in my mind than body lie my pains.
Reading I hate, and with unwilling ear
The voice of comfort or of health I hear;
Friends or physicians I with pain endure,
Who strive this languor ot my soul to cure.
Whate'er may hurt me I with joy pursue;
Whate'er may do me good with horror view.
Inconstant as the wind, I various rove;
At Tibur, Rome; at Rome, I Tibur love.
Ask how he does; what happy arts support
His prince's favor, nor offend the court;
If all be well, say first, that we rejoice,
And then, remember, with a gentlest voice
Instil this precept on his listening ear,
'As you your fortune, we shall Celsus bear.'

1· 9· *To Claudius, Introducing a Friend, Septimius*

Septimius, Claudi

Claudius, Septimius clearly deems that he
Of all men knows how much you make of me.
He dares to ask me with insistent prayer
To try to praise, commend him to your care
As worthy in your home to bear a part,
To share in Nero's love who reads the heart.
He fancies me your own familiar friend,
Lends me more grace than to myself I lend.
I urged a thousand pleas to be excused;
Yet feared, if I persistently refused,
To seem less influential, and to own
Myself a fraud who serve myself alone.
So I, that greater blame I might not bear,
Have smoothed my brow, to serve my crony dare
But if, because to praise my friend I've tried,
You laud my bashfulness now laid aside,
Enroll him in your staff: 'tis understood,
I'd have you confident he's brave and good.

I· 10· *To Fuscus, with Greetings from The Country*

urbis amatorem Fuscus

Town-lover Fuscus, I salute you, I,
A country lover—unlike certainly
On this one point alone, but on all others
Twins almost, in our thoughts and feelings brothers;
When one says "No," the other too says, "No";
We nod together "Yes"—old doves all know.

You keep the nest while I extol the brooks,
The rocks arrayed in moss, the groves, the rooks
Of the delightful country. In a word,
I live, I am a king, soon as I've stirred
And left behind those things that you extol
Up to the skies with the applause of all,
And, like a priest's slave fled beyond recall,
Cakes I reject; 'tis bread my hunger wakes,
Now choicer to my taste than honeyed cakes.
Ought ways of living Nature's ways express,
And first a site whereon a house to place
Is to be sought for, know you any spot
More genial than the country can be got—
The blissful country? Nowhere, if you please,
Are winters milder, or more grateful breeze
Tempers the Dog-star's rage, the Lion's run
When stung to fury by the scorching sun.
Is there a place where envious care less oft
Breaks rudely in upon our slumbers soft?
Smells grass less fragrant, shines with duller laughte
Than Libyan mosaics? Is the water

That strives to burst the pipes in every quarter
More limpid than the waters hurrying sped
In babbling wimples down the sloping bed?
Why, mid a peristyle of varied hues
A grove is reared and nursed with care profuse;
A house with distant prospect too is prized.
Drive Nature with a pitchfork from your door,
Return she will each time, yea, o'er and o'er,
And working silently in forms disguised,
Will burst the squeamish notions you hold fast,
And in the contest victor prove at last.

The connoisseur that fails to compare
Sidonian purple and the fleeces fair
That drink their color from Aquinum dye
Will not incur a loss more certainly,
A loss that cuts more deeply, than the man
That never false from true distinguish can.
One overmuch elated with success
A change of fortune plunges in distress;
Whate'er you fancy, you'll resign such things
With much regret. From grandeur keep aloof:
A man may live beneath a humble roof
Happier than kings and favorites of kings.
The stag, victorious in fight, in course
Drove from the common pasturage the horse,
Until the horse, at last forced to submit,
Called in the help of man and took the bit;
But, when he had subdued his foe by force,
The rider from his back he couldn't divorce,
Nor from his mouth the bit. So, if in dread
Of Want, one has one's freedom forfeited—

Freedom more precious than a mine outspread—
A master he will carry for his greed,
And always be a slave, because indeed
He knows not how to make a little do.
Suit not one's means one's lot—'tis like the shoe:
Be it too large, 'twill cause the man to fall;
Be it too small, his foot 'twill surely gall.
If satisfied, Aristius, with your lot,
You'll live the life a wise man lives, I wot;
Nor let me go unchastened when the while
You deem I pile too much nor cease to pile.
His master or his slave is each man's hoard,
And ought to follow, not to pull, the cord.

Beyond Vacuna's smouldering fane of note,
These lines I penned—happy but for the thought
That you were not with me the while I wrote.

I · 11 · *To Bullatius, on There Being No Place like Home*

quid tibi visa Chios

Do the famed islands of th' Ionian seas,
Chios, or Lesbos, my Bullatius please?
Or Sardis, where great Croesus held his court?
Say, are they less, or greater than report?
Does Samos, Colophon, or Smyrna, yield
To our own Tiber, or to Mars's field?
Would you, fatigued with trials of lands and seas,
In Lebedus, or Asia, spend your days?
You tell me Lebedus is now become
A desert, like our villages at home,
Yet there you gladly fix your future lot,
Your friends forgetting, by your friends forgot;
Enjoy the calm of life, and safe on shore,
At distance hear the raging tempest roar.
A traveller, though wet with dirt and rain,
Would not forever at an inn remain,
Or chill'd with cold, and joying in the heat
Of a warm bath, believe his bliss complete.
Though by strong winds your bark were tempest toss'd,
Say, would you sell it on a distant coast?
Believe me, at delicious Rhodes to live,
To a sound mind no greater bliss can give,
Than a thick coat in summer's burning ray,
Or a light mantle on a snowy day,
Or to a swimmer Tiber's freezing stream,
Or sunny rooms in August's mid-day flame.
While yet 'tis in your power; while Fortune smiles,
At Rome with rapture vaunt those happy isles,
Then with a grateful hand the bliss receive,

If heaven an hour more fortunate shall give.
Seize on the present joy, and thus possess,
Where'er you live, an inward happiness.
  If reason only can our cares allay,
Not the bold site, that wide commands the sea;
If they, who through the venturous ocean range,
Not their own passions, but the climate change;
Anxious through seas and land to search for rest
Is but laborious idleness at best.
In desert Ulubrae the bliss you'll find,
If you preserve a firm and equal mind.

I· 12· *To Iccius, Advice on Adjusting Himself to His Career in Sicily*

fructibus Agrippae

Iccius, the fruits of fair Sicilia's lands
Placed by Agrippa in your trusty hands
If you enjoy aright, not Jove's great power
Could in your bosom greater affluence shower;
Hush then vain murmurs—throw complaints aside.
He ne'er is poor, whose wants are well supplied.
Possessed of health and food and raiment, know
Arabia's treasures can no more bestow.
If, with the choicest viands on your board,
Wild herbs and roots your homely fare afford,
That fare were still the same, though fortune rolled
Into your lap a flood of liquid gold,
Or because Nature shifts not at the call
Of wealth, or virtue forms you all in all.
That swine consumed Democritus' corn
While far on fancy's wings his soul was borne,
Seems now no longer strange,—when you retain,
Plunged in the murrain and mid pest of gain,
Your old pursuits; and, spurning earth's low clime,
Can soar to speculate on themes sublime:
As,—what dark cause confines the swelling tides;—
What in their course the varying seasons guide;—
Whether yon stars in heaven's wide concave roll
Drifted by chance or urged by strong control;—
What mystic influence bids the queen of night
Now veil her orb and now disclose her light;—
What that discordant union which appears
To link the world and regulate the spheres;—

Whose system best with nature's truth agrees,—
Which halts Stertinius or Empedocles.
However this may be—whether your wish
Tend more to slice the leek or slay the fish,—
Admit Pompeius Grosphus to your heart,
And what he asks with willing zeal impart.
Grosphus will put no base or mean request;
And friendship's a cheap market—when the best
Are overlooked. But now, to let you know
How matters of more public interest go,—
Agrippa has subdued Cantabria's fields;
To Claudius Nero's sword Armenia yields;
Low on his knees Phraates has implored
The grace of Caesar as his rightful lord;
Fled from Italian plains is Famine grim,
And Plenty pours her horn replenished to the brim.

I· 13· *To Vinius Carrying His Master's Poetry to Augustus*

ut proficiscentem docui

This volume, Vinius, must (as I before
Expressly charged you and repeat once more)
Sealed as it is, be placed in Caesar's hands;
Provided first (observe my strict commands)
He be in health—if cheerful be his look,
Or if, in short, he ask you for the book;
Nor, overzealous to fulfil your trust,
Let pert officiousness create disgust.
  If chance, my papers, an unwieldy load,
Prove galling, rather leave them on the road
Than, when arrived whither your steps are bound,
Bolt them with eager rudeness on the ground;
Lest saucy punsters on your name refine
And swear Asella is right asinine.
  Go, plod your weary way o'er hill and moor;
And, when you shall have reached the destined door,
Heave not your bundle with an awkward air,
Just as a clown beneath his arm would bear
A lambkin, or as Pyrrhia, maudlin fool,
Bears on the stage her pilfered pack of wool;
Or burgess, at my lord's, with sheepish look
His hat and sandals. Bear not so my book.
  Though much entreated, halt not by the way;
Nor to each curious knave that sifts you, say
That on your back a precious burden lies,
Worthy to charm great Caesar's ears and eyes.
  Go! Fare thee well, but hark ye have a care
Of stumbles, lest you mar your fragile ware.

I· 14· *To Villius, His Steward, Urging Him to Be Content With His Lot*

vilice silvarum

Dear Bailiff of the woody wild domain
Where peace restores me to myself again,
(A sprightlier scene, it seems, your taste requires,
To Varia though it send five sturdy sires
The lords of five good households) let us see
If I from thorns and briars can better free
My mind, or you my farm; and which is found
In fairer culture, Horace or his ground.
Me though my Lamia's deep and tender grief
(Mourning with an anguished heart that scorns relief
A brother lost—a brother snatched away
In manhood's prime) tempts to prolong my stay;
My restless soul still thither casts from Rome
A wistful look, as to her proper home;
And, like the racer, pants for her discharge
To burst the barrier and to roam at large.
A country life's the haven of my rest;
To you no mortal but in town seems blest.
No wonder, when another's lot alone
Attracts our wishes, if we loathe our own.
Differing in taste, our folly is the same,
While each absurdly thinks the place to blame,
Nor sees the fault in all his mind to lie—
The mind which never from itself can fly.
Erewhile a city drudge, your silent prayer
Was all for country quiet, country air.
A Bailiff now, your taste more squeamish grows,
And pants for town, the bagnios and the shows.

For me, you know that free from vain caprice,
Consistent with myself, and of a piece,
Whene'er for Rome cursed business bids me start,
I quit the country with a heavy heart.
  Fancy, methinks, has tinged with various dyes
Things to our view, and here the difference lies.
What you abhor as dreary trackless dells,
I hail as shades where tranquil silence dwells,—
And deprecate the life which you would choose:
The greasy cookshops, and the steaming stews
Give you (I see) a yearning wish for town,
And make you view with a fastidious frown
That little nook of mine, which would produce
Sooner perhaps than the grape's luscious juice,
Pepper or frankincense;—no tavern nigh
Which may with brimming cup your thirst supply,—
No minstrel-wench to whose soft rebeck's sound
You may with thumping footstep beat the ground.
And yet you're fain to ply your rustic toil,—
To turn with busy spade the unbroken soil,
Or tend the steer unharnessed from the plough
And feast with leaves fresh-gathered from the bough.
Oft, swoln with rain, the brook augments your care,
Which mounds must teach the sunny mead to spare.
  Now learn how much we differ: I who drest
So smart, with perfumed locks and silken vest,—
I who (you know) the venal jilt could please
And Cynara's favors won without the fees,—
I who from midnoon with convivial souls
Would sit carousing o'er Falernian bowls,—
Now praise the frugal meal and sober glass,
With slumbers near a fountain, on the grass.

Nor think, I blush, now that the blood runs cool,
At follies past, but still to play the fool.
There none my privacy with rancor spy,
Nor scan my comforts with malignant eye;
The neighbors do but smile and archly nod
To see me turn the stone or bruise the clod.
Among the city slaves you fight to gnaw
Their stinted meal—that way your wishes draw;
Meanwhile the town-drudge envies you the use
Of what those gardens, groves, and herds produce.
Thus the slow ox, it seems, in earnest now
Would wear the saddle, and the pack-horse plow.
My counsel is that each contented sit,
And ply in peace the craft for which he's fit.

I· 15· *To Vala, Asking after a Vacation Spot*

quae sit hiems

By my physician's learn'd advice I fly
From Baia's waters, yet with angry eye
The village views me, when I mean to bathe
The middle winter's freezing wave beneath;
Loudly complaining that their myrtle groves
Are now neglected: their sulphureous stoves,
Of ancient fame our feeble nerves to raise,
And dissipate the lingering cold disease,
While the sick folks in Clusium's fountain dare
Plunge the bold head, or seek a colder air.
The road we now must alter, and engage
Th' unwilling horse to pass his usual stage:
'Ho! whither now?' his angry rider cries,
And to the left the restive bridle plies.
'We go no more to Baiae; prithee hear:'—
But in his bridle lies an horse's ear.
Dear Vala, say, how temperate, how severe,
Are Velia's winters, and Salernum's air:
The genius of the folks, the roads how good:
Which eats the better bread, and when a flood
Of rain descends, which quaffs the gather'd shower,
Or do their fountains purer water pour?
Their country vintage is not worth my care,
For though at home, whatever wine I bear,
At sea-port towns I shall expect to find
My wines of generous and of smoother kind,
To drive away my cares, and to the soul,
Through the full veins, with golden hopes to roll;
With flowing language to inspire my tongue,

And make the list'ning fair one think me young.
With hares and boars which country's best supplied?
Which seas their better fish luxurious hide?
That I may home return in luscious plight—
'Tis ours to credit, as 'tis yours to write.
When Maenius had consumed, with gallant heart,
A large estate, he took the jester's art:
A vagrant zany, of no certain manger,
Who knew not, ere he dined, or friend, or stranger:
Cruel, and scurrilous to all, his jest;
The ruin'd butcher's gulf, a storm, a pest.
What e'er he got his ravening guts receive,
And when or friend or foe no longer gave,
A lamb's fat paunch was a delicious treat,
As much as three voracious bears could eat;
Then, like reformer Bestius, would he tell ye,
That gluttons should be branded on the belly.
But if, perchance, he found some richer fare,
Instant it vanish'd into smoke and air—
"By Jove! I wonder not that folks should eat
At one delicious meal a whole estate;
For a fat thrush is most delightful food,
And a swine's paunch superlatively good."
Thus I, when better entertainments fail,
Bravely commend a plain and frugal meal;
On cheaper suppers show myself full wise,
But if some dainties more luxurious rise—
"Right sage and happy they alone whose fate
Gives them a splendid house and large estate."

I· 16· To *Quinctius, Some Reflections Suggested by the Poet's Country Place*

ne perconteris

Ask not, good Quinctius, if my farm maintain
Its wealthy master with abundant grain,
With fruit or pastures; ask not, if the vine
Around its bridegroom elm luxuriant twine,
For I'll describe, and in loquacious strain,
The sight and figure of the pleasing scene.
  A chain of mountains with a vale devide,
That opens to the sun on either side:
The right wide spreading to the rising day,
The left is warm'd beneath his setting ray.
How mild the clime, where sloes luxurious grow,
And blushing cornels on the hawthorne glow!
My cattle are with plenteous acorns fed,
Whose various oaks around their master spread;
Well might you swear, that here Terentum waves
Its dusky shade, and pours forth all its leaves.
A fountain to a rivulet gives its name,
Cooler and purer than a Thracian stream;
Useful to ease an aching head it flows,
Or when with burning pains the stomach glows.
  This pleasing, this delicious soft retreat,
In safety guards me from September's heat.
  Would you be happy, be the thing you seem,
And sure you now possess the world's esteem;
Nor yet to others too much credit give,
But in your own opinion learn to live;
For know, the bliss in our own judgment lies,
And none are happy but the good and wise.

Nor, though the crowd pronounce your health is good,
Disguise the fever lurking in your blood,
Till trembling seize you at th' unfinish'd meal—
Idiots alone their ulcer'd ills conceal.
 Should some bold flatterer soothe your listening ear,
'The conquer'd world, dread sir, your name reveres,
And Jove, our guardian god, with power devine
Who watches o'er Rome's happiness and thine,
Yet holds it doubtful whether Rome or you,
With greater warmth, each other's good pursue.'
This praise, you own, is sacred Caesar's fame;
But can you answer to your proper name,
When you are call'd th' accomplish'd, or the wise,
Name, which we all with equal ardor prize?
Yet he who gives to-day this heedless praise,
Shall take it back tomorrow if he please,
As when the people from some worthless knave
Can tear away the consulship they gave;
'Lay down the name of wisdom, sir, 'tis mine;'
Confused I leave him, and his gifts resign.
 What if he said, I hanged my aged sire,
Call'd me a thief, a slave to lewd desire,
Shall I be tortured with unjust disgrace,
Or change the guilty colors of my face?
False praise can charm, unreal shame control—
Whom, but a vicious or a sickly soul?
Who then is good? QUINCTIUS. Who carefully observes
The senate's wise decrees, nor ever swerves
From the known rules of justice and the laws:
Whose bail secures, whose oath decides a cause.
HORACE. Yet his own house, his neighbors, through his art
Behold an inward baseness in his heart.

Suppose a slave should say, 'I never steal;
I never ran away—'—'No human blood I shed—'
—'Nor on the cross the ravening crows have fed.'—
'But, sir, I am an honest slave, and wise.'
—'My Sabine neighbor, there, the fact denies:
For wily wolves the fatal pit-fall fear;
Kites fly the bait, and hawks the latent snare;
But virtuous minds a love of virtue charms:
The fear of chastisement thy guilt alarms.
When from my stores you steal one grain of wheat,
My loss indeed is less, your crime as great.'

Your honest man, on whom with awful praise
The forum and the courts of justice gaze,
If e'er he made a public sacrifice,
Dread Janus, Phoebus, clear and loud he cries;
But when his pray'r in earnest is preferr'd,
Scarce moves his lips, afraid of being heard:
'Beauteous Laverna, my petition hear;
Let me with truth and sanctity appear:
Oh! give me to deceive, and, with a veil
Of darkness and of night my crimes conceal.'
Behold the miser bending down to earth
For a poor farthing, which the boys in mirth
Fix'd to the ground; and shall the caitiff dare
In honest freedom with a slave compare?

Whoever wishes, is with fear possess'd;
And he, who holds that passion in his breast
Is in my sense a slave; hath left the post
Where Virtue placed him, and his arms hath lost:
To purchase hasty wealth his force applies,
And overwhelm'd beneath his burden lies.

Say, is not this a very worthless knave?

But if you have the most untoward slave,
Yet kill him not, he may some profit yield,
Of strength to guard your flock and plough your field,
Or let him winter in the stormy main,
By imports to reduce the price of grain.
The good, the wise, like Bacchus in the play,
Dare, to the king of Thebes, undaunted say,
'What can thy power? Thy threat'nings I disdain.
PENTHEUS. I'll take away thy goods. BACCHUS. Perhaps you mean
My cattle, money, movables, or land.
Well, take them all. PENTHEUS. But, slave, if I command,
A cruel jailer shall thy freedom seize.
BACCHUS. A god shall set me free whene'er I please.
HORACE. Death is that god the poet here intends,
That utmost bound, where human sorrow ends.

I · 17 · *To Scaeva, on How to Get on in the World*

quamvis, Scaeva, satis

Tho' with the great to deal, my Scaeva! well
You wot, and need no monitor to tell,
Take some poor hints from one who must in turn
Frankly admit he has much to learn;
As if the blind should point the road. Yet see
If something worth your thought fall e'en from me.
 If after dawn one hour of calm repose,
With snug retirement, please; if taverns, shows,
And dust and brawls and rumbling carts offend—
No more! To quiet Ferentinum bend
Your steps; there fix the heaven of your rest;
For not Ambition's sons alone are blest,
Nor fares he ill who, making peace his own,
Steals from the cradle to the grave unknown.
 But, would you serve your kindred, would you share
Yourself a somewhat more indulgent fare,
Go, seek some lordly board without delay!
"To supper with what appetite you may!"
When one, who hated courtiers from his heart,
Growl'd out—"If Aristippus knew the art
To dine content on potherbs, he would spurn
To court the great." "Aye," quoth the sage in turn;
"And he, who knew the great man's smile to gain,
By my advice your potherbs would disdain."
Declare now which of these contending schools
You favor: or (compliant with the rules
Of eldership) hear, tried by reason's test,
Why Aristippus' system likes mine best.
For thus with keen retort, as history shows,

He parried off the snarling Cynic's blows:
"I act the zany fairly with a view
To serve myself—to please the rabble you.
I pay my court (what's nobler?) that a steed
May bear me, purple clothe, and monarchs feed.
You beg scant offal, smaller than the small,
Then brag forsooth you have no wants at all!"
All states of life the supple sage became;
All hues of fortune found him still the same,
On higher things his eye was mostly bent;
With present things his heart was still content.
Not so the churl, whom hardihood of limb
In mantle of coarse drugget wraps; on him,
'Twere marvel, if, for sufferance only fit,
A change of circumstance with ease could fit.
The one ne'er tarries for his fine-spun vest;
But, in whatever garb chance offers drest,
Saunters among the throng and boasts the art
In either character to top his part.
Cloth of Milesian texture t'other flies
As a mad dog or asp. He starves, he dies
If you restore him not his rug. Restore,
And let him live the fool he was before!
  If to direct the helm of state, and show
To shouting multitudes the captive foe,
Above all earthly majesty raised high,
Soars to the throne of Jove and tempts the sky;
Of chiefs and statesmen, sure, to win the grace
Holds not in glory's scale the lowest place.
To make the port of Corinth, we are told,
Falls to the lot of none except the bold.
Who doubts his powers had best sit still. Agreed!

But what of those more venturous who succeed?
Lies there not gallant firmness at the root?
Why here, or nowhere, hangs the point we moot.
This dreads an enterprise which, he conceives,
Unless all virtue be an empty name,
The palm of honor is th' adventurer's claim.
They who their own distress forbear to din
In their rich patron's ear more favor win
Than the importunate. It differs much
To grasp the prize, and modestly to touch
The *present.* Yet here lies the source, the end
From which our efforts spring, to which they tend.
The teasing fool, who clamors every hour:
"My mother starves; my sister lacks a dower;
My fields, alas! are little worth to sell,
Yet insufficient to maintain me well"
Says, in effect, "Please, gentle folks, to show
Compassion on the poor your alms bestow!"
Then chimes some other to the self same tune:
"Oh, pity me! let me too share the boon!"
Had but the crow in silence deigned to eat,
His rivals had been less and more his meat.
Whoe'er, when kindly summon'd on a ride
Forth to Brundisium by his patron's side,
Or fair Surrentum, all the way complains
Of rugged roads, sharp winds, and pelting rains;
Or (which is worse) deplores due measure
His ransack'd baggage and his rifled treasure,
Apes the sly jilt who ever and anon
Sobs for her necklace lost, her bracelet gone;
Until, the trick grown stale, her genuine grief
And real losses gain but small relief.

None care, when they have once found out the cheat,
To lift the canting cripple from the street.
Tho' many an unfeign'd tear his eyes let fall,
By great Osiris let him swear, and bawl:
"Help, cruel neighbors, help! 'tis truth I tell!"
"Seek elsewhere, knave!" cry they; "We know thee well."

I· 18· *To Lollius, Advice on Getting Along with the Great*

si bene te novi

Lollius, if well I know your heart,
Your liberal spirit scorns an art
That can to sordid flattery bend,
And basely counterfeit the friend;
For such the difference, I ween,
The flatterer and friend between,
As is betwixt a virtuous dame
And women of uncertain fame.
  Behold, in opposite excess,
A different vice, though nothing less;
Rustic, inelegant, uncouth,
With shaggy beard, and nasty tooth,
That fondly would be thought to be
Fair virtue, and pure liberty:
But virtue in a medium lies,
From whence these different follies rise.
  Another, with devotion fervent,
Is more than your obsequious servant;
Admitted as an humble guest
Where men of money break their jest,
He waits the nod, with awe profound,
And catches ere it reach the ground
The falling joke, and echoes back the sound.
A school-boy thus, with humble air,
Repeats to pedagogue severe;
Thus players act an underpart,
And fear to put forth all their art.
  Another in dispute engages,
With nonsense armed, for nothing rages,

'My word of honor not believed?
'Or my opinion not received?
'And shall I, whether right or wrong,
'Be forced, forsooth, to hold my tongue?
'No: at a price so base and mean,
'I would a thousand lives disdain.'
  But what's the cause of all this rage?
Who's the best actor on the stage,
Or to which road you best may turn ye,
If to Brundisium lies your journey.
Now, Lollius, mark the wretch's fate
Who lives dependent on the great.
If the precipitating dice,
If Venus be his darling vice,
If vanity his wealth consumes,
In dressing, feasting, and perfumes,
If thirst of gold his bosom sways,
A thirst which nothing can appease,
If poverty with shame he views;
And wealth with every vice pursues,
My lord, more vicious as more great,
Views him with horror, and with hate:
At least, shall o'er him tyrannise,
And like a fond mamma advise,
Who bids her darling daughter shun
The paths of folly she had run.
'Think not,' he cries, 'to live like me;
'My wealth supports my vanity;
'Your folly should be moderate,
Proportioned to a small estate.'
  Eutrapelus, in merry mood,
The object of his wrath pursued,

And where he deepest vengeance meant,
Fine clothes, with cruel bounty, sent;
For when the happy coxcomb's dressed,
Strange hopes and projects fill his breast;
He sleeps till noon, nor will he, listless
Of fame and fortune, leave his mistress.
Lavish he feeds the usurer's store,
And when the miser lends no more,
He learns the gladiator's art,
Or humbly drives a gardener's cart.

Strive not, with mean unhandsome lore,
Your patron's bosom to explore,
And let not wine or anger wrest
Th' intrusted secret from your breast.

Nor blame the pleasures of your friend,
Nor to your own too earnest bend;
Nor idly court the froward muse,
While he the vigorous chase pursues.
Humors like these could fatal prove
To Zethus' and Amphion's love,
Until Amphion kind complied,
And laid the offensive lyre aside.
So to your patron's will give way,
His gentle insolence obey,
And when he pours into the plain
His horses, hounds, and hunting train,
Break from the peevish muse away,
Divide the toils, and share the prey.

The chase was by our sires esteemed;
Healthful, and honorable deemed.
Thy swiftness far the hound's exceeds;
The boar beneath thy javelin bleeds,

And who, like thee, with grace can wield
The weapons of the martial field,
Or with such loud applause as thine
Amidst the youthful battle shine?
In the destructive war of Spain
Early you made your first campaign,
Beneath a leader, who regains
Our eagles from the Parthian fanes,
Who boundless now extends his sway,
And bids a willing world obey.
Lollius, though all your actions rise
From judgment temperate and wise,
Yet oft at home you can unbend,
And even to trifling sports descend.
Your little boats with mimic rage,
Like Actium's mighty fleets engage;
Your lake like Adria's ocean spreads,
The adverse war your brother leads,
Till Victory her wings display,
And crown the conqueror of the day.
Caesar, who finds that you approve
His taste, shall your diversions love.
If my advice regard may claim,
Be tender of another's fame,
And be the man with caution tried
In whose discretion you confide.
Th' impertinent be sure to hate;
Who loves to ask, will love to prate.
Ears, that unfold to every tale,
Intrusted secrets ill conceal,
And you shall wish, but wish in vain,
To call the fleeting words again.

With cautious judgment, o'er and o'er,
The man you recommend explore,
Lest, when the scoundrel's better known,
You blush for errors not your own.
Then frankly give him up to shame,
But boldly guard the injured fame
Of a well-known and valued friend,
With vigor and with zeal defend;
For, be assured, when he's defamed,
At you the envenom'd shaft is aim'd.
When flames your neighbor's dwelling seize,
Your own with instant rage shall blaze;
Then haste to stop the spreading fire,
Which, if neglected, rises higher.

Untried, how sweet a court attendance!
When tried, how dreadful the dependence!
Yet, while your vessel's under sail,
Be sure to catch the flying gale,
Lest adverse winds with rapid force,
Should bear you from your destined course.

The grave, a gay companion shun;
Far from the sad the jovial run;
The gay, the witty, and sedate,
Are objects of each other's hate,
And they who quaff their midnight glass,
Scorn them, who dare their bumper pass,
Although they loudly swear, they dread
A sick debauch, and aching head.

Be every look serenely gay,
And drive all cloudy cares away.
The modest oft too dark appear,
The silent, thoughtful and severe.

Consult with care the learned page;
Inquire of every scienced sage,
How you may glide with gentle ease
Adown the current of your days
Nor vex'd by mean and low desires,
Nor warm'd by wild ambition's fires,
By hope alarm'd, depress'd by fear,
For things but little worth your care:
Whether fair Virtue's hallow'd rules
Proceed from nature, or the schools;
What may the force of care suspend,
And make you to yourself a friend;
Whether the tranquil mind and pure,
Honors and wealth, our bliss insure,
Or down through life unknown to stay,
Where lonely leads the silent way.

When happy in my rural scene,
Whose fountain chills the shuddering swain,
Such is my prayer—Let me possess
My present wealth, or even less,
And if the bounteous gods design
A longer life, that life be mine.
Give me of books the mental cheer,
Of wealth, sufficient for a year,
Nor let me float in Fortune's power,
Dependent on the future hour.
To Jove for life and wealth I pray,
These Jove may give or take away,
But, for a firm and tranquil mind,
That blessing in myself I'll find.

I· 19· *To Maecenas, Answering His Unfair Critics*

prisco si credis

If, dear Maecenas, versed in classic lore,
To what Cratinus taught in days of yore
Your credence yield, the water-drinker's song,
Cold as his heart, can never flourish long.
From that time forth when Bacchus of his grace
Amid the Fauns and Satyrs deign'd to place
True poets as possest, the dulcet Nine
Have every morn, 'tis whisper'd, smelt of wine.
The praise, which father Homer oft bestows
On brimming goblets, proves he loved his dose.
Ennius ne'er pour'd the war song, till his soul
Had suck'd inspiring rapture from the bowl.
"That sober folks turn poets, Heav'n forefend!
"Such to the courts and Libo's Font I send."
This edict past, our wits without delay
Tope wine by night and breath its fumes by day.
Strange notion! What? If barefoot, with grim frown
And the coarse texture of a scanty gown,
One ape old Cato, would he body forth
All Cato's probity and patriot worth?
The Moor who toiled in rival repartees
To match in powers of tongue Timagenes,
At last a victim to defeated pride,
Bursting with sullen envy, drooped and died.
So, if I look but pale, some ape shall seek
With cummin-dose to bleach his rosy cheek.
Models mislead, when copiers fix their view
On faults alone. How oft, ye servile crew
Of mimics, when your bustling pranks I've seen,

Have ye provoked my smiles—how often my spleen!
 Peace to all such! a vacant walk I found,
A bold advent'rer in unbeaten ground.
Let cowards lag behind! The brave explore
New paths, and rush where foot ne'er trod before.
I first held forth to Latium's fond regard
The stern Iambics of the Parian bard,
Copying his verse—his spirit, not each thought
And phrase with death to poor Lycambes fraught.
Nor thou with scantier wreath my brows array,
As loth to change the structure of his lay:
A verse in which warm Sappho urged her suit,
To which Alcaeus tuned his warbling lute,
Albeit, distinct in manner and in style,
In tart lampoons he studies to revile
No perjured sire-in-law, with keen abuse
Weaves for no false betrothed the fatal noose.
His song to Roman ears by me alone—
By me the Latian minstrel—was made known;
Proud that those lays are conned (unseen before)
By liberal eyes, by liberal hands turn'd o'er.
 Ask you why some at home my page applaud,
Yet cry it down ungraciously abroad?
I coax no fickle rabble for their votes
With bribes of tempting treat and cast off coats;
I brook to hear no noble bards rehearse,
That they in turn may deign to hear my verse;
I court no desk—no pedant-tribes caress;
And hence—hence flow those tears of bitterness
If I aver my shame, with modest look,
To spout in crowded theatres a book
Whose claim to notice is so poor, and swear

I blush to publish trifles light as air.
Their answer is, "Pshaw, Horace! now you jeer
And keep those dainties back for Jove's own ear,
Vainly convinced (if truth be told) that few
Can pour such nectared streams of song as you!"
At this to sneer outright my courage fails;
So, rather than encounter desperate nails,
"Let's waive that tender topic!" I exclaim,
And crave a truce; for oft has this mock-game
To dudgeon led and bickering broils, and they
To furious conflict and the bloody fray.

I · 20 · *To His Book, About to Make Its Own Way in the World*

Vertumnum Ianumque

For mart and street you seem to pine
With restless glances, book of mine!
Still craving on some stall to stand,
Fresh pumiced from the binder's hand.
You chafe at locks, and burn to quit
Your modest haunt and audience fit
For hearers less discriminate.
I reared you up for no such fate.
Still, if you must be published, go;
But mind, you can't come back, you know!
"What have I done?" I hear you cry,
And writhe beneath some critic's eye;
"What did I want?" when scarce polite,
They do but yawn and roll you tight.
And yet, methinks, if I can guess
(Putting aside your heartlessness
In leaving me, and this your home)
You shall find favor, too, at Rome.
That is, they'll like you while you're young,
When you are old, you'll pass among
The Great Unwashed,—then humbled and sped,
Be fretted of slow moths, unread,
Or to Ilerda you'll be sent,
Or Utica for banishment!
And I, whose counsel you disdain,
At that your lot shall laugh amain,
Wryly, as he who, like a fool,
Thrust o'er the cliff his restless mule.

Nay! there is worse behind. In age
They e'en may take your babbling page
In some remotest slum to teach
Mere boys their rudiments of speech!
  But go. When on warm days you see
A chance of listeners, speak of me.
Tell them I soared from low estate,
A freedman's son, to higher fate.
(That is, make up to me in worth
What you must take in point of birth);
Then tell them that I won renown
In peace and war, and pleased the town;
Paint me as early gray, and one
Little of stature, fond of sun,
Quick-tempered, too,—but nothing more.
Add (if they ask) I'm forty-four,
Or was the year that over us
Both Lollius ruled and Lepidus.

II · 1 · *To Augustus, Explaining the Modern Literary Attitude Toward the Ancient Greeks*

cum tot sustineas

Seeing affairs so many and so great
You, Caesar, bear alone, the Roman State
Protecting by your arms from moral flaws,
Raising it fair and bettering it by laws,
Against the public welfare I'd transgress
Should I your time waste with a long address.

Romulus, Father Bacchus, Castor, Pollux,
Their mighty deeds achieved, attained abodes
Within the heavenly quarters of the gods;
But they lamented that, while still they strove
The lands of earth and mankind to improve,
Wars bitter to repress, lands to allot,
Cities to found, the gratitude they got
With their deserts and hopes accorded not,
The hero that beat down the Hydra fell,
And by the toil assigned to him by Fate
Subdued the monsters known to all so well,
Found death alone could Envy subjugate.
For he that overbears all lesser heads
Them scorches by the brilliant light he sheds:
For love, till he is dead, the man must wait.

To you, while still on earth with us you live,
We haste betimes all honors due to give,
And altars raise where by your name to swear,
Acknowledging your like has risen ne'er,
Nor e'er will in the coming times arise.
But this your people, though they're just and wise
In you esteeming—yea, and only you—
Before our captains, and the Grecian too,
By no means use like principle and plan
In estimating aught else, thing or man,
For they despise and hate as nothing worth
All save whate'er they see removed from earth,
The span of life assigned thereto fulfilled:
The ancient things they hold of such account
As to insist that on the Alban Mount
The Tables the Decemvirs framed and willed
As law, to strike misdoers all with fears,
The treaties that our kings with Gabii struck
And with the Sabines, men of stubborn pluck,
On equal terms, the pontiffs' books, the seers'
Old rolls, the Muses spake to Roman ears.

Now, if it is because the ancientest
Of Grecian writings also are the best
That Roman writers in like scales are weighed,
Then clearly there is little to be said:
Inside the olive there is nothing hard,
Outside the nut, too, there is nothing hard.
We've scaled the very top of Fortune's hill:
We paint, we sing, we wrestle with more skill
Than do the Greeks, anoint them as they will.
If poems, as do wines, improve with age,

I fain would know how many years must run
Before our works have higher value won.
If, say, a writer reached his latest stage
A century ago, shall I be told
To rank him with the perfect and the old
Or place him with the worthless and the new?
Some limit fix to shut disputes from view.

"A writer that has lived a hundred year
Is old and is a classic, 'twould appear."

Well, in which category shall we place
A man that has a month, a year, lived less?
Among the ancient poets, or with them
That this and future ages may condemn?

"O, such a one may honourably appear
Among the ancients—one that's in arrear
But a short month, or e'en a whole round year.

Of your concession I myself avail,
And, as the hairs were of a horse's tail,
I pluck away, first one, then one, the years,
Till, foiled, he falls, like a fast-shrinking heap,
The man that will his eyes on annals keep
And judges excellence by lapse of years,
Admiring only what has met its doom,
Sacred to Libitina and the tomb.

Ennius, wise, brave, a second Homer too,
As critics wont to say, but little seems
To care what fortune may at last pursue

His promises, Pythagorean dreams.
Nay, is not Naevius in all our hands,
And holds he not our memory with bands
As strong as if he wrote but yesterday?
So sacred to us every ancient lay.
When one the question which is better moots,
Pacuvius is a sage of olden time,
And Accius is yclept a bard sublime;
Afranius' gown, 'tis said, Menander suits;
Plautus is said vivacity to claim,
Like Epicharmus of Sicilian fame;
Caecilius in dignity excels;
And Terence by his art applause compels.
These mighty Rome to memory commits,
And these to gaze upon she crowded sits
Within a narrow theatre; and these
As poets she esteems and counts alway
From Livius' age down to the present day.

Sometimes indeed aright the public sees,
Sometimes it blunders. If it so admire
The ancient bards as to find nothing higher
To praise, and nothing with them to compare,
It errs; but, if it think they sometimes are
O'ermuch archaic, often harsh, and tame,
Its view is wise, and is with mine the same—
A judgment favored by the Heaven high,
I don't attack the works of Livius, I,
And think they should be quashed—Orbilius,
My master stern, well I remember it,
Read them to me when I was but a chit—

But I do wonder polished they're esteemed,
And beautiful, and all but perfect deemed—
Works where if chance some elegant expression
Forth flashes, or some lines are with discretion
More neatly turned than commonly befell,
That accident unfairly will avail
To puff the poem and ensure its sale.

I cannot bear to hear a poem blamed,
Not just because 'tis thought to have been framed
Or coarse in texture or devoid of grace,
But just because it wears a modern face;
That not excuse, but preference and praise,
Are claimed from us for bards of ancient days.
Should I express a doubt whether some play
Of Atta's treads the boards in proper way,
The elders almost all would straight exclaim
That from the earth has wholly perished shame,
Since I'm with blame attempting to degrade
A piece that dignified Aesopus played
Or skilful Roscius: either that they deem
There's nothing right but what themselves esteem,
Or that they look on it as a disgrace
To yield to juniors, and, when old, confess
That what they learned erstwhile as beardless boys
Must now be put away with other toys.
Indeed, who praises Numa's Salian hymn,
And entertains the strangely foolish whim
To seem the only man to understand
Its meaning—which he can no more command
Than I do—does not favor and applaud

Departed geniuses, but takes the road
Our writings to attack, and in his spite
Hates us and our performances outright.
Yet, had the Greeks held novelty in hate
As we it hate, what work of ancient date
Would now exist, or even what there be
To be perused and thumbed by you and me?

As soon as Greece, her wars brought to an end,
Began her time on idle things to spend,
And by prosperity slide to excess,
Now horses, now athletes, she would caress,
Artificers in marble, ivory,
And bronze, she fancied, and she let her eye
And mind on pictures rest, and took delight
Now in musicians, now in actors wight.
But what she keenly sought she put away
Quickly, quite sated, as a child will play
Under her nurse's eye, unstable aye.
Pleasing or hateful, what in all the range
Should you suppose to be exempt from change?
Such was the nature of the times of peace.
At Rome for long it was a pleasant way,
A habit, to be up by dawn of day,
Wide to the wall the mansion door to throw,
The clients to advise on points of law,
Money to lend, secured by names of weight,
To learn from elders and to juniors state
The means whereby one's havings to increase,
And how to make indulgence wasteful cease.
Now have the fickle people changed their mind,
And, fired with one desire, are all inclined

To write; alike the boys and fathers grave,
Their hair enwreathed with bays that learned wave,
Their poems dictate while they dine and rave.
But I myself, who writing verse disclaim,
Am found more false than man of Parthian name:
I'm up before the sun, prompt for my task,
And call for pen and paper and my desk.
He fears to steer a ship that knows not how;
A man untrained not southernwood, I trow,
Dares give a patient—'tis the doctors' part
To treat the patient by the doctors' art;
A workman's tools are for the workman's hands:
But we, though one has learnt the art or not,
We scribble poems—a promiscuous lot.

And yet how great, how worthy, points commands
This foible, this mild madness, gather hence:
A poet rarely lusts for pounds or pence;
Verses he loves—there centre his desires;
Pulse and brown bread he is content to eat;
He laughs at losses, flight of slaves, and fires;
He'll never form designs or counterfeit
A partner or a youthful ward to cheat;
A slack and sorry soldier in the field,
Good service to the city he will yield—
Grant you that small things too assist the great.
The poet forms youth's tender lisping mouth,
E'en now he turns its ear from words uncouth,
And later too he moulds the youthful breast
With friendly precepts; rudeness, envy's pest,
And passion's gusts he checks; right worthy deeds
He tells; by noble instances he feeds

The rising generations through his art;
Consoles the poor, and cheers the sick at heart.
The hymn of prayer, how would they come to know it,
The modest maids and boys, had not a poet
The Muses sent? The chorus calls for aid,
And feels the favor of the gods as prayed:
Persuasively the prayer it learned it pours,
And rains of heaven it earnestly implores,
Averts diseases, dangers dreaded stops,
And peace obtains, and seasons rich in crops.
By hymns are soothed the gods above, and so
By hymns are also soothed the gods below.

The husbandmen of old, right sturdy men,
With little pleased, on storing of their grain
Kept festival, recruiting wearied frames—
Yea, wearied minds, which heavy hardships bore
In hope of respite from their labors sore—
Together with the sharers of their toil,
Their faithful wife and children, and the while
Took care to satisfy aright the claims
Of goddess Earth with offering of a swine,
Of god Silvanus with a bowl of milk,
And of the Genius with flowers and wine—
Who aye reminds that life is short for ilk.
Thus custom the Fescennine licence bred,
Which rustic taunts in verse alternate shed;
And this free habit, welcomed year by year,
Expressed itself in friendly sportive vein
Until the jest now charged with bitter pain
Began to turn to open rage and rear
Its head against good houses, one by one,

Nor were there means its menaces to shun.
The folk that were assailed with bloody tooth,
What could they do but nurse their grief, in sooth?
Those unassailed grieved for the common good;
Nay, more, a law was passed, with penalty,
Forbidding any man should branded be
With verse abusive: so they changed their mood,
Reduced by terror of the cudgel's strokes
To civil speech and e'en delightful jokes.

Greece captive captured her rough conqueror,
And gave her arts to Latium, rude before.
So came that coarse Saturnian verse to pall,
And elegance expelled offensive gall;
But yet some rustic traces long remained,
And others to this day are still retained.
For late the Roman was to turn his wit
To scan the works by Grecian authors writ;
And, now at peace, when Punic wars were done,
He 'gan to search what useful might be won
From Thespis, Aeschylus, and Sophocles.
This too he tried, their writing to translate
In worthy fashion, and perceived elate
The good results, in high hopes to excel:
For tragic spirit shows he passing well,
And happily his boldest strokes oft tell:
But in his ignorance he deems a blot
Disgrace, and sticks to what at first he wrote.

An easy job is Comedy, because
Its subjects from our daily life it draws,
'Tis thought; but, less the indulgence it obtains,

The more it calls for unremitting pains.
Just see how Plautus' self supports the part
Of love-sick youth, of father close of heart,
Of artful pandar; mark how grand a sight
Dossennus makes as greedy parasite—
With sock how slack he runs about the boards;
His anxious care but to increase his hoards
By picking up a coin: that business done,
Succeed the play or fail—why, all is one.

Whom glory in her airy car has borne
Upon the stage, he finds himself forlorn
When listless prove the audience; when they prove
Attentive, then his spirits upward move:
So slight, so small, the thing that can abase
Or elevate the man that covets praise.
Farewell the stage, if I am rendered lean
By losing palms, or if, to my amaze,
The winning of them make me plump and sheen.
This too will often drive away in fright
A daring poet—daring as may be—
This, namely, that the great majority,
Inferior in rank and moral tone,
Men that nor learning nor acumen own,
Men ready to put up a desperate fight
Should e'er the knights express dissent in aught,
Call for a bear or boxers to be brought,
E'en in the very middle of the play:
For such delight the lowest plebs alway.
But now the pleasure of the knights likewise
Has passed away from ear to wandering eyes
And vain amusements. For four hours or more

The curtain is kept down, while swiftly pour
Across the stage both horse and foot galore;
Then kings unfortunate are dragged around,
Their hands behind their back securely bound,
Chariots and carriages and wagons, ay,
E'en ships, are rushed, and captive ivory,
And captive Corinth. Were he here to spy,
Democritus would laugh at the riffraff
Agape at a white elephant or giraffe—
A panther with a camel so combined
As form of two a beast of different kind,
Attention more than on the sports below
Upon the people round he would bestow,
As furnishing a far more varied show,
While on the writers the remark he'd pass,
They told their story to a stone-deaf ass.
For what strength of lungs can overpower
The din our theatres upon us shower?
You'd think Garganus' forests were a-roar,
Or waves were thundering on the Tuscan shore,
In such a noise we view our works of art,
Our shows, the wealth from every foreign part
Wherewith bedecked the actor, on appearing,
Is overwhelmed with a clapping and with cheering
And has he spoken yet? No, not a word.
What is it, then, that such delight has stirred?
His woolen robe tinged with Tarentine dye,
With hue of violets set up to vie.

But, lest you think I damn with faintest praise
Such work as I myself decline to try,
While others handle it successfully,

A simple statement may distrust erase:
Quite fit to walk the tight rope seems to me
The bard that by illusions grieves my breast,
That irritates, and soothes again to rest,
And with unreal fears, like a magician,
Fills it, and, carrying me o'er land and sea,
At Thebes or Athens fixes my position.

But come, give also some brief heed to those
That rather on their readers would repose
Than bear fastidious spectators' looks,
Would you desire to furnish well with books
Your gift right worthy of Apollo's name,
And spur our bards with greater zeal to aim
To gain Mount Helicon with all its charm.

True, oft we poets do ourselves much harm—
My own vineyards I'm cutting, to my cost—
By offering you a book when you're engrossed
Or else fatigued; by taking it to heart
If any friend has dared a single part,
A single verse, to censure; by once more
Reciting passages without encore;
By grumbling that our toil is seen by none,
Nor with how fine a thread our work is spun;
By hoping that, as soon as you have heard
We are composing verses, you'll be stirred,
Unasked, obligingly for us to send,
Force us to write, and so our troubles end.

But, after all, 'tis well worth while to know
What kind of temple-keepers care bestow

Upon your merit proved in peace and war—
A charge indeed too valuable far
To be entrusted to a bard unfit.
The famous Cherilus was a favorite
With great King Alexander, and he owed
The royal coins he got, the pieces broad,
Philippi, to his verse, rough, misbegot.
But, just as ink, when handled, makes a blot
And stain, so poets oft expend their pains
In smearing splendid deeds with blots and stains.
That self-same king, who, with a lavish hand,
On verse so preposterous had spent
So large a sum, by edict did command
No artist save Apelles should him paint,
No sculptor save Lysippus bronze should mould
In likeness of King Alexander bold.
But, should you now transfer that judgment great
In viewing works of art so delicate
To books and to the Muses' gifts, you'd swear
That he was born in thick Boeotian air.

But neither do your poets well beloved,
Vergilius and Varius disgrace
The judgment of them that you have approved
Nor yet the many gifts they have received—
With credit to the giver, all confess—
Nor do the busts in bronze, it is believed.
The features of our famous men express
More truly than the poet's work displays
Their character and mind. Nor should I lays
That creep along the ground prefer to write
Than deeds of arms to sing, to tell how lie

Countries and streams, and castles perched on height,
And barbarous realms, and wars compelled to die
O'er all the world beneath your auspices,
The barrier that Ianus compasses,
Of peace the guardian, and Rome, whose name
Beneath your rule the Parthian renders tame,
Were strong as is my wish my feeble wit.
But neither does your majesty permit
Mean verse, nor dares my modesty essay
A part my powers refuse to let me play.
Officious zeal unwisely plies a friend,
And most so when it can itself commend
By art poetic; for one sooner learns
And easier remembers such concerns
As men deride than those men favor lend
And venerate. I care not for the zeal
That makes my life a burden; I don't feel
The smallest wish to be exposed in wax,
Or here or there with countenance that lacks
The least resemblance, or to be bepraised
In verses fashioned in a style debased,
Lest I should blush for shame at the award—
The stupid gift—and, stretched beside my bard,
Within a box, be carried to the yard
Where people deal in spices, pepper, incense,
And all things wrapped in sheets of written nonsense.

II · 2 · *To Florus, an Excuse for Writing Poetry No Longer*

Flore, bono claroque

Florus, the illustrious Nero's faithful friend,
What if some one, who wished a slave to vend,
Should thus with you about the purchase treat:
"He's a fine lad, from head to foot complete;
Eight thousand sesterces, and he's your own;
Quick, at a nod, at once your will is done!
Talks Greek, learns anything you wish with ease;
Just like moist clay you'll mould him as you please.
Then he's a singer too, his voice so fine,
Tho' all untaught, will charm you o'er your wine
But why this praise? 'Tis but the common tale
Of pedlars seeking for their wares the sale.
I under no necessity am laid,
And though not rich, yet all my debts are paid.
No dealer'd put him to you half so low,
And 'tis not every one should have him so.
I own that once he made a trifling slip,
And hid himself, as usual, from the whip.
That he won't run away I don't pretend
In all things else I'll warrant and defend."
If then, with open eyes, you buy the slave,
It seems to me that you can fairly have
No claim for damages, yet you dispute,
And vex the seller with a tedious suit.
All blame, before you left me, to prevent,
I told you I was dull and indolent.
Yet say, of what avail was this to me,
If still you murmur at so just a plea;
Nay more, complain, because I did not send

Th' expected poems, I've deceived my friend.
   One of Lucullus' soldiers, as 'tis said,
By service hard a little sum had made.
One night, as weary, fast asleep he lay,
Some pilfering scoundrel stole the whole away.
He, with himself and foes alike outraged,
Fierce as an hungry wolf in fight engaged,
Dislodged a garrison well fortified,
And took the place with richest stores supplied.
The man, praised loudly for a feat so bold,
Received beside a good round sum in gold.
About this time ('twas dangerous to perform,)
The Praetor wished a certain fort to storm.
When thus the daring hero he addressed,
In words that might have fired a coward's breast:—
"Go, go, my friend, where valor leads the way,
And large rewards shall your deserts repay!
Go, and may victory on your footsteps wait!
Astonishment! And so you hesitate?"
Whom the shrewd rustic drily answer'd thus:
"He, he will go, who's lately lost his purse."
   Brought up at Rome, it chanced I there was taught
What ills on Greece Achilles' anger brought.
Athens, the seat of ev'ry art refined,
Then gave a little polish to my mind;
Taught me geometry, and bid me rove,
In search of truth, through Academus' grove.
But ah, unhappy times soon call me far
From these sweet scenes; the rage of civil war
Drove me unskilled to arms, that strove in vain,
Th' unequal fight 'gainst Caesar to maintain.
But when Philippi clept my soaring pride,

And sent me home, with ruin by my side,
Compelled by want, I tried to court the muse;
But now, when blest with more than I can use,
What dose would cure a madness so absurd,
Unless my ease to writing I preferred?
  The years revolving steal from us our powers:
My jests, loves, sports, my taste for festive hours
They've torn away; and now my poems, too,
They strive to wrest. What would you have me do?
In fine, with various humors men admire;
You lose the measure suited to the lyre;
He most is pleased with the Iambic strain;
A third delights in Bion's bitter vein.
Thus I 've three guests of different tastes to dine.
How shall I suit you? That, which you decline,
Another calls for; and, what pleases you,
Is sour and odious to the other two.
  Beside, mid all the cares and toils of Rome,
Can I write verses? One entreats I'd come,
And be his bail; another humbly prays,
Business, I'd quit, and listen to his lays,
And though they live at different ends of town;
(A special distance you must surely own,)
Both, must I see. "Still in the streets there's nought,
That, as you walk, need interrupt a thought."
Here drives a builder with his busy throng
Of mules and porters; there an engine strong
Heaves a vast stone or beam; in sad array,
Funerals contend with waggons for the way.
Next a mad dog, or miry pig you meet;
Now go, compose we verses in the street.
Votaries of Bacchus, poets ever love

To shun the crowd, and court the shady grove.
In such a din can I then hail the muse,
Or trace the path of beauty she pursues?
  Even at Athens, calm as it appears,
A genius who has studied seven long years,
If through the streets, with books and cares grown grey,
Profoundly lost in thought, he bend his way;
Mute as a statue, as he walks along,
He shakes with laughter all the gathering throng.
Shall I then, midst this ocean of affairs,
This very storm of business and of cares,
To modulate harmonious strain aspire,
And suit their measure to the sounding lyre?
  Two brothers, one for rhetoric renowned,
The other in the wiles of law profound,
Conspired at Rome by unremitting praise,
In every speech each other's fame to raise;
The one a perfect mutual to the other,
And he, in turn, a Gracchus to his brother,
And equal folly fires the poet's brain,
I strike the lyre, soft elegy his strain.
What wonderous genius glows in every line?
'Twas surely polished by the tuneful nine.
Now mark with what parade and pride we claim
Appollo's temple to enshrine our fame;
Then following after learn, if time allows,
Why we the wreath intwine around our brows.
Like Samnites, who engage by candle light,
We deal alternate blows in harmless fight.
In his opinion I, Alcaeus shine,
And he, at least Callimachus in mine.
If more than this his high ambition claim,

I will his pride with great Mimnermus' name.
Thus, while I court the public with my muse,
To sooth each rival every art I use;
My studies done, my rhyming frenzy o'er,
Against the scribbling tribe I shut my door.
Bad poets are to all a standing jest:
And yet they write with self-complacence blest;
Admire the jingle of their senseless lays,
And if you're silent, e'en themselves will praise.
He, who from every fault his piece would free,
Must of himself a rigid critic be.
Such terms, as but with little splendor shine,
Such as enfeeble, or degrade the line,
He from his poem boldly will erase,
However reluctant they may quit their place;
From uncouth phrase, and long oblivion take
Words, our old Catos and Cethegi spake;
To these new terms of sanctioned usage join,
And ancient force with modern grace combine.
Flowing and full he'll pour his verse along,
And Latium bless with rich tide of song;
Polish the rough, th' exuberant confine,
And blot the unmeaning; till the perfect line,
Wrought by laborious patience into ease,
By graceful negligence shall seem to please.
Just as the dancer, trained by toilsome art,
Now plays the Satyr's, now the Cyclops' part.
Stupid I'd rather be, a thousand times,
While still delighted with my own dull rhymes,
Than, cursed with finer taste, forever be
Tortured to mend the many faults I see.
An Argian once, of no mean name, deceived

By a strange frenzy of his brain, believed,
While in the empty theatre, he heard
Fine Tragedies, and all delight appeared.
And still, in other things, was sound of mind,
A worthy neighbor, as a husband kind,
A master not severe, enough of wit,
To shun a precipice or open pit.
His friends to cure him every mean explored,
And hellebore at length his wits restored.
Come to himself, "By heavens, my friends," he cried,
"Is this to cure? 'Twere better I had died,
Than thus to lose by your officious love,
Those sweet illusions, that my fancy wove."
'Tis wisdom then no longer to engage
In trifles suited to a younger age;
No more the concord of sweet sounds to swell,
But learn the harmony of living well;
Thus then I oft commune with my own mind;
If, from repeated draughts, you could not find
The burning fever of your thirst allayed,
You'd tell your doctor, and implore his aid;
But when, the more you gain, you crave the more,
Say is there none, whose aid you dare implore?
You'd throw aside prescriptions, that you found
Of no avail, to soothe an aching wound.
Perchance some one has told you, folly flies
The man, whom Jove with stores of wealth supplies;
But when with added treasures you receive
No added wisdom, will you still believe?
If gold with prudence could your breast inspire,
Could calm anxiety, subdue desire;
Well might you blush, if in the search of pelf

One lived on earth, more eager than yourself.
  If that is ours, for which our gold we pay,
And use gives property, as lawyers say;
That field is yours, whose fruits supply your board,
And Orbius' steward owns you as his lord.
You give him money, and receive its worth,
In wine, grapes, eggs, in pullets, and so forth;
Thus by degrees a farm you may possess,
Bought at three hundred pieces, more or less.
The same, whether at once the fee you buy,
Or daily what may each day's wants supply.
Thus he, who long since paid the purchase down
Of all the lands, he fondly calls his own,
The fruits that feed him, and the word that warms,
Still buys, though proudly boasting of his farms;
As if to any here belonged the power
To call his own, that which each fleeting hour,
Sold, giv'n, or torn by force, or death away,
May change its owner, and new lords obey.
If then earth's strongest tenure is so frail;
What can your houses, what your stores avail?
Why add, with anxious labor, field to field?
Will death, subdued by gold, to bribery yield?
Heir treads on heir, as wave rolls over wave,
And all distinction's levelled in the grave.
  Gems, Tuscan statues, marble, ivory,
Plate, paintings, vests of rich Getulian dye,
Though these the objects, most with ardor crave,
There are, who have not, nor desire to have.
Why of two brothers, one more dearly loves
Perfumes, ease, pleasures, than all Herod's groves;
Though rich, the other with incessant toil

Early and late, labors to tame his soil;
That Genius knows, who rules our natal star,
Fashions our tempers, makes us what we are,
Bids, at his pleasure, still new humors rise,
Lives in our life, and only with us dies.
Careless of what a thankless heir may say,
My little store shall bless the passing day.
Yet the distinction shall in me be seen
The social, open hearted man between,
And prodigal; the frugal, and the mean.
For wide the difference is, to waste profuse
The wealth you want, the wit to turn to use;
And without grudging to enjoy your store,
Nor meanly pinch yourself, to make it more,
But, as a boy, the fleeting holiday,
To seize each moment, as it wings its way.
Avert, ye gods, forever from my door
Those loathsome miseries, that haunt the poor.
If I'm unchanged, 'tis all the same to me,
If boat or barge convey me o'er life's sea.
What, though the north wind rarely swell our sails,
We do not always buffet southern gales,
Last of the first, first of the last, in health,
In genius, beauty, virtue, birth, and wealth.
You say you're free from av'rice; grant it true,
Have all your other vices fled you too?
Does vain ambition never swell your breast;
No rage, no fear of death, disturb your rest?
Smile you at witches, prodigies, and dreams,
And ghosts, that vex the midnight air with screams?
With grateful calm your added years survey?
Do you the errors of your friends forgive,

And as you longer, better learn to live;
As age approaches, do your passions cease,
And mildest feelings soothe your soul to peace?
What boots it to extract a single thorn,
If by so many still your breast be torn?
If ignorant to act, resign your part
To those, who'll play it with more taste and art.
You've sported, ate, and drank enough; now quit
The table, sober; lest the taunting wit
Of sportive youth, with better grace absurd,
Should jeer, and drive you reeling from the board.

Jubilee Hymn
(Carmen Saeculare)

Written especially to be sung by a picked chorus of boys and girls at the great festival celebrated by the Emperor in 17 B. C.

JUBILEE HYMN

Phoebe silvarumque potens

Choir of Youths and Virgins

Phoebus, and Cynthia o'er the chase
Presiding, Heaven's eternal grace
Whom, as passed times, the future shall adore,
Grant what this sacred season we implore

Now when the sibyl's lives command
That youths and maids, a chosen band,
Shall to the gods, whom our seven hills delight,
A choral hymn alternately recite.

Choir of Youths

Indulgent sun whose various ray
Now spreads and now withdraws the day,
Another and the same, may years to come
No prospect yield thee more august than Rome.

Choir of Virgins

Your aid, mild Ilithyia, give
To matrons, and their pangs relieve,
Whether you choose Lucina for your name,
Or rather that of Genitalis claim.

To pregnant wives give large increase,
The laws that favor wedlock bless,
Those laws ordained to multiply our race,
Which fathers with peculiar honors grace.

Both Choirs

Oft as the allotted term of years
Return and a new age appears,
May it restore much grateful songs and plays,
Three shining nights and three distinguished days.

To Parcae whose resistless will
Events infallibly fulfill,
Whose word once spoke immutable shall last,
With future blessings still improve the past.

Let earth with corn and flocks o'erspread
Weave yellow wreaths for Ceres' head.
Let wholesome streams, sweet air and grassy food
Cherish the herds, the flocks and tender brood.

Choir of Youths

With bow unstrung and favoring ear,
Kindly the suppliant youths, Apollo, hear!

Choir of Virgins

Horned queen of stars, the maids attend
Who to thy throne with humble homage bend.

Both Choirs

If Rome was reared by your command;
If Trojans sought the Etruscan land,
Enjoined by you to leave their native shore,
And foreign realms, with prosperous course, explore,

Whom safely through devouring flame
The chief, immortalized by fame,
Led to a fairer soil, a happier coast,
A nobler empire than in Troy they lost;

Let youth with probity be blest;
To age, ye gods, give needful rest,
And crown the Romans with a numerous race,
With large increase of wealth and every grace!

Let Caesar in his vows succeed,
Who bids the milk-white victim bleed—
Caesar who triumphs o'er his stubborn foes,
But generous mercy to the suppliant shows.

The Mede now fears by sea and land
The Albanian axe and Caesar's hand.
Scythians and Indians, late so haughty, wait
From Rome's revered decrees to learn their fate.

Now honor, truths and ancient shame,
And peace our savage passions tame.
Virtue unveils her face, secure from scorn,
And Plenty scatters fruits with plenteous horn.

Choir of Youths

The prophet-god with golden bow,
Dear to the Nine, who well can show
The healing power of every herb and plant,
And sprightly health to languid mortals grant;

If he survey with gracious eye
His own high towers that pierce the sky,
Will add fresh glories to our envied name,
And spread from age to age the Roman fame.

Choir of Virgins

Cynthis, adored on Aventine
And Algidus, with looks benign
Regards these rites, the priestly vows receives,
And what we beg, with kind indulgence gives.

Both Choirs

We who have sung in sacred lays
Apollo's and Diana's praise
Will have returns with just presage that Jove
Allows our prayers, and all the powers above.

The Art of Poetry

Random ideas on the writing of poetry (chiefly dramatic) and on the training of the poet. Probably the last work of Horace, published in 13 B. C. when the poet was fifty-two.

THE ART OF POETRY

Suppose a painter wished to couple a horse's neck with a man's head, and to lay feathers of every hue on limbs gathered here and there, so that a woman, lovely above, foully ended in an ugly fish below; would you restrain your laughter, my friends, if admitted to a private view? Believe me, dear Pisos, a book will appear uncommonly like that picture, if impossible figures are wrought into it—like a sick man's dreams—with the result that neither head nor foot is ascribed to a single shape, and unity is lost.

'But poets and painters have always had an equal right to indulge their whims.' Quite so: and this excuse we claim for ourselves and grant to others: but not so that harsh may mate with gentle, serpents be paired with birds, lambs with tigers.

Frequently grave openings, that promise much, have one or two purple patches tagged on, to catch the eye and enhance the colour. Thus, for example, we get descriptions of 'Diana's grove and altar', 'the moving waters hurrying through fair fields', or get a picture of the Rhine, or of a rainbow; but all the time there is no place for these scenes. Perhaps you know how to limn a cypress; but what avails this if your sailor, who has paid to have his portrait painted, is represented as struggling hopelessly to shore from a wreck? A wine-jar was designed: why, when the wheel goes round, does it come out a pitcher? In short, be your subject what you will, only let it be simple and consistent.

Most of us poets—O father, and sons worthy of your father,— are misled by our idea of what is correct. I try to be terse, and end by being obscure; another strives after smoothness, to the sacrifice of vigour and spirit; a third aims at grandeur, and drops into bombast; a fourth, through an excess of caution and a fear of squalls, goes creeping along the ground. He who is bent on lending variety to a theme that is by nature uniform, so as to produce an unnatural effect, is like a man who paints a dolphin in a forest or a wild boar in the waves. If artistic feeling is not there, mere avoidance of a fault leads to some worst defect.

The humblest bronze-smith who lives near the Aemilian training school will depict you nails, and imitate waving hair in metal, yet fail in his work because he cannot represent the figure as a whole. Now, if I wanted to compose a work, I should no more wish to be like that smith than to live admired for my dark eyes and dark hair while I had a crooked nose.

You writers, choose a subject that is within your powers, and ponder long what your shoulders can and cannot bear. He who makes every effort to select his theme aright will be at no loss for choice of words or lucid arrangement. Unless I am mistaken, the force and charm of arrangement will be found in this: to say at once what ought at once to be said, deferring many points, and waiving them for the moment.

Careful and nice, too, in his choice of words, the author of the promised poem must reject one word and welcome another; you will have expressed yourself admirably if a clever setting gives a spice of novelty to a familiar word.

If by chance some abstruse subject needs new terms to

make the meaning clear, it will be right to frame words never heard by old-fashioned folk like the Cethegi, and the license will be allowed if not abused; new and lately-minded words will be accepted if drawn from a Greek source, provided this be done sparingly. Why should a Roman grant to Caecilius and Plautus a privilege denied to Virgil and Varius? Why am I myself, if I can capture a phrase or two, grudged this freedom, seeing that the works of Cato and Ennius have enriched the mother-tongue and broadcasted new names for things? It has always been and always will be permissible to circulate a word stamped with the hall-mark of the day.

As forests suffer change of leaves with each declining year, so the earliest-invented words are the first to fall: an elder generation passes away and new-born words, like youth, flourish and grow. Death claims both us and our works. What matter if the sea, let into the heart of the land, shelters our ships from the north winds—a right royal work; or the marsh, long barren and fit for boats alone, feeds neighboring cities and groans under the plough-share; or the river, taught a better channel, has changed its course once ruinous to crops? The works of men's hands must perish, much less can the glory and charm of words endure undecaying. Many a word long disused will revive, and many now high in esteem will fade, if Custom wills it, in whose power lie the arbitrament, the rule, and the standard of language.

Homer has shown in what metre the deeds of kings and captains and the sorrows of war may be written. First came the voice of lament, in couplets unequally paired; then the joy of the successful lover: but who the author was that first published the dainty measures, critics dispute, and the matter is still unjudged.

It was fury that armed Archilochus with his own device, the iamb; this metre comedy and stately tragedy adopted, as fitted for dialogue, drowning the din of the audience, and born for action.

The Muse has assigned to the lyre the work of celebrating gods and heroes, the champion boxer, the victorious steed, the fond desire of lovers, and the cup that banishes care.

In works of geniuses are clearly-marked differences of subject and shades of style. If, through ignorance, I fail to maintain these, why hail me poet? Why from a false shame, do I prefer ignorance to knowledge? A subject for comedy refuses to be handled in tragic verse; the banquet of Thyestes disdains to be rehearsed in lines suited to daily life and right enough for comedy. At times, however, even Comedy exalts her voice, and an angry Chremes rants and raves; often, too, in a tragedy Telephus or Peleus utters his sorrow in the language of prose, when, poor and in exile, he flings aside his paint-pots and his words a yard long, in eagerness to touch the spectator's heart with his lamentable tale.

It is not enough for poems to be fine; they must charm, and draw the mind of the listener at will. As the human face answers a smile with a smile, so does it wait upon tears; if you would have me weep, you must first of all feel grief yourself; then and not till then will your misfortunes, Telephus or Peleus, touch me. If the part assigned you is not in character, I shall fall asleep or laugh.

Sad words suit a gloomy countenance, menacing words an angry; sportive words a merry look, stern words a grim one. For Nature shapes first our inner thoughts to take the bent of circumstance; she moves to gladness or drives to anger, bows the heart to earth and tortures it with bitter grief. After, with the tongue her aid, does she express emotion.

If a speaker's words are out of gear with his fortunes, all Rome, horse and foot, will guffaw. It will make a world of difference whether god or demigod be talking; an old man well on in years or a stripling in the first flush of youth; a wealthy dame or some bustling nurse; a roving trader or a son of the soil; a Colchian or an Assyrian; one reared in Argos or in Thebes.

Either stick to tradition or see that your inventions be consistent. If when writing a play you introduce yet again the 'far-famed Achilles', make him impatient, hot-tempered, ruthless, fierce; he must disown all laws: they were not made for *him;* his appeal will be to the sword. In like manner let Medea be high-hearted and unconquerable, Ino tearful, Ixion a traitor, Io a wanderer, Orestes forlorn.

If you bring on to the stage a subject unattempted yet, and you are bold enough to create a fresh character, let him remain to the end such as he was when he first appeared—consistent throughout. It is hard to treat a hackneyed theme with originality, and you act more wisely by dramatizing the *Iliad* than by introducing a subject unknown and hitherto unsung. I shall aim a poem so deftly fashioned out of familiar matter that anybody might hope to emulate the feat, yet for all his efforts sweat and labor in vain. Such is the power of order and arrangement; such the charm that waits upon common things. The common quarry will become your own by right, if you do not dally in the cheap and easy round; if you do not, an all too faithful translator, essay to render your author word for word; if you do not—a mere copyist—take a plunge into some narrow pit from which diffidence or the conditions of the work itself forbid you to escape.

Nor should your exordium be like that of the cyclic poet of old: 'I'll sing the fate of Priam, and the famous war of Troy'. What will this writer produce worthy of such mouthing? It will be a case of 'mountains in labor and—a mouse comes out!' Much better he who makes no ill-judged effort: 'Sing me, O Muse, the tale of that hero who, after the capture of Troy, surveyed the manners and cities of mankind.'

His aim is to fetch not smoke from a flash but light from smoke, that afterwards he may bring you marvels of the picturesque—Antiphates and the Cyclops, Scylla and Charybdis. He does not date 'the Return of Diomede' from Meleager's death, nor the Trojan war from the twin eggs: he ever hurries to the crisis and carries the listener into the midst of the story as though it were already known; what he despairs of illuminating with his touch he omits; and so employs fiction, so blends false with true, that beginning, middle, and end all strike the same note.

Now hear what I, and the world at large, expect. If you want an appreciative audience that will sit quiet till the curtain drops and the call for 'cheers' begins, you must observe the characteristics of each age and assign a fitting grace to natures that shift with the years. The child who can just talk and feel his feet with confidence longs to play with his peers; is quick to anger, as quick to cool; his moods change hourly. The beardless boy, his tutor out of the way, finds delight in horses and dogs and the turf of the sunny plain. Pliant as wax to vice, he is gruff with his counsellors, slow to provide for his own best interests, lavish with his money; high-spirited, passionate, ready to discard his fancies. With manhood comes a change of tastes: his aim now is money and friendship; he will be the slave of ambition, and will shun doing what, later on, he might wish to undo.

Many are the discomforts of age, partly because the old man, ever amassing, shrinks from his gains and dares not enjoy them; partly because he handles everything in chill and listless fashion,—irresolute, a laggard in hope, lazy, greedy of long life, cross-grained, querulous, one who extols the past as it was 'when I was a boy'; a censor and critic of the rising generation. The years as they come bring many blessings: many do they take as they go. Lest an old man's part be given to a youth, or a man's part to a boy, we shall do wisely to dwell on the attributes proper to each period of life.

An action either takes place on the stage, or is announced as having taken place off it. What finds entrance through the ear strikes the mind less vividly than what is brought before the trusty eyes of the spectator himself. And yet you will not present incidents which ought to be enacted before the scenes, and will remove from sight a good deal for the actor to relate on the stage by and by—so that, for example, Medea may not butcher her boys or savage Atreus cook human flesh in front of the audience, Procne turn into a bird or Cadmus into a snake. Anything you thrust under my nose in this fashion moves my disgust—and incredulity.

A play which is to be in demand and, after production, to be revived, should consist of five acts—no more, no less. A god must not be introduced unless a difficulty occurs worthy of such a deliverer; nor should a fourth actor be forward to speak. The Chorus should discharge the part and duty of an actor with vigor, and chant nothing between the acts that does not forward the action and fit into the plot naturally. The Chorus must back the good and give sage counsel; must control the passionate and cherish those that fear to do evil; it must praise the thrifty meal, the blessings of justice, the laws, and Peace with her unbarred gates. It will respect confidences and implore heaven that prosperity may revisit the miserable and quit the proud.

In days gone by the pipe, not as now bound with brass and rival of the trumpet, but soft and simple with its few stops, was useful to accompany the Chorus and give its note. It could fill with sound the not yet overcrowded benches, to which of course the people would gather, readily counted (for they were few)—a thrifty folk, chaste and honest. When victorious nations began to extend their boundaries, and an ever-widening wall to compass their cities, and people were free to enjoy themselves uncensored on feast days with early revels, a greater license was granted to rhythms and tunes. What taste could you expect in some unlettered rustic, out for a holiday, when in company with a townsman—clown and gentleman together? So the piper added movement and wanton gestures to his art of old, and would trail his robes as he strutted about the stage; so were new notes added to the lyre; bold eloquence brought with it a language unknown before; and wise saws, prophetic of the future, would match the oracles of Delphi.

The poet who competed in tragic verse for a paltry goat soon made the rustic satyrs doff their garments and ventured on coarse jests without loss of dignity, sure that the spectator, fresh from the sacrifice, drunk and subject to no law, must needs be held by the charms and enticements of novelty.

It will be well so to commend to your audience the quips and laughter of Satyrs, so to pass from grave to gay, that no god or hero that is to be staged—so conspicuous of late in royal gold and purple—should in his discourse sink to the level of tavern-talk; or again, while shunning the ground, catch at clouds and emptiness. It is beneath the dignity of Tragedy to blurt out trivial verse: like a matron bidden to dance on holy days, the Muse, if she has to move among saucy Satyrs, will show a due reserve.

If I write Satyric plays, I shall not choose only bald and everyday terms; nor so try to vary from tragic diction that none can guess whether Davus is the speaker, or bold Pythias who won a talent by wiping her master's eye, or Silenus—guide, philosopher, and friend of a god.

In my judgment, when woodland Fauns are brought on to the stage they should be careful not to languish in love-verses, like city exquisites, nor rap out filthy and shameful jests. For those who possess horse, father, or estate take offence; nor do they receive with favor or award a crown to everything the purchaser of fried peas and chesnuts may approve.

A long syllable following a short is termed an 'iambus'—a lively foot; hence the word 'trimeter' was given to iambic lines, since, uniform from first to last, they yielded six beats. Not so long ago, to permit of a slower and more sedate movement, the iambus granted the staid spondee a share in its native rights, with the proviso that it kept its place in the second and fourth feet, in friendly fashion. The iambic foot is rarely found in the much-vaunted trimeters of Accius, and brands those ponderous lines which Ennius launched on to the stage with the dishonoring charge of over-hurry and carelessness in workmanship or, worse, of ignorance of the poetic art.

It is not every critic that notices false rhythms; and it is true that needless indulgence is given to Roman poets. Am I, therefore, to run riot and break the rules? Or shall I assume that the public will mark my slips? If so, then, wary and safe within the hope of forgiveness, I have indeed escaped censure, praise I have deserved not.

Do you, my friends, study the Greek masterpieces: thumb them day and night.

'But', some one answers, 'your forebears praised the measures and pleasantries of Plautus.' True: they admired both far too tolerantly, not to say foolishly, if only you and I know how to distinguish vulgarity from wit, and are quick with fingers and ears alike to catch the right cadences.

Thespis is said to have discovered Tragedy—a form of poetry hitherto unknown—and to have carried his plays about in tumbrils, to be chanted and performed by actors with faces smeared with lees. After him Aeschylus, inventor of the mask and comely robe, laid his stage on short planks, teaching his company how to talk grandiloquently and strut with buskined feet. Next came the Old Comedy, praised by all; but freedom degenerated into license and violence, to be checked by law; to law it yielded, and the Chorus, robbed of its power to hurt, fell silent—to its shame.

Our own poets have left no style untried; not the least of their merits was when they boldly forsook the footsteps of Greece and celebrated, in comedy and tragedy alike, our national deeds. Latium would not be mightier in valor or feats of arms than in letters, if only her poets, one and all, did not scorn the long labor of the file. Do you, O Bisos, sprung from Numa, censure the poem that has not been pruned by time and many a cancellation—corrected ten times over and finished to the finger-nail.

Because Democritus believes that genius is happier than miserable art, and shuts the gates of Helicon on all sane poets, a good few will not cut their nails or beard, but court solitude and shun the baths. The fact is, a poet may win a poet's name and reward if only he has never entrusted to Licinus, the barber, a pate that not three Anticyras could cure!

What a fool I am to get rid of the bile when spring comes on! But for that, no poet would write better. But nothing is worth that! I'll serve as a whetstone which, though it cannot cut of itself, can sharpen iron. Though I write nothing, I'll teach the business and duty of a writer; show where his materials may be found; what it is that trains and moulds a poet; what becomes him, what does not; whither knowledge tends, and whither error.

The secret of all good writing is sound judgment. The works of the Socratics will supply you with the facts: get these in clear perspective and the words will follow naturally. Once a man has learned his duty to friend and fatherland, the just claims of parent, brother, or guest on his love, the obligations of a senator or judge, or the duty of a general sent on active service, he will infallibly know how to assign to each character its fitting part. I shall bid the clever imitator look to life and morals for his real model, and draw thence language true to life. Sometimes a play, tricked out with commonplaces and with characters well-drawn, even though it be void of charm, force, or artistic skill, delights the populace and holds their interest far better than 'lines without sense, and tuneful trifles.'

It was the Greeks, aye the Greeks, covetous of praise alone, that the Muse endowed with quick wit and rounded utterance. Our Roman youths by long calculations learn how to divide the shilling into a hundred parts. 'Come, young Albinus, tell me this: take a penny from sixpence, and what is over? You ought to know?' 'Fivepence.' 'Good! you'll hold your own some day. Now add a penny: what's the result?' 'Sevenpence.' Ah, once this canker of avarice, this money-grubbing, has tainted the soul, can we hope that poems will be written worthy of cedar-oil and to be treasured in polished cases?

The poet's aim is either to profit or to please, or to blend in one the delightful and the useful. Whatever the lesson you would convey, be brief, that your hearers may catch quickly what is said and faithfully retain it. Every superfluous word is spilled from the too-full memory. Fictions made to please should keep close to the truth of things; your play should not demand an unlimited credence; it will not do to describe how a living boy is ripped from Lamia's belly after she has just eaten him. Elder folk rail at what contains no serviceable lesson; our young aristocrats cannot away with grave verses: the man who mingles the useful with the sweet carries the day by charming his reader and at the same time instructing him. That's the book to enrich the publisher, to be posted over seas, and to prolong its author's fame.

Yet some faults there are that we can gladly overlook. The string does not invariably give the note intended by mind and hand; we listen for a flat, and often get a sharp; nor does the arrow always hit the target. But whenever beauties in a poem form a majority, I shall not stumble at a few blemishes that are due to carelessness or that the weakness of human nature has failed to guard against.

How, then, do we stand? A copyist who continually makes the same blunder, in spite of constant warning, gets no quarter; a harpist who is forever fumbling with the same string is laughed at; so, too, I rank the slovenly poet with

Choerilus, whose occasional fine lines, though surprising, move one to mirth. Am I, then, to be indignant whenever good Homer nods?

'Yes, but it is natural for slumber to steal over a long work. Poetry is like painting: one piece takes your fancy if you stand close to it, another if you keep at some distance. One courts a dim light, another, challenging keen criticism, will fain be seen in the glare; this charms but once, that will please if ten times repeated.'

Hope of the Pisos! although you have your father to guide your judgment aright and are yourself wise to boot, cherish this lesson and take it home: that only in limited fields is mediocrity tolerable or pardonable. A counsel or second-rate pleader at the bar may not rival Messalla in eloquence, nor possess the knowledge of Cassellius; yet he has his value; but mediocrity in poets has never been tolerated by the gods, men, or—booksellers. Just as, at some pleasant banquet, ugly music, coarse perfume, and poppy seed mixed with Sardinian honey offend the taste, because the meal could have passed without such things: so a poem, created to give delight, if it fails but a little of the highest sinks to the lowest. One who is ignorant of games will abstain from the weapons of the Campus; and if he knows nothing of ball, or quoit, or hoop, will hold aloof, lest the thronging onlookers laugh with none to check them; yet he who is no poet, presumes to write verses! 'And why not? Is he not free, of gentle birth, rated at a knight's income, with nothing against him?' *You,* I know, will say and do nothing 'against the grain'—such is your resolve, such is your good sense. If, however, you should one day produce something, pray submit it first to Maecius the critic, to your father, to me; and then put back the manuscript in your desk and let it stand for over a decade. The unpublished may be cancelled; but a word once uttered can never be recalled.

Orpheus, seer and bard in one, weaned savage forest-tribes from murder and foul living; whence the legend that he tamed tigers and fierce lions. It was said, too, that Amphion, founder of Thebes, moved stones by the sound of his lyre and drew them where he would by the magic of his entreaty. This was the poets' wisdom of old—to draw a line between the Man and the State, the sacred and the common; to build cities, to check promiscuous lust, to assign rights to the married, to engrave laws on wood. Thus did praise and honour come to divine poets and their lays. Following upon them, noble Homer with impressive art depicted the character of heroes and their wrath, while Tyrtaeus with his songs kindled men's hearts to warrior deeds; in verse were oracles delivered, and the path of life shown forth, while the favor of monarchs was courted by Pierian strains, and festivals were devised to sweeten human toil. This I say lest perchance you should be ashamed of the lyric Muse, and of Apollo lord of song.

Whether a good poem be the work of nature or of art is a moot point. For my part I fail to see the use of study without wit, or of wit without training: so true is it that each requires the other's aid in helpful union.

The athlete who is eager to reach the longed-for goal has endured and done much in boyhood, has borne heat and cold, has abstained from women and wine; the flute-player who plays at the Pythian games has first learned his lesson and trembled before a teacher. Nowadays people think it enough to say: 'I make wonderful poems; devil take the hindmost! it's a shame for me to be outdone and to own I really do not know what I have never learned.'

As a crier collects a crowd to buy his wares, so a poet, rich in land and rich in investments, bids flatterers flock to him for their profit. If there is one who can provide a costly feast, who will go bail for a poor man and rescue him from the law's grim toils, I shall be surprised if, for all his wealth, he is clever enough to distinguish the false friend from the true. Whether you have given another a present, or mean to do so, never call him, when filled with joy, to listen to your verses; for he will be sure to cry, 'Splendid! bravo!' He will change color over them, drop tears of pleasure, leap, beat upon the floor.

Hired mourners outstrip in word and action those whose sorrow is real: so is the sham admirer moved far more than the honest one. Wealthy folk, when keen to mark whether a man be worthy of friendship, are said to ply him with many a bumper and put him to the ordeal of wine; so, if you write poems, you will never fail to detect the spirit that lurks beneath the fox's skin.

In days gone by, whenever you read a piece to Quintilius he would exclaim, 'Correct this, I pray, or that.' If you replied that you could do no better, that you had tried twice or thrice in vain, he would bid you cut out the ill-turned lines and bring them to the anvil again. If you chose rather to defend than to mend the faulty line, not a word more would he say, or waste his efforts. Henceforth you might hug yourself and your works, alone, without a rival.

A kind and sensible critic will censure verses when they are weak, condemn them when they are rough; ugly lines he will score in black, will lop off pretentious ornaments, force you to clear up your obscurities, criticize a doubtful phrase, and mark what needs a change—in fact prove another Aristarchus. He will not say, 'Why should I take my friend to task for mere trifles?'—it is such trifles that will bring into sad scrapes the poet who has been fooled and flattered unfairly.

As men shun the patient troubled with itch, jaundice, insanity, or moonstruck frenzy, so wise men dread to touch a mad poet, and avoid him: boys jostle him and fools pursue. If, spouting his lines and roaming, head in air (like a fowler watching thrushes), your bard falls into a pit or ditch, he may bawl, 'Help, neighbors, help!' but there's no one to pull him out. Should somebody minded to assist throw a rope, I shall say, 'Who knows whether he has not thrown himself there on purpose, and does not want to be saved?' And then I shall relate the Sicilian poet's end: 'Empedocles, wishing to be thought a god, in cold blood leapt into the blazing Etna.' Suffer poets to destroy themselves if they choose; he who saves a man against his will as good as murders him. No first attempt this; if pulled back straightway, he'll never become like other folk nor lay down his desire for a theatrical ending. Nobody quite knows why he fashions verses; possibly he has fouled his father's grave or violated some sacred boundary, and so lost caste. Well, he's mad; that's clear; and like a bear that has managed to break its prison bars this pitiless reciter stampedes scholar and dunce alike. Once he has captured his victim, he sticks till he slays him with reading—like a leech that will never let go till gorged with blood.